ITALY
AND ITS INVADERS

ITALY
AND ITS INVADERS

Girolamo Arnaldi

Translated by Antony Shugaar

HARVARD UNIVERSITY PRESS

Cambridge, Massachusetts

London, England

2005

for Lucrezia

in the shared memory of Sara

Originally published as *L'Italia e i suoi invasori;*
© 2002, Gius. Laterza e Figli

This translation of *L'Italia e i suoi invasori* is published by arrangement with Gius.
Laterza & Figli S.p.A., Rome-Bari.

Library of Congress Cataloging-in-Publication Data

Arnaldi, Girolamo.
[Italia e i suoi invasori. English]
Italy and its invaders / Girolamo Arnaldi; translated by Antony Shugaar.
p. cm.
Includes bibliographical references and index.
ISBN 0-674-01870-2
1. Italy—History. 2. Italy—History, Military. 3. Italy—Foreign relations.
I. Shugaar, Antony. II. Title.

DG473.A7613 2005
945—dc22   2005050770

CONTENTS

PREFACE

THIS BOOK makes no claims. I would not want anyone to think, in particular, that I believe I have found the central theme, still being sought, of Italy's history, and that I am trying to identify it in the series of foreign invasions that have punctuated that history. If I had set out with that goal in mind, I would have been committing an act of desecration toward Italy's national identity—a terribly fragile identity, as is often noted. It was Rosario Romeo who warned me of this pitfall when, many years ago, I spoke to him about this project, which I was already planning to undertake. But if, for an Italian like Mario Luzi, "Italy is an illusion, indeed, a mirage, the stuff of wishes," the fact remains that for foreigners Italy has for many centuries been (unfortunately for us Italians) a wish come true.

But I should say that this book does make one claim: to be readable. If I had finished it before he died, I would have sent it to Indro Montanelli for his opinion. Montanelli, a respected Italian journalist and author of popular histories, died in 2001. He often said that "academic" historians, at least Italian academic historians, are incapable of writing readable books. It is up to the reader to say whether I have been successful or not. In any case, I believe that the task is easier, or at least less difficult, the further you move away from topics that you have approached as a scholar—because it is for those topics, where you flatter yourself that you have shed new light on a tiny particle of truth, that you can publish only after perusing *all* sources, after anticipating *all* possible objections and reading *every*-

thing that has been written on the subject by those who have come
before you.

Now, it is easier to be readable once you venture into the vast
spaces that surround the little field that you have tilled and cultivated yourself. It is likewise easier, once you leave the grounds of
your own garden, to lapse into platitudes or, what is worse, in the attempt to avoid that risk, to indulge in up-to-date winks and nods, or
ill-considered judgments (worse still if they are revisionist in nature),
in violation of the historian's ethical code, even in the writing of
popular history.

All I can say is that although it is true that I enjoyed myself while
writing this book (in the original sense of the Italian term *divertirsi,*
to indulge in a temporary diversion from one's usual labors), it is
also true that it demanded a very serious commitment in ethical and
civic terms, for I clearly understood that it might very well wind up
in the hands of a greater number of readers than the few dozen who
usually read my writings.

I have borrowed the title from an old English book. On 15 February 1887, Antonio Labriola wrote to Benedetto Croce: "I don't know
how much progress you have made in your understanding of the
English language. I would recommend that you purchase the four
volumes of [Thomas] Hodgkin *(Italy and Her Invaders):* an excellent
book in its information and its form, as well as in its illustrations. I
have seen only one volume, but it is a first-class book. There is a degree of self-interest in my recommendation. Since the book costs 2
pounds 8 shillings, I cannot afford to buy it—and you, rich as an
Englishman, would let me read it."

The title, but nothing more than the title. Certainly not the chronological approach, considering that Hodgkin stopped at the year
814, while I begin with the Sack of Rome in AD 410 and continue all
the way up to a pseudoconquest, that of the Piedmontese during the
Risorgimento, and a true liberation, that of the English and Americans in the Second World War. Nor do I speak of "invaders" in the
strict sense of the word. Perhaps I should have said "foreigners,"

since I also write about the "ultramontane" students (that is, students from north of the Alps) in Bologna and even about Christina of Sweden, the Protestant queen who converted to Catholicism and came to live, and die, in Rome. It is in fact in the choice of content that I have been particularly creative. Some of the choices were unavoidable: How could I leave out the Longobards or Naples and Milan under the Spaniards? Others were less so. And it may be that in some cases I strayed from my theme, writing pages that would be better suited to a project that, I repeat, I would never have dared to undertake: the history of Italy in a nutshell.

The story line is punctuated by quotations of all sorts: from contemporary historical sources, modern historians, but also literary texts. These quotations become increasingly numerous as the story moves forward. I could not say whether this disparity is due to the fact that the true invasions are those treated in the first few chapters, or whether it is due to my growing lack of professional expertise as I move away from the familiar territory of the Middle Ages, which might have led me inadvertently to make more frequent use of quotations from the writings of others, as I prudently stood aside.

1

FROM THE SACK OF ROME TO ODOACER, "KING OF THE NATIONS"

AT THE TURN of the fifth century, Milan, too vulnerable to attack from the north, lost its standing as capital of the Western Roman Empire. The city that took its place was not Rome, which would have had every right to aspire to the role, but Ravenna:

> For this city of Ravenna lies in a level plain at the extremity of the Ionian Gulf [Adriatic Sea], lacking two stades [ca. 360 meters] of being on the sea, and it is so situated as not to be easily approached either by ships or by a land army. Ships cannot possibly put in to shore there because the sea itself prevents them by forming shoals for not less than thirty stades [ca. 5.5 kilometers], consequently the beach at Ravenna, although to the eye of mariners it is very near at hand, is in reality very far away by reason of the great extent of the shoal-water. And a land army cannot approach it at all; for the river Po . . . , coming from the boundaries of Celtica, and other navigable rivers together with some marshes, encircle it on all sides and so cause the city to be surrounded by water.[1]

No longer interested in Milan by this point, and having failed to penetrate into Ravenna, the king of the Visigoths, Alaric (ca. 370–410) marched on Rome.[2] It is said that on the road to the Eternal City Alaric met a monk who begged him to go no further. Alaric supposedly replied that he had no choice, that he was obeying an inner voice that was ordering him to go to Rome. Although the story is certainly fictitious, it reflects the welter of anxieties, hopes, and fears engendered by that threatening march on the city, which lasted years and years and produced a continual alternation of rumors, sometimes alarming, sometimes reassuring, among contemporaries.

Wealthy Romans buried their treasures. Ancient divinatory practices came back into fashion: dreams, the flights of birds, and comets in the sky were all scrutinized. Those of a more hopeful frame of mind worked to strengthen the city walls. The walls of Rome had originally been built by Aurelian (270–275) after the city had recklessly sprawled for eight centuries outside the original circle of walls built in the sixth century BC, traditionally attributed to King Servius Tullius. In the view of Saint Paulinus, bishop of Nola (351–431), however, it was nonsensical either to rely on the few remaining Roman legions to challenge the invaders on the field of battle, or to seek shelter inside the walls. Much better to rely on the protection of the saints—for instance, to place oneself in the merciful hands of Saint Felix, patron saint of his town of Nola—and to rely on their intercession. Even some generals agreed with him. One of them drew the withering irony of a patriotic poet, Claudian, who dedicated the following *jaculatoria* to him:

> May Saint Thomas serve as a shield for your breast, and may Saint Bartholomew accompany you to war; may the protection of the saints defend the Alps against barbarian attack; may Saint Susanna lend you her strength, and may the protection of Saint Tecla ensure the victory of Rome's troops.

Others, just as disheartened as that general at the prospect of waging a defensive war against the invader, were convinced instead that it was best to resume praying to the old pagan deities, since the new Christian God and his court of saints were beginning to look less invincible than advertised. A rumor spread through Rome that at Narni, sacrifices made to the pagan gods had brought on a number of lightning bolts that had chased away the looming barbarian threat. At that point, even Pope Innocent I (401–417) agreed to a compromise, at the explicit request of the city prefect, the emperor's representative in Rome and the chairman of the Senate: Let sacrifices be made to the gods, but in the privacy of the home, not in public. The pagans objected that carried out in that way, the sacrifices would produce no effect: either sacrifices were to be offered in the light of day, in the presence of the Senate, or else one might just as well do nothing at all. In the end, the idea was abandoned.

It was inevitable that in the final dramatic days, with Alaric approaching the gates of Rome, buried disagreements from the history of the previous hundred years, from Constantine (306–337) on, should come to the surface. Justified by the need to rejuvenate the empire, the conversion to Christianity seemed to have done nothing more than predispose the people's souls to resignation and surrender. Observance of the evangelical principle "Whosoever shall smite thee on thy right cheek, turn to him the other also" (Matthew 5:39) was considered by many to be incompatible with the safety of the *respublica,* then in a state of grave peril. It was thought unlikely that the tombs of the apostles Peter and Paul would have the virtue of protecting Rome against the attack of the invaders.

A last-ditch effort was made to mollify Alaric with gifts of gold, silver, and spices—in very large quantities. Aristocrats and the wealthy did their best to protect their estates from the special tax levied to pay the agreed tribute. There were some who preferred to donate their gold to the poor, rather than to their homeland. The temples of the pagan gods, with their statues made of precious metals, paid the price. Even the statue of the goddess Virtus, the personification of military valor, was melted down along with the others.

Saint Jerome (ca. 348–420), who was living in Bethlehem at the time, recorded the echoes of such events that reached him, magnified by the great distance:

> I hear from the West the terrible news that Rome is besieged, that her citizens have been obliged to purchase their salvation in heavy gold, and, already plundered of all their possessions, they have been besieged anew because, having lost their goods, they must now lose

their lives. My words strangle in my throat. My sobs stop me from dictating these words. Behold, the city that conquered the world has been conquered in its turn. Rome is dying of hunger before it can die by the sword. There are but few survivors, who will be led away in chains. The ravenous hunger of the besieged is nourished with an unclean food. The Romans are eating one another.

The Visigoths, under Alaric's command, entered Rome through the Salarian Gate on the night of 24 August 410. They remained for three days. The massacres, fires, and looting especially affected the wealthier quarters—the Caelian and Aventine Hills. Damage was distributed equally to pagan and Christian Rome. The marks of the fire that raged in the hall of the Senate are perhaps still visible. Included in the loot carried off by the invaders was the solid-silver ciborium, a gift from Constantine, which had been on the main altar of the basilica that bore his name (later Holy Savior, and finally Saint John Lateran). Many Romans, in both Rome and the rest of Italy, among those who had the means to do so, hastily abandoned their homes and fled to Egypt, to other parts of Africa, to the East, spreading news of the event as they went.

Some Christian authors, in reaction to the insinuations being made in pagan milieus, did their best to minimize the importance of the event. It was necessary to explain to the faithful how such a thing could have happened without the responsible parties' being punished on the spot by the Lord. Orosius was an Iberian priest who at the behest of Saint Augustine (354–430) wrote *Historiarum adversus paganos libri septem (The Seven Books of History against the Pagans)* in Africa seven years later. Writing with an openly apologetic intent, and admitting that he had not witnessed the events himself, he mentioned the far more devastating conquest of Rome by the Gauls in 390 BC, the last conquest before the Sack of AD 410:

> Let anyone, if he can, compare some of the disturbances of this age with this disaster, although he does not weigh equally the story of a past disaster with a calamity in the present! . . . . As the Gauls departed there had remained within the circuit of the former City a re-

pulsive mass of shapeless ruins, and on all sides the echo of the unfortunate voices of those wandering over obstructions and not
knowing that they were among their own possessions resounded
and kept ears alarmed. Horror shook men's minds; the very silence
terrified, for the material of fear is loneliness in open spaces. Hence
the Romans considered, voted, and attempted to change their
homes to inhabit another town, and even to be called by another
name. Behold the times in comparison with which the present is
weighed; behold the times for which our memory sighs; behold the
times which strike us with penitence because of our *elected* religion
or rather because of our *rejected* religion. Truly these two captivities
are similar and comparable to each other, the one raging for six
months and the other running its course in three days.[3]

Also, still on the subject of damage done to Rome in the pre-
Constantinian period, Orosius, over the period of time that elapsed
between the Gauls and the Visigoths, discourses at length on the fire
set in the city, not by foreign invaders, but by an emperor, Nero,
who in AD 64 "made a fire of the city of Rome as a spectacle for his
pleasure; for six days and seven nights the blazing city caused astonishment to his royal eyes." This is the same Nero, perhaps by no coincidence, who was also "the first at Rome to torture and inflict the
penalty of death upon Christians."[4]

Orosius concludes that those responsible for what happened in
410 were not the barbarians, but the sins of the Romans, who had
drawn down upon themselves the wrath of God. And in fact, once
the invaders had left, a succession of lightning bolts finished the job
they had begun. In his view of events, distorted by the thrust of his
polemic, the account of the Visigothic incursion culminates in a description of the solemn removal by Alaric's warriors of the sacred
vases from St. Peter's Basilica, which had been concealed out of pre-
caution in a house for nuns:

> This building, as they say, was far from the sacred places and with
> half the City in between. And so, to the great wonder of all, the gold
> and silver vessels, distributed one to each individual and raised above

their heads, were carried openly; the pious procession was guarded on all sides for their protection by drawn swords; a hymn to God was sung publicly with Romans and barbarians joining in; in the sacking of the City, the trumpet of salvation sounded far and wide, and invited and struck all, even those lying in hidden places; from all sides they came together to the vessels of Peter, the vessels of Christ; a great many, even pagans, mingled with the Christians in profession, although not in faith; and in this way they escaped temporarily that they might become more confused; the more thickly the Romans in their flight came together, the more eagerly the barbarians surrounded them as their defenders.[5]

The others (the aliens, the enemies) were not, in other words, in Orosius's eyes Alaric's soldiers, but the Romans who had obstinately remained pagans and who were seeking safety in St. Peter's Basilica, taking advantage of the right of asylum, mingling with the crowd of psalm singers made up of both Christian Romans and barbarians. Concerning Alaric's soldiers, Orosius neglects to point out a detail of some importance: the Visigoths were Christians, it is true, but Arians, and therefore heretics in the view of the Church.

With a different depth of understanding, and of faith, Saint Augustine did nothing to minimize the events, but he urged believers to remember that it is only in exceptional circumstances that God metes out punishments and rewards in this life. It is in the afterlife that individuals receive their just deserts. He recalled, moreover, that neither losing your life nor, to an even greater degree, losing your material possessions could be considered evils in any absolute sense, at least to a Christian worthy of the name. As for the fate that was looming over the Roman Empire, it was necessary to understand that even if it had become Christian, it was still an "earthly city," whereas for believers in Christ the true homeland was the "celestial city," of which even the Church itself was only a partial foreshadowing on this earth.

And so with his treatise *City of God (Civitas dei),* written in the wake of the Sack of Rome in 410, Augustine clearly showed his intent to hold at arm's length the *respublica,* which over the previous century had showered the Church with advantages and privileges of all sorts. That did not mean, however, that Christians, under cover of the distinction between the "earthly city" and the "celestial city," should desert the cause of the empire en masse at the moment of greatest danger (on the night of 31 December 406, a coalition force of Vandals, Alani, and Suebi had crossed the frozen Rhine River at Mainz, destroying the city and then going on to sack defenseless Gaul, up to the Pyrenees). Owing in part to the fact that the Germans were either still pagans (most of them) or else converts to Arian Christianity (the leadership), the fifth century witnessed the growing spread and consolidation of a new type of patriotism, both Roman and Catholic.

In sharp contrast with this attitude, the isolated but significant voice of Salvianus (or Salvian the Presbyter) should be mentioned, a monk from the island of Lerinum (the Îles de Lérins, off Cannes), who wrote a treatise around AD 440 entitled *De gubernatione Dei (On the Government of God)*—that is, Providence—in which he claimed that although it was true that in religious terms the Romans were undeniably superior to the barbarians, whether pagans or heretics, it was also unquestionable that in moral terms the barbarians, uncouth though they might be, were far preferable. It was no accident that many Romans would go to live near the barbarians, tolerating their bad manners and foul odors. If they did so, and many chose this path, it was because they "prefer to live free in an apparent slavery, rather than to be slaves in apparent liberty."

The presence in Italy and throughout the West of so many representatives of a humanity so different from that to which they were accustomed led many to question the excellence, heretofore unquestioned, of "civic" life. The fashion of wearing trousers and leather boots, as the barbarians did, became so common that several laws were passed against it. They were nothing but palliatives, however.

From Ravenna, where he was besieged, the western emperor

Honorius (384–423) had been unwilling or unable to prevent the Sack of Rome. More than a century later, he was described as a poor idiot:

> At that time they say that the Emperor Honorius in Ravenna received the message from one of the eunuchs, evidently a keeper of the poultry, that Rome had perished. And he cried out and said, "And yet it has just eaten from my hands!" For he had a very large cock, Rome by name; and the eunuch comprehending his words said that it was the city of Rome which had perished at the hands of Alaric, and the emperor with a sigh of relief answered quickly: "But I, my good fellow, thought that my fowl Rome had perished." So great, they say, was the folly with which this emperor was possessed.[6]

Honorius's half sister, Galla Placidia (ca. 389–450), who had stayed in Rome, was taken prisoner by the Visigoths in 410.[7] They took her with them in an enclosed litter as they marched south in a futile quest to reach Africa—the breadbasket of Rome, the land of plenty dreamed of by every barbarian (though only the Vandals ever managed to set foot there)—and following the death of Alaric (who was buried, along with his horse, in the riverbed of the Busentinus—the Busento River, which had been diverted from its course), in their long march northward, back up the peninsula, led by Athaulph, the new king. In January 414, at Narbonne, in southern France (Languedoc-Roussillon), where the Visigoths had made a halt on their march, in the house of a Roman notable, the blond Athaulph wed the dark-eyed and dark-haired captive princess. His wedding gift: five traysful of jewels looted from Rome four years before. But those, the bridegroom assured her, were days best forgotten.

It is again Orosius who tells how and why:

> For I myself also heard a man of Narbo . . . relating at Bethlehem, a town in Palestine, to the most blessed priest, Jerome, that he was a very close friend of Athaulf at Narbo, and that he often learned from him under oath what he was accustomed to say when he was

in good spirits, health, and temper: that he, at first, was ardently eager to blot out the Roman name and to make the entire Roman Empire that of the Goths alone, and to call it and make it, to use a popular expression, *Gothia* instead of *Romania,* and that he Athaulf, become what Caesar Augustus had once been. When, however, he discovered from long experience that the Goths, by reason of their unbridled barbarism, could not by any means obey laws, nor should the laws of the state be abrogated without which the state is not a state [*sine quibus respublica non est respublica*], he chose to seek for himself the glory of completely restoring and increasing the Roman name by the forces of the Goths, and to be held by posterity as the author of the restoration of Rome, since he had been unable to be its transformer. For this reason, he strove to refrain from war; for this reason, to be eager for peace, being influenced in all the works of good government, especially by the persuasion and advice of his wife, Placidia, a woman, indeed, of a very keen mind and very good religiously. While he was very zealously occupied in seeking and offering this very peace, he was killed in the city of Barcelona in Spain by the treachery, as it is said, of his own men.[8]

Concerning this passage by Orosius—its reliability and, if we choose to accept it, the real nature of Athaulph's plans for a restoration—historians and authors have waxed argumentative and fanciful. Even if we accept that Athaulph believed that the son born to him and Galla Placidia might become emperor one day, thereby putting an end to the ferocious battles between Romans and Goths, we have no idea what Galla Placidia thought of it. Perhaps she remembered that her father, the emperor Theodosius (ca. 347–395), had given his niece Serena (whom he adopted as a daughter) as a bride to Stilicho (ca. 365–408), a valiant general and the son of a Vandal and a Roman woman. In those days, people couldn't afford to be too picky. Mixed marriages of convenience were the order of the day, even though the Church disapproved of them because in most cases the Arian husband refused to convert to Catholicism before marrying a

Catholic bride. To mitigate the sufferings of princesses married against their will, there was the intimate comfort of faith, the awareness that they were serving the cause of the empire, and the attractions of a simpler, less ceremonious, and less tedious life than the one they were used to living at court, dominated by the obsession with etiquette. Honorius, however, reacted with acts of open hostility to those interested peace feelers, and the Visigoths set off again, headed for Spain, sacking the cities they encountered along the path of their march. From Spain, Galla Placidia, widowed and bereft of her son, who had lived only a few months, was sent back to Ravenna, in exchange for a shipment of grain.

In Italy, a second marriage awaited her, perhaps even less welcome than the first: this time the bridegroom was a Roman general, the supreme commander Constantius, to whom she bore a son, Valentinian. But the years she had spent among the barbarians—her favorite corps of bodyguards was composed of Visigoths—aroused the suspicions of the citizens of Ravenna, in the grip of a fit of xenophobia, and of her stepbrother, who forced her into exile in Constantinople. She returned from there, after Honorius's death, with the support of the eastern emperor Theodosius II (401–450), whose soldiers took advantage of this opportunity to sack Ravenna—"invaders," even though they called themselves Romans. By now, Galla Placidia was the *Augusta,* summoned to rule at the side of the Valentinian III, who with the title of Caesar appeared to be officially designated to succeed to the throne.

Galla Placidia had not forgotten the son she had borne to Athaulph. He was named Theodosius, like his grandfather; he had been born, had died, and had been buried in Barcelona. His name appears among those of the other family members, living and dead, in the dedication for the church of St. John the Evangelist in Ravenna, built by the empress to fulfill a vow made during a storm at sea. But from the mosaics that adorn the walls of her so-called mausoleum—which she also in all likelihood ordered built, in the part of the city where the imperial palace stood and with which her name remains linked (though she was almost certainly never buried there)—there wafts an air of hope that no longer has anything to do with the plans for reconciliation between Romans and barbarians, the outlook for a "Romania," or land of the Romans, rejuvenated by the introduction of the intact forces of the Goths, with the dreams, in short, that had animated her adventurous youth. It is a Christian hope for the advent of the kingdom of God, established in the face of a shattered world.

Shortly before Galla Placidia died, her daughter Honoria, who in the wake of an indiscretion had been forced into reparatory marriage with an elderly senator, secretly sent a slave with a message to Attila, king of the Huns (ca. 395–453), asking him to come free her. Accompanying the request was a ring bearing the seal of the venturesome princess. She had indulged in a typically headstrong undertaking, driven by the most personal motives imaginable. In fact, however, Honoria, perhaps without even being clearly aware of it, was following in her mother's footsteps, proposing once again the traditional policy of openness toward the barbarian world, and this time toward a ruler who had actually earned the title "Scourge of God." Ammianus Marcellinus (ca. 330–ca. 400), who was practically the last Roman historian, speaks of the Huns as small, stout men with strong heads, with horrible, beardless faces in which it is difficult to recognize human features.[9] When Attila stepped forward and claimed the princess's hand, only Galla Placidia's prestige saved Honoria from the savage wrath of Valentinian III (419–455). But when the time came to stem the advance of the "Scourge of God," after Attila had destroyed Aquileia in 452 and was on the march toward Rome, the task fell, according to tradition, at any rate, to Pope Leo I (440–461), who hastened to the banks of the river Mincius. The days of imperial princesses, wives of supreme commanders of Roman barbarian descent and mothers of "child emperors," were coming to an end. An era was beginning of "bishops who were defenders of the cities" (*defensor urbis* was a specific civic office, not an honorific), who stood alone in protecting the lives and possessions

of their faithful at a delicate juncture in the transition from the rule
of the Romans to that of the barbarians, a transition that was by this
point definitive.

—⁂—

ODOACER (CA. 434–493) was the first barbarian sovereign to rule
over Italy. It happened in AD 476. There was a time when great importance was attributed to this date, as if it were a watershed between antiquity and the Middle Ages. And there was good cause: it
was no small matter that even Italy, whose territory encompassed
Rome, should become the seat of a barbarian reign, as had happened to all the other provinces of the Western Roman Empire before it. But it is a mistake to imagine that for the people of the time,
either in Italy or elsewhere, the advent of Odoacer necessarily came
as a shock. In fact, Arnaldo Momigliano has spoken of the "noiseless
fall of an empire."[10]

Odoacer himself seems to have helped muffle what noise there
was. Once he had deposed the very young emperor Romulus
Augustulus and sent him into exile in Campania, he persuaded the
Senate to send the imperial insignia to Constantinople. It hardly
seemed necessary to him for the West, in the state to which it had
been reduced, to have an emperor of its own. For himself he requested only the title "patrician," the same that had been held by
Horestes (d. 476), the barbarized Roman general (former secretary
of Attila!) and father of the deposed Romulus Augustulus. It is true
that Odoacer was a Scirian, not a Roman; but before Horestes there
had been other non-Roman commanders in chief and patricians: for
instance, Ricimer (d. 472), the son of a Suebian prince and a
Visigothic princess, who had disposed as he pleased over the thrones
and the lives of five western emperors.

The gold coins stamped in Italian mints continued to bear the
name of the eastern emperor Zeno (ca. 476–491), even after 476.
Odoacer confined himself to stamping his own name on silver and
bronze coins, used only for daily transactions. An incurable optimist

would have had sound reasons to conclude from the vantage p
of Constantinople that the situation of the empire not only had not
worsened, but had actually improved. From the death in 395 of
Theodosius I on, the two parts of the empire, the eastern and the
western, had always been under different rulers. Now, thanks to
Odoacer's initiative, there was once again only one emperor, just as
in the good old days before the invasions.

Similarly, the inhabitants of the peninsula must not have paid
much attention to the deposition of some mere "small-time Augustus," not a successor to, but a ridiculous counterfeit of, the real Augustus, the first in the series. Perhaps the fact that he was called
Romulus might have caused some brows to furrow. A wise man, in
fact, had predicted that the Roman Empire would survive for twelve
centuries—as many centuries as Rome's founder had seen vultures
on the Palatine Hill. That span of time was now coming to an end.
And the potential coincidence was striking: a Romulus at the beginning, another at the end. But to calm people, to persuade everyone
that, after all, nothing much had happened, there was the account of
events as they had unfolded between August and September of 476.

The Scirian Odoacer was a barbarian, but not precisely an invader,
in the sense that he had not forced his way in a spectacular manner
across any border at the head of an armed people bent on conquer-
ing new lands because—as was so often the case—that people was
being prodded from behind by the incursions of another, more powerful people intent on taking the land the first inhabited. In the case
of Odoacer and his people there had been, as in so many other
cases, a peaceful infiltration across the borders. He had been in Italy
for many years now. He had fought at Ricimer's side. Last of all, he
was an almost familiar presence, not an unknown figure sweeping
down on the peninsula from the forests or the steppes of northern
or eastern Europe.

The dynamics of the revolt against Horestes by the Germanic
forces quartered in Italy, culminating in the proclamation of
Odoacer as king, would also have come as little or no surprise. It

was unclear of what and whom he had become king: certainly not of Italy, because the Romano-barbarian kingdoms that sprang up in this period took their names from the invading peoples (Franks, Burgundians, Vandals, Visigoths), not from the province invaded (Gaul, Spain, Africa); nor would he have been king of the Scirians, because the group of mutineers was anything but homogeneous, including not only Scirians, but also Heruli and Rugians. They were just one of the fragments into which the agglomeration of Germanic peoples had broken down that had belonged to the empire of the Huns after the death of Attila. An appropriate title that certain sources attribute to Odoacer is, instead, *rex gentium,* where the Latin *gentes* referred to the non-Romans—in a word: the barbarians stationed, or settled, in Italy.

What the rebels were demanding was simply that they too be accorded the status of *hospites. Hospitalitas,* or "hospitality," is a term that in modern parlance refers to an attitude of cordial and spontaneous generosity, but in those harsh days it had taken on a special meaning, which could only by quite a stretch be brought into line with its current usage. Many barbarian peoples had penetrated into the territory of the empire, and there was no real possibility of evicting them. Moreover, they could come in handy for filling the gaps that epidemics and wars had produced in local populations, as well as for pushing back potential new and even more catastrophic waves of barbarian invaders appearing at the borders. The imperial authorities had long ago come to the conclusion that it was best to negotiate with them.

The settlement of barbarians in the lands of the empire that they already occupied had been legalized through a procedure that involved making available to these so-called *hospites* a portion of the houses and lands in a given province. The clauses of the *foedus,* or "treaty," that was stipulated varied from case to case. A fairly common formula called for the assignment to the *hospites* of one third of the houses and lands, or the fruits of the earth (in Latin, *fruges*), a distinction that amounted to very little, since the ones who worked the land were still exclusively the Roman *coloni*. Often, however, the split was even more favorable to the *hospites*.

Between 395 and 476, the western emperors established roughly one hundred treaties with the barbarians who had settled in the provinces. They deluded themselves into believing that they were being clever in favoring one group of invaders over another. When barbarians allied with the Romans died fighting in battle, killing other barbarians, it was thought that a twofold benefit had been obtained. But all this wasted guile served only to stave off the inevitable, not to solve the problem, at least as far as the West and Italy were concerned.

We do not know whether in 476 Odoacer satisfied his supporters at the expense of large landholders alone, or whether small and medium-sized properties were also parceled out. From northern Italy, where they were probably concentrated at first, the Germanic forces scattered across the rest of the country. But the literal application of the pact of *hospitalitas* would necessarily have led to a definitive fragmentation of the groups of *hospites,* and that in turn would have conflicted with their natural tendency to remain united, lest they be overwhelmed by the more numerous indigenous population.

2

OSTROGOTHS, ROMANS OF ITALY
AND ROMANS OF THE EAST

THEODORIC, king of the Ostrogoths (493–526), was the founder of the first Romano-barbarian kingdom to exist on Italian territory. He cannot, any more than Odoacer, be considered an "invader" in the full sense of the term, because his arrival in Italy was approved, if not actually encouraged, by the eastern emperor Zeno, when he saw that the time had come for an endgame with Odoacer. Unlike Odoacer, however, he was the king of a specific people, with a history behind it, and he descended from a family of ancient Germanic nobility, the Amali.

Even though their rule lasted less than fifty years, the Ostrogoths sank roots into Italy. The words that have passed from their language into Italian cover a vast range of social relations and contexts: nouns such as *arengo* (meeting, gathering place), *astio* (rancor), *stia* (henhouse), *stecca* (stick), *briglia* (bridle), *nastro* (ribbon), *fiasco* (flask), *stanga* (bar), *forra* (gorge); a verb like *smaltire* (to digest); an adjective like *sghembo* (crooked). Place names such as Goito, Godego, and Gottolengo point to so many Ostrogothic settlements. The Gothic term for "victorious" gave the city of Rovigo its name.

The unusual form of the mausoleum in which he was buried in Ravenna led to the formulation, many years ago, of a hypothesis, quite venturesome, to tell the truth: that when the time came to plan his own tomb, the Ostrogothic king at first thought of a building that would be circular in plan, of which many existed in the provinces of the Roman Empire, but that he then changed his mind and decided to give to at least the upper section of his funerary monument an imprint that harkened back to his ethnic origins.[1] The roof or vault of the mausoleum in Ravenna, then, would be nothing other than the reproduction in stone of a large field tent, similar to those used by his people's chiefs during the time of the migrations of peoples. If the hypothesis is accurate (and it is doubtful, at best), then Theodoric's rethinking of his tomb might be linked to the fact—this much is certain—that his relations with the Romans of Italy, begun under more auspicious circumstances, had been progressively deteriorating, until the final break.

At first, the *hospitalitas* operation went forward in a relatively painless manner, because it was kept under control by a very experienced Roman who had worked with Odoacer and who busied himself finding accommodations for the new arrivals in the houses and fields vacated by the soldiers of the Scirian king. Cassiodorus (ca. 490–ca. 580), the Roman who served as Theodoric's spokesman and devoted rivers of eloquence to rendering the image of the new kingdom acceptable, offered an idyllic description of coexistence between Romans and Goths in the Italian countryside:

> Usually, closeness is a cause for friction among men. This time, however, shared possession of the land engendered harmony. It happened that the fact that both peoples lived together caused them to have a single will. The sharing of revenue, which was something unheard of and praiseworthy in every way, produced a union with their masters. With a share of his own landholding, the Roman landlord obtained a defender that assured that his property would remain safe. A single law, fairly established, protected, at the same time, both one and the other. By necessity of things, those who are confined within the boundaries assigned to them wind up loving one another.[2]

Had the era of Romano-barbarian peace truly begun?

To keep from offending the sensibilities of the *hospites*, the word "barbarian" was banished from the official vocabulary. On the bricks used for the restoration of public buildings in the Eternal City, fallen into disrepair during the last years of the Western empire, Theodoric had the following words inscribed: "During the reign of our lord Theodoric, for the good of Rome." The educated Romans who, following the example of Cassiodorus, agreed to collaborate with the Ostrogothic king pushed their zeal to the point of believing, or pretending to believe, that he was a sort of philosopher-king—much like the one Plato had called for—merely because he had been educated at Athens, while he was being held there as a hostage. In any case, studies flourished again, including Greek studies. It was during these years that Anicius Manlius Severinus Boethius (ca. 480–524), another of Theodoric's Roman collaborators, began work on his project of translating into Latin the classics of Greek philosophy. In an era in which bilingualism, which had characterized the centuries of Greco-Roman Hellenism, was vanishing, the few surviving bilingual men of letters became translators, lending to those who were no longer bilingual their valued skills as "experts in one language or the other" *(utriusque linguae periti)*. As for Boethius, he did not accomplish much, but the works that he did manage to translate constituted in practical terms all of Greek philosophy that was available in the West during the High Middle Ages.

In theory, religion—so important in those times for every aspect of social life—should have been a complicating factor in the coexistence between the two ethnic groups. The Ostrogoths were, in fact, Arians. But Theodoric took care to ensure that his compatriots lived in separate quarters, with their own houses of worship, built specially and not confiscated from Catholics. Moreover, the schism in effect between the churches of Rome and Constantinople relegated to a secondary level, in a certain sense, the contrast in faith between Catholic Romans and Arian Ostrogoths.

Cassiodorus also felt a "concern to place the barbarians," in this case the Ostrogoths, in a specific historical context, emphasizing "everything that could be said in [their] favor . . . and rendering them worthy of ruling the Romans."[3] With his *Historia Gothorum* (History of the Goths), to use his own words, "he made the history of the

Goths Roman."⁴ Cassiodorus's History of the Goths has been lost, but a summary of it has survived, composed by Jordanes, who was no longer a Roman, but rather a Goth of Latin culture who lived in the sixth century. This text is sufficient to show us that Cassiodorus had attempted, by manipulating the oral traditions of the Goths, to emphasize their supposed antiquity, identifying them arbitrarily with the Geti, a people of southern Russia mentioned by Herodotus as early as the fifth century BC. The Goths are judged to be more civilized than all the other Germanic peoples and are even compared to the Greeks. Their raids into Asia Minor took on an epic status: "Along the way, they devastated Troy and Ilium, which were just beginning to recover after the war with Agamemnon."⁵

Not satisfied with ruling over Italy, Theodoric was working to make his realm the center of a constellation of Romano-barbarian kingdoms, with Rome at the center. Except for the central role of Rome and the very different way in which he brought it about—two substantial exceptions—this was the project that Charlemagne would undertake successfully three hundred years later. The instruments of Theodoric's plan were the matrimonial ties that he established, by capitalizing on the special regard that the Germanic world seemed to have for Amalian bloodlines, with the various ruling dynasties, in more than one case at odds with one another. He himself married Audofleda, sister of Clovis, king of the Franks (481–511); his sister Amalfrida was married to Thrasamund, king of the Vandals (496–511); his niece Amalberga, the daughter of Amalfrida, was married to Hermanfrid, king of the Thuringians; his first daughter, Arevagni, was married to Alaric II, king of the Visigoths (484–507); his second daughter, Theodegotho, was wed to Sigismund, king of the Burgundians (516–524); his third daughter, Amalasuntha, was espoused to the Eutharic the Amal. "This importance placed on female collaboration in the political field is characteristic of the Germanic world."⁶

Although the Frankish defeat of the Visigoths, at Vouillé in 507 (Alaric II, Theodoric's son-in-law, died in battle), allowed him to annex Provence, it also undermined his hegemonic policies focused on a dynastic and family-based structure, a policy that had earned him the honor of being called the "propagator of the Roman name" in the formerly Roman empire, and the "tamer of the nations," that is, the barbarians. The Franks, in fact, did not mean to play by his rules, which involved "exalting in his dealings with the Romans the superiority of his own rule over the *gentes* [that is, barbarians—*Trans.*], and in his dealings with the barbarians the magnificence and wonderful strength that the Goths derived from their involvement with all that was prestigious in the Roman way of life."[7]

In 519, the new eastern emperor, Justin (514–527), accepted the conditions set by Pope Hormisdas (514–523) to put an end to the schism between the churches of Rome and Constantinople. This move, although it was religious in nature, had immediate political repercussions in Italy. The Romans of Italy began to consider the eastern Romans as friends again, while they started looking with suspicion at the Ostrogoth "heretics." The Ostrogoths, in turn, were certainly aware of the news arriving from Constantinople about the persecutions to which their Arian coreligionists residing in the empire were being subjected.

The reactions of the Romans of Italy against a number of abuses committed by the Ostrogothic government led Theodoric to forbid them officially to bear arms. The order was greeted with outrage. The Ostrogoths were welcome precisely because they defended the Romans' security. It was quite another matter, and unacceptable, to be told that as Romans they no longer had the right to move about armed.

Theodoric realized that part of the Roman Senate had become hostile to him. Suspicious by nature, in 523 he gave credence to accusations against certain senators, and in particular against the patrician Albinus, accused of exchanging letters with the court of Byzantium, charges that had been made by Severus, a native of Africa. Boethius, who had since the previous year held the office of *magister officiorum*—that is, coordinator of all public activities—had tried for his part to keep the matter under wraps, convinced as he was that it was a frame-up; in contrast, the *referendarius* Ciprianus (or Cyprian), whose job it was to keep the king advised of important current affairs, had taken it upon himself to keep the matter alive. Caring little for the reliance that Theodoric placed on Ciprianus, Boethius, when Albinus was brought before the *Consistorium principis,* the supreme governing council comprising a group of Gothic chiefs and high Roman officials, boldly took up his defense: "The accusation of Ciprianus is false, but if Albinus did it, then I and the entire Senate unanimously did it too. It is false, O Lord."[8]

Ciprianus, however, reiterated his view of matters, and on the basis of Boethius's incautious self-accusation the investigation was widened to include him and the entire Senate, where the only one who defended him was the presiding officer, Symmachus, who was also his father-in-law (he had married Symmachus's daughter Rusticiana). Son-in-law and father-in-law paid for their courage with their lives.

In prison in Pavia, Boethius was driven by necessity alone to speak about himself in *The Consolation of Philosophy*—something that was otherwise normally disagreeable, according to Dante: "so that under the pretext of consolation he might defend himself against the perpetual infamy of his exile, by showing it to be unjust, since no other apologist came forward."[9]

And in light of the predictable outcome of the "purely political trial"[10] of which he had been both the protagonist and the intended victim, he set out a picture of relations between Romans and Ostrogoths that differs somewhat from that depicted in Cassiodorus's letters. Cassiodorus's portrayal, then, emerges from this comparison not so much invalidated as completed and partially corrected:

How often have I withstood Conigastus to his face, whenever he has attacked a weak man's fortune! How often have I turned by force Trigulla, the overseer of the Emperor's household, from an unjust act that he had begun or even carried out! How many times have I put my own authority in danger by protecting those wretched people who were harried with unending false charges by the greed of barbarian Goths which ever went unpunished! Never, I say, has any man depraved me from justice to injustice. My heart has ached as bitterly as those of the sufferers when I have seen the fortunes of our subjects ruined both by the rapacity of persons and [by] the taxes of the state. Again, in a time of severe famine, a grievous, intolerable sale by compulsion was decreed in Campania, and devastation threatened that province. Then I undertook for the sake of the common welfare a struggle against the commander of the Imperial guard; though the king was aware of it, I fought against the enforcement of the sale, and fought successfully. Paulinus was a man who had been consul: the jackals of the court had in their own hopes and desires already swallowed up his possessions, but I snatched him from their very gaping jaws. I exposed myself to the hatred of the treacherous informer Cyprian, that I might prevent Albinus, also a former consul, being overwhelmed by the penalty of a trumped-up charge. Think you [Boethius here addresses Philosophy in person] that I have raised up against myself bitter and great quarrels enough?[11]

The image of the "last of the Romans" (Boethius was not, however, the only one to be called this), shut up in the prison tower of Pavia and consoled by Philosophy, an image appearing in a miniature that decorates a number of illuminated manuscripts of the *De consolatione philosophiae,* is symbolic of the end of the peace between Romans and barbarians in Italy, an illusion that was cultivated for about twenty years by Cassiodorus and others like him, both Goths and Romans.

Pope John I (523–526), on a mission to Constantinople in 525 at the behest of Theodoric, along with a delegation of bishops and senators, had interceded in favor of the empire's Arian subjects and had obtained the repeal of certain discriminatory provisions. He was unable, however, to procure for those Arians who had been forced to convert the right to profess their original faith once again. John was greeted in Constantinople with full honors (it was the first time that a pope had visited the city), but upon his return to Ravenna John was held in isolation, awaiting the king's pleasure. Before Theodoric could decide on his next step, John died, in May 526. The delicate balance that the Ostrogothic king had been working to preserve was now lost. After two months of bitter struggle over who would be John's successor, in the wake of a death that was widely considered to have been that of a martyr, Pope Felix IV (526–530) was elected "by the will [*arbitrio*] of Theodoric," as King Atalaric (516–534), son of Amalasuntha, would later openly state in his words of thanks to the Romans for having honored his grandfather's preferences.[12]

Theodoric refused to admit defeat and set about organizing a naval expedition, with no less an objective than Constantinople itself. His death, in August 526, rendered moot the great question of whether the planned attack would succeed. An expedition did take place ten years later, but in the opposite direction. This time, Byzantium sent a fleet to attack Italy. The result, after a war that lasted almost twenty years, was the end of the Ostrogothic kingdom and the restoration of the empire on the peninsula. No longer charged with the mission of becoming the capital of the Romano-barbarian West, in order to draw it back into Rome's ideal sphere of influence, as Theodoric had attempted to do, Italy would now become under Justinian (527–565, nephew of and successor to Justin) a province just like all the others—though for only a short time, as we shall see—an outlying satellite of the true center of imperial power: the New Rome of the East.

A legend that was widespread among the Romans of Italy claimed that Theodoric was seized by the devil and hurled into the crater of Lipari. In the Germanic legend, Dietrich von Bern, as Theodoric of Verona was known (so dubbed because it was in Verona that he had defeated Odoacer in 489, and where he had often lived, in a palace that he had built for himself), is the very personification of a dignified, austere, and patient hero who when put to the test was invincible.

Having secured Africa from the Vandals (533–534) and having thus won control of the sea, Justinian saw his chance to intervene in Italy in the midst of the groundswell of outrage among the Roman population, and among some Goths as well, that followed the killing of Queen Amalasuntha (who was regent after Theodoric's death on behalf of her son Atalaric and who followed a policy of peaceful coexistence with the Romans) at the orders of Theodatus (534–536, Theodoric's nephew as the son of his sister Amalfrida, and chief of the Gothic nationalist forces). In 535, two Byzantine armies—one marching from Dalmatia, the other from Sicily—simultaneously launched an invasion of Italian territory.

From the very outbreak of hostilities, the Romans of Italy realized that the other Romans (those of the east) who had come from far away to free them from the Ostrogoths were likewise foreigners, and not only because they spoke a foreign language—that is, Greek—but also because they had an exotic appearance, which contrasted to some degree with their desire to be welcomed as brothers (supposing, though it is only a supposition, that they indeed wished to be and took the time to express this wish). They were irremediably "other."

The adjective "Byzantine" with which historians from this point on identify what had hitherto been the Eastern Roman Empire was not coined until much later. It derives from Byzantium, the name of the fortress that stood on the spot where Constantine, in AD 330, had founded his new capital: Constantinople. But the Byzantines of the time, who had never heard of this name that we moderns are accustomed to use for them, continued to refer to themselves as *romaioi* ("Romans," in Greek). The emperors who sat on the throne of Constantinople until 1453, when the city was conquered by the Osmanli, or Ottoman Turks, and the Byzantine Empire ceased to exist, all considered themselves legitimate successors of the Caesars of ancient Rome. In reality, as early as the sixth century in the empire over which they ruled, the only Roman aspects that survived were the political organization (though it too was undergoing a radical transformation) and the conception of the state. But the state, by this point, had been almost entirely grecized with regard to language and culture and was dominated by elements that were in part or entirely eastern. The empire's finest soldiers had for many years been recruited in the provinces of Asia Minor, especially in Isauria.

Relations between the Romans of Italy and the Romans of the east during the years of the Gothic-Byzantine war (535–553) had many of the qualities of a dialogue between deaf people, set against the background of an immense collective tragedy in the wake of which Italy lay drained and depopulated, even though the figure of more than fifteen million dead cited by Procopius has only exclamatory value. Procopius meant us to understand that a great many had died. During the war, Rome suffered four sieges and changed hands five times. An incessant counterpoint to the ups and downs of the war were the sufferings of the *ordo senatorius,* which was decimated and scattered to the winds.

Procopius himself cannot completely gloss over the difficulties, suspicions, friction, and misunderstandings that plagued relations between the local population and the imperial army. For the Romans of Italy, both armies were an endless source of problems:

> The commanders of the Roman army, as well as the soldiers, were plundering the possessions of their [Italian] subjects, and they did not shrink from any act of insolence and licentiousness whatsoever. . . . As for the Italians, the result of the situation for them was that they all suffered most severely at the hands of both armies. For while, on the one hand, they were deprived of their lands by the enemy [the Ostrogoths], the emperor's army, on the other hand, took all their household goods. And they were forced besides to suffer cruel torture and death for no good cause, being hard pressed as they were by the scarcity of food. For the soldiers [of Justinian], though utterly unable to defend them when maltreated by the enemy, not only refused to feel the least blush of shame at existing conditions, but actually made the people long for the barbarians by reason of the wrongs they committed.[13]

Of course, the Ostrogoths tried to gain every possible advantage from the disappointment of the Romans of Italy—as the reader can see, we hesitate to call them outright "Italians," even though the Greek text uses *italiotai* and reserves the term *romaioi* for the Romans of the East. The memory of the tragic deaths of Boethius and Symmachus began to fade among the Romans of Italy. Many of them began to feel a degree of nostalgia for the good rule of Theodoric. Totila, king of the Ostrogoths (541–552), wrote to the Roman Senate around 544:

> Has it really come to pass that you are ignorant of the good deeds of Theoderic and Amalasuntha, or that they have been blotted from your minds with the lapse of time and forgetfulness? No, indeed; neither one of these is true. . . . But was it because you had been informed by hearsay or learned by experience the righteousness of the Greeks toward their subjects that you decided to abandon to them as you did the cause of the Goths and Italians? At any rate, you, for your part, have, I think, entertained them royally, but you know full well what sort of guests and friends you have found them, if you have any recollection of the public accounts of Alexander.[14]

About this Alexander and his deeds, it is once again Procopius who tells us that:

> The Byzantines indeed went so far as to call him by the name "Snips," because it was an easy feat for him to cut off the edge all around a golden coin, and while thus making it as much smaller as he wished, still to preserve the circular shape it originally had. For they call the tool with which such work is done "snips." This Alexander . . . summoned the Italians . . . to face an investigation, laying to their charge the wrongs they had done Theoderic and the other Gothic rulers, and compelling them to pay whatever gains they had made, as he alleged, by deceiving the Goths.[15]

It seemed unbelievable, but this imperial officer criticized the Romans of Italy for having enriched themselves at the Ostrogoths' expense, and demanded that their ill-gotten gains be returned to the coffers of the empire!

The two mosaics in the apse of the church of San Vitale in Ravenna depict, respectively, Justinian and the empress Theodora (d. 548), each with a retinue, as they offer bread and wine for the Mass of consecration for the basilica, a Mass that was held in the time of the archbishop Maximian, perhaps in 547. The long war with the Ostrogoths had not yet ended, even if the two mosaics are presented as a celebratory monument to the victory won by Justinian over Theodoric's successors. As had already happened in once-Vandalic Africa and later the section of Spain that had once been Visigothic, extending from Cartagena to the Atlantic, now all of Italy, with the Old Rome, became Roman once again. In theory, it was all that was needed to give life to a slightly diminished version of the former Western Roman Empire. But Justinian did not consider it wise to create a successor to Romulus Augustulus.

ONE SALIENT aspect of the centuries (how many?) of transition from the ancient world to the Middle Ages consists, in Italy as well, of the abandonment of the cities by all those who were able to flee, to escape the risks of the frequent changes in regime following the invasions. The large landholders retired to the countryside, to live in sumptuous dwellings, the *villae,* which were sometimes even fortified, where the owners were surrounded by small armies of slaves and *coloni.* Since ancient civilization had been, by definition, an urban civilization, the crisis of the cities is one of the clearest indicators of the arrival of new times, characterized by different forms of settlement and, above all, different forms of social organization. One episode of the Gothic-Byzantine war offers enlightenment on the subject.

In an effort to win for the Gothic cause the support of the less fortunate classes in the local population, King Totila, in the decisive phase of the conflict, expropriated the large landholdings that constituted the economic foundation of the senatorial aristocracy. He also declared those living in servitude on those large landholdings free from all bonds. He then armed them and inducted them into his army. He also authorized marriage between slave men and free women and between slave women and free men, thus striking at the roots of the structures of a society based on slavery. In Lucania, however, the *coloni* took sides against Totila and in favor of the large landholders, demanding the restitution of the lands to their traditional owners. Clearly, they believed that the large landholders alone were capable of assuring them a minimal level of safety and a living.[16]

Even though it is hard to say to what degree we can generalize from this episode, the choice of the Lucanian *coloni* still preserves its exemplary value on the boundary between an age in which a strong state authority guaranteed, and therefore gave a meaning to, the distinction between free men and slaves, and the new era of the High Middle Ages, in which a single individual, whatever his legal status, could find needed protection only by entering into a relationship of personal dependency with someone with greater material resources and therefore greater power. The "liberty" offered by the Ostrogothic king was a meaningless piece of flattery that no longer fooled anyone.

Alongside the *villae* of the *beati possidentes* (blessed landowners), the monasteries represented another, radically different alternative for those who wished to leave the cities behind them.

The Rule of St. Benedict was written between 530 and 560, during or shortly after the Gothic-Byzantine war. The extraordinary success that it was to enjoy, beginning in the ninth century, was due to the fact that Benedict had been able to adapt the original ideal of monasticism, as it had developed over the previous two centuries, especially in the Libyan desert and in Egypt, to the situation in central Italy in those decades of terribly grave political and social crisis. His rule allowed monks to work in the fields, in contrast with the prohibitions made by previous monastic legislators. He justified this change by the critical condition, the poverty, in which those monks lived. Those who worked the land, moreover, needed special treatment in the area of fasting and the scheduling of the daily meal. Benedict did not hesitate to modify the rigid observances of monasticism at its origins.

Without distinguishing between *extranei* and *hospites,* as the author of the so-called *Rule of the Master* had done—a work that Benedict had always before him, "in content and in structure," while drawing up his own rule—Benedict ordered that *all those* who knock at the monastery's gates

> shall be welcomed as Christ because he will say: I WAS A GUEST AND YOU MADE ME WELCOME. . . . It is most especially in the reception of the poor and of pilgrims that attentive care is to be shown, because in them Christ is all the more received. Dread is enough of itself to secure honour for the rich. . . . No one, who is not authorized to do so, shall associate or speak at all with guests; but should he meet or see them, let him, as we have said, pass on, after greeting them most humbly, . . . saying that he is not allowed to speak with a guest.[17]

Peregrini, as we shall see, still meant "foreigners, strangers." For them, as for *pauperes,* the warmest welcome was reserved. Around them too, however, the calamities of the time demanded that a barrier of silence be erected.

3

THE LONGOBARDS IN WAR AND PEACE
AND THE ORIGINS OF THE TEMPORAL
DOMINION OF THE POPES AND OF VENICE

ITALY'S RETURN to the political nexus of the Eastern Roman Empire lasted only fifteen years. In 569, the first real invaders entered Italy, crossing the Julian Alps from their base of operations in Pannonia: the Longobards led by King Alboin (d. 572). They had come to stay, bringing their women and children.

They certainly knew the way: Longobard forces had fought in Italy on the side of the empire during the Gothic-Byzantine war. It is, however, anything but certain that the invasion took place according to a preexisting plan that called for the occupation of the Po Valley and Tuscany and an in-depth infiltration along the Apennine ridge, to prevent any potential Byzantine offensives in response, starting from the coastal cities of southern Italy. In any case, the Longobards never occupied all of Italy. Alongside a "Longobard" Italy there continued to exist, until the very end, a "Roman" Italy, which meant a Greco-Byzantine Italy.

Two present-day Italian regions, Lombardy and Romagna, still preserve in their names an artifact of this division. Before shrinking to its present-day boundaries, Lombardy for centuries corresponded to the entire Po Valley. In the twelfth century, the league of Bergamo, Brescia, Verona, Cremona, Bologna, Modena, Milan, Mantua, and others was called the Lombard League. And the term "Lombards" was used to describe Italian merchants active in northern Europe from the twelfth century on and, in particular, in the first half of the fourteenth century, to the degree that traces remain in the place names of the most important cities north of the Alps.

But neither in Lombardy nor in Romagna did Longobard or Byzantine domination last, at least not as long as in southern Italy. In Benevento, the capital of a duchy and, beginning in 774, a Longobard principality that survived for two and a half centuries after the fall of the kingdom of Pavia, the church of Santa Sofia commemorates the memory of its builder, Prince Arechi II (d. 787), who, as his successor Adelchis would say in 866, "following the example of his ancestors, ruled with nobility and honor what remained of his people."[1]

According to Paulus Diaconus, or Paul the Deacon (720/730–ca. 799), who wrote the story of that people when the Longobard king of Italy had already ceased to exist, King Authari (574–590) ventured beyond Benevento, as far as Reggium, "the last city of Italy. . . . And since it is said that a certain column is placed there among the waves of the sea, that he went up to it sitting upon his horse and touched it with the point of his spear saying: 'The territories of the Langobards will be up to this place.'"[2]

The anecdote reflects an intention that, though it may actually have been conceived, was nevertheless not carried out. Calabria and Apulia (now known as Puglia) remained Byzantine possessions until the Norman Conquest.

Both the part of Italy that had become Longobard and the part that remained imperial were ruled by people from outside and from far away. For the imperial rulers, there was the aggravating circumstance, if we may use the terminology, that the "exarch" set up in Ravenna was an official answerable to a power based outside the peninsula. Byzantine civil functionaries, commanders, and military garrisons in Italy, whatever their number may have been in any given period and circumstance, were subject to routine rotation. As a result, leaving aside the cases of individuals who might have married a local and therefore wound up settling in Italy, there was no issue of intermingling with the native population.

The Longobards, in contrast, tended to put down roots in Italy. They had been the most numerous, as well as the politically and militarily dominant group, in the array of different peoples that had streamed into Italy in 569: roughly two hundred thousand people. Once they had settled on Italian territory, they began to define themselves as a distinct people, endowed with a "sharply stratified . . . nucleus of historic and mythical traditions"³ that differentiated them from the other Germanic peoples. Immediately there developed for them the problem of intermingling with the Romans of the peninsula. In contrast with Pannonia, their previous base of operations, a virtually deserted land, Italy was an urbanized and densely populated place, even after the terrible losses inflicted during the two decades of the Gothic-Byzantine war. In Pannonia, in contact with the empire, under whose banners they had fought on numerous occasions, the Longobards had learned to imitate Byzantine goldsmith work. But their ordinary eating utensils, unearthed by archaeologists, along with their buckles and bracelets made of precious metals, still had a Germanic style. Once they were in Italy, however, they adopted for their everyday use the utensils employed in the country that was destined to become their permanent home after so much wandering.

One of the essential innovations that their new environment suggested in time to the invaders was the use of writing, which allowed them to record in Latin (thereby obliging them to make use of local scribes) the saga of their origins, and in particular the element that served as its basic structure, that is, the list of kings, once they decided to establish one, as well as—and this was even more important in practical terms—their ancient customs, handed down up to this point only through oral tradition. Once they were fixed in written form, those customs acquired a vague patina of Roman-ness. Legal historians disagree about the depth of that patina. Their "runes," graphic characters that were peculiar to the primitive Germanic world, could be used only for brief inscriptions on stone or on weapons, often in a magical context. They certainly could not have been used for a codex of laws like that drawn up under King Rothari in 643 and called, in Roman style, the Longobard Edict.

The Longobards took control of Italy by force. The "dukes" (this term, too, was a nod to Roman style, and designated the chiefs of the larger groupings into which the invading army split after the conquest) chose to reside in the most important cities, reduced to shadows of their former selves, in most cases—but still cities, sharply different from the surrounding territory, if for no other reason than that each was the see of a bishop, and now the seat of a Longobard duke.

In competition with the old Roman cities, however, new centers of power, such as Seprio, a formerly Byzantine castle set high above the valley of the river Olona, reflected the disruption of the old territorial organization and the ensuing barbarization of the countryside. Castelseprio, set as an outpost guarding a stretch of the northern boundaries of the Longobard kingdom of Italy, became in this period far more important than Milan, the former capital of the Western empire.

Under the Longobards, the old mechanism of *hospitalitas,* so celebrated in its day by Cassiodorus, who saw in it a sort of panacea capable of ensuring the peaceful coexistence of Romans and the barbarian invaders, no longer functioned at all. Or perhaps we should say that it was put into effect only in a confused way, once the harsh initial collision between the native inhabitants and the new arrivals had produced devastating effects. According to Paul the Deacon, who was especially interested in what happened at the highest levels of society, those hardest hit were also those with the most to lose: the rich and powerful. About the second Longobard king, Cleph (572–574), he says that "of many powerful men of the Romans some he destroyed by the sword and others he drove from Italy."[4] But the worst happened after Cleph's death:

> After his death the Langobards had no king for ten years but were under the dukes. . . . In these days many of the noble Romans were killed from love of gain, and the remainder were divided among their "guests" and made tributaries, that they should pay the third part of their products to the Langobards. By these dukes, . . . the

greater part of Italy . . . was seized and subjugated by the Langobards [after] the churches were despoiled, the priests killed, the cities overthrown, the people who had grown up like crops annihilated.[5]

Paul the Deacon was writing two centuries after the events occurred. His descriptions are based on a contemporary source that has since been lost. That source may have been discussing a limited area of Longobard Italy. It is therefore possible that things went differently in other areas.

Many place names still in use that include the word *fara* (Fara d'Alpago, Fara Vicentina, Fara d'Adda, Fara Sabina, and so on), scattered all over, go back to so many minor Longobard settlements, a clear indicator of the capillary nature of the conquest. A *fara* was a small nucleus of warriors, perhaps belonging to the same clan, which constituted the core of a duchy. Among the Longobards, as among the Germans in general, blood relations had great political and social importance.

The disappearance, in documents written during the Longobard era, of the word *domus* (meaning city residence), replaced by *casa,* which for an ancient Roman had been a country hut made of straw and wood, and the presence of the Germanic word *sala,* to indicate a room made of masonry, both clearly show that the more socially elevated part of the population belonged to the invading people.

The economic quality of life was on the whole quite low. Longobard kings generally neglected the minting of coins in base metals used for small payments. This tells us a great deal about the nature of day-to-day transactions. Neither the stones of Castelseprio and the other sites explored by archaeologists since the end of the Second World War nor the few written documents tell us anything about the thousands of ways in which, day by day, the Longobard invaders and the vanquished Romans adapted to coexistence. The intermingling can be said to have been completed by the eleventh century, when in Tuscan documents the term *lambardi* (a variant of *lombardi*), which, over and above the other meanings mentioned earlier, was taken to indicate "the minor rural aristocracy, . . . vassals, chatelains, and militias"—that is, "a new development of an essentially social nature," which had nothing to do with the "methods of the barbarian settlement and deployment and the episodes of the Longobard conquest."[6]

The harsh initial impact was followed by a process of reciprocal adaptation. The Church, tied in so many ways to the world of the rich and powerful, bore the full brunt of the first phase. It survived the ordeal, however, and found itself in a position to encourage the development in the second phase, reinforced by its strong hold on the masses of faithful of Roman descent. It was necessary, however, to take into account the other interested party: the Longobards. On the eve of the expedition into Italy, Alboin had promised, out of political calculation, to convert his people to Arianism. In the Byzantine strongholds, a fifth column of Arian Goths facilitated the task of the invaders. But the Longobards, behind the appearance of the mass baptism, had remained pagans deep down; you don't turn Christian from one day to the next. As for the Catholic clergy, its voice would have had some possibility of being heard, in theory, because it was a schismatic clergy, obstinately rejecting the condemnation of the so-called Three Chapters imposed by Justinian at the fifth ecumenical council (Constantinople, 553). This decision, which had at first been rejected by the papacy and then reluctantly accepted, wound up indirectly reopening for discussion a decree of the fourth ecumenical council (Chalcedonia, 451), which had opted for the thesis according to which Christ was a person with two distinct natures, divine and human, and not with an exclusively divine nature, as the "Monophysites" claimed. The fact that Catholic bishops and priests were also schismatics warded off suspicions that they were agents of the Byzantine enemy, working from within the Longobard kingdom. With the passage of time, however, the stubborn persistence of the Three Chapters schism in the dioceses of northern Italy became a serious stumbling block to the creation of a climate of reciprocal trust between the kingdom and Rome.

Sermons from the pulpit were not particularly useful. They were rendered all the more useless from the very beginning by the difficulties of communicating, given the differences in language. Only the occurrence of miracles, in the narrowest sense of the word, would have sufficed to persuade the invaders, who were still—as we have said—profoundly pagan, that the god of the Romans was much more powerful than all their gods put together. But if miracles were to be requested, saints were necessary, and in the Italy of the time saints were apparently in very short supply. It was precisely to react to the defeatism of his contemporaries and to provide evangelizers with an arsenal of irrefutable arguments that Pope Gregory the Great (590–604) wrote the four books of the *Dialogues*. In these books he reviewed the stories of a great number of relatively recent Italian saints (especially from central and southern Italy), both bishops and abbots. One whole book was devoted to a man said to have performed more miracles than all the others put together: Benedict of Nursia. Gregory even praised Benedict's monastic rule, though only in passing.

About Paulinus, bishop of Nola in the fourth century, Gregory writes that a widow came to him to ask for money to ransom her son, taken prisoner by the son-in-law of the king of the Vandals.[7] Since Paulinus did not possess such a sum, he offered to travel to Africa with the widow, pretending to be her slave. When they reached their destination, the widow proposed to the king's son-in-law that he exchange her son for Paulinus. The Vandal looked at this man of noble appearance and asked him what he knew how to do. "I possess no arts," Paulinus answered, "but I do know how to cultivate a vegetable garden." A deal was struck. Mother and son returned to Italy; Paulinus stayed behind and became a gardener.

One day Paulinus said to his master: "Make the necessary arrangements immediately. Consider how to safeguard the kingdom of the Vandals, because your father-in-law the king will die very soon." Paulinus's master informed the king, who asked to see the man who had spoken these words. The meeting took place at the son-in-law's table. As soon as the king sat down, Paulinus came in with a basket of fresh vegetables. The king immediately began to tremble because the night before he had seen him in a dream; Paulinus had been in the company of other judges, and together they had been judging the king and stripping him of his scepter. He must be someone important, not just an ordinary gardener! At the insistent questioning of his master, Paulinus confessed who he was. The king's son-in-law asked him to tell him what he wanted. He was ready to grant his wishes. Paulinus replied: "There is only one thing that you can do for me: release all the prisoners from my region." And the king's son-in-law immediately ordered a search carried out throughout Africa. And then, to the great joy of the venerable Paulinus, he set them all free, sending them back home in ships loaded with grain.

A few days later, the king of the Vandals died and thus lost the scepter with which, by the will of God, he had held the faithful in submission. And the prophecy of Paulinus thus came true; and he, who alone had offered to go into slavery, recovered his own liberty along with that of many others, a faithful imitator of the one who had taken the form of a servant, in order that we might not remain enslaved to sin.

At the beginning of the seventh century, there was an acceleration in the gradual process of adjustment. The conversion of the Longobards to Catholicism seemed to be at hand. A few Romans from the old ruling class began to cooperate with the invaders, in positions of renewed prestige, as had been the case under the Goths.

—⁂—

ENCOURAGEMENT was given by Theodolinda, a Bavarian Catholic princess who was married to two Longobard kings in succession: Authari and Agilulf (590–616). It was during her lifetime that Catholic churches began to be built inside a number of Longobard castles. In 602, the abbot of a Trentine monastery gave Catholic baptism in Monza to Adaloaldus, son of Theodolinda and Agilulf. A legend flourished in time concerning Theodolinda:

But after these events, king Flavius Authari sent ambassadors to Bavaria to ask for him in marriage the daughter of Garibald their king. The latter received them kindly and promised that he would give his daughter Theudelinda to Authari. . . . He desired to see his betrothed for himself and bringing with him a few but active men out of the Langobards, and also taking along with him, as their chief, one who was most faithful to him, he set forth without delay for Bavaria. And when they had been introduced into the presence of king Garibald . . . and he who had come with Authari as their chief had made the usual speech after salutation, Authari, since he was known to none of that nation, came nearer to king Garibald and said: "My master, king Authari has sent me especially on this account, that I should look upon your daughter, his betrothed, who is to be our mistress, so that I may be able to tell my lord more surely what is her appearance." And when the king, hearing these things, had commanded his daughter to come, and Authari had gazed upon her with silent approval, since she was of a very beautiful figure and pleased him much in every way, he said to the king: "Since we see that the person of your daughter is such that we may properly wish her to become our queen, we would like it if it please your mightiness, to take a cup of wine from her hand, as she will offer it to us hereafter." And when the king had assented to this that it should be done, she took the cup of wine and gave it first to him who appeared to be the chief. Then when she offered it to Authari, who she did not know was her affianced bridegroom, he, after drinking and returning the cup, touched her hand with his finger when no one noticed, and drew his right hand from his forehead along his nose and face. [Theudelinda], covered with blushes, told this to her nurse, and her nurse said to her: "Unless this man were the king himself and thy promised bridegroom, he would not dare by any means to touch thee. But meanwhile, lest this become known to thy father, let us be silent, for in truth the man is a worthy person who deserves to have a kingdom and be united with thee in wedlock." For Authari indeed was in the bloom of youth. . . . Then Authari, when he had now come near the boundaries of Italy and had with him the Bavarians who up to this time were conducting him, raised himself as much as he could upon the horse he was managing, and with all his strength he drove into a tree that stood near by, a hatchet which he carried in his hand and left it fixed there, adding moreover these words: "Authari is wont to strike such a blow." And when he had said these things, then the Bavarians who accompanied him understood that he was himself king Authari.[8]

The years of Theodolinda, while perhaps not actually the "summer of the dead," were also hardly the harbinger of a coming spring.[9] The Romans that we find in positions of importance had been educated under the old regime. They were survivors, rather than up-and-coming individuals. The road that lay ahead until the Longobards could absorb the values embodied by the "vanquished Romans" and win appreciation for the values that they embodied in their turn had a steep uphill grade. They would not, moreover, have time to reach the end of that difficult road.

Conversion to Roman Catholicism, an indispensable condition first of all for peaceful coexistence, and then for complete union with the Roman population, took place only gradually. It can be said to have been completed only toward the end of the seventh century. And not in the sense that the Longobards had in the meantime all become good Christians (for that matter, the Romans weren't either!), but rather in the sense that the ethical and religious principles shared by their ruling classes, which were beginning to inspire the additions made to the edict of Rothari by his successors, were roughly identical with the principles that were being preached from the pulpits. At the beginning of the eighth century, the concept of sin began to appear in Longobard legislation.[10]

The kings of Pavia by this point were fond of portraying themselves as devout builders of churches, generous founders and benefactors of monasteries, zealous scouts for and purveyors of saints' relics. King Liutprand (712–744), also, hearing that the Saracens had laid waste Sardinia and were even defiling those places where the bones of the bishop St. Augustine had been formerly carried on account of the devastation of the barbarians and had been honorably buried, sent and gave a great price and took them and carried them over to the city of Ticinum [Pavia] and there buried them with the honor due to so great a father.[11]

And again:

He was indeed a man of much wisdom, very religious and a lover of peace, shrewd in counsel, powerful in war, merciful to offenders, chaste, modest, prayerful in the night-watches, generous in charities, ignorant of letters indeed, yet worthy to be likened to philosophers, a supporter of his people, an increaser of the law. At the beginning of his reign he took very many fortresses of the Bavarians. He relied always more upon prayers than upon arms, and always with the greatest care kept peace with the Franks and the Avars.[12]

At this point, the story is interrupted, probably owing to the death of the author, who, even though he knew just how things had turned out for his people with the catastrophe of 774 (he began work just after 786–787), reiterates right up to the end the point that was closest to his heart—that is, to defend against "the rejection of the Longobards by the Popes of his time . . . the equal worth of a different origin and . . . assuring equal care and love of God toward them."[13] But before the infamy of being *nefandissima gens* that Gregory the Great (590–604) had pinned on them at the very start could be removed,[14] it was not enough for the last remnants of paganism and Arianism to be stripped away, or for the Three Chapters schism to be entirely reabsorbed, with a return to Roman obedience on the part of the Catholics of the Longobard kingdom. It was also necessary that they remain at peace with their neighbors, contentedly respecting the boundaries that had been established in 680, when the empire, even though it was traditionally so reluctant to acknowledge *faits accomplis*, officially gave up all claims to the territories that had been occupied until then by the Longobards. But "this patience was not found in Liutprand's successors. Not Ratchis [744–749], who began his reign in harmony with the Pope. . . . Nor Aistulf [749–756] who, with total consistency, but failing to muster sufficient forces and consensus, attempted the only alternative that was theoretically possible: a full attack. . . . And not Desiderius [757–774], who practiced a policy aiming in several directions, . . . and was finally left virtually alone to stave off the attack of the Frankish army. Desiderius was defeated, and with his defeat the experience of the Longobard kingdom came to an end (774)."[15]

In a certain sense, if they failed to exercise the "patience" that might have been advisable, it was precisely because of their awareness that they were now ready to sweep away all that remained of the Byzantine dominions in central and northern Italy, in a first step toward the achievement of the goal that, at least according to Paul the Deacon, had been expressed by King Authari a little less than two centuries earlier on the beach of Reggium. It would seem to be a genuine anachronism to attribute to eighth-century Longobards the intention—as Gregory the Great, mentioned above, did not hesitate to do (and perhaps at the time he had his own good reasons for doing so)—of wanting to make him "the bishop not of the Romans but of the Longobards" themselves, "agreements with whom are like swords, and their favor like a punishment."[16] Was it not perhaps true that King Liutprand had ordered to be written very clearly, in his additions to the edict, that the pope was "chief of the churches and priests of all the world"?[17]

The popes, at least to judge by appearances, had no special interest in defending the status quo on the peninsula. The emperors and the patriarchs of Constantinople, in fact, lost no opportunity to support or promote, jointly, theological or disciplinary positions that were in conflict with the teachings of the Roman Church. Moreover, it was precisely during the reign of Liutprand that the emperor Leo III Isauricus (717–741), who was practically his contemporary—in order to cover the expenses of the war against the Arab Muslims, who had gone so far in 717 as to threaten the very capital of the empire—ratcheted up the tax burden on the southern and island possessions of Saint Peter, which had enjoyed an especially favorable treatment up to that time. The refusal of Gregory II (715–731) to submit to this measure, which he considered unfair, triggered a conflict with the imperial government—for once on different grounds from the usual ecclesiastic and religious ones. The features of the conflict, however, remained familiar. After having tried twice, in vain, to eliminate the pontiff physically, Leo did his best to have him dethroned, and therefore concocted a trial against him (the pope) for the crime of *lèse majesté*. But the army corps sent from Ravenna to Rome found, at just the strategic moment, that its path was blocked by mixed Longobard militia from the realm of Tuscia and the duchy of Spoleto. Gregory had not hesitated to request their help.

Later, for reasons that have not been entirely understood, Leo undertook a systematic campaign to destroy sacred images ("iconoclasty") in all the provinces of the empire, including those in Italy. In this case as well, Gregory refused to accept the imperial dictates in the area of worship and further rejected the trade-off that was proposed: if Gregory agreed to the campaign, Leo said that he was willing to dismiss the charges of *laesa maiestas*. In contrast with other "new ideas," this campaign against sacred images profoundly disturbed the populace of Byzantine Italy, which rose up against the imperial authorities, expelling the dukes appointed by Constantinople and electing local dukes in their place. The slow but inexorable process of "estrangement"[18] between the Old and the New Rome thus experienced a sudden acceleration. There was a moment at which the Longobards seemed to be taking advantage of the favorable opportunity to step forward and to support the people of the peninsula in open revolt against the imperial power, destroyer of sacred images, thus prompting the enthusiasm of the papal biographer who already envisioned Longobards and Romans "bound together, almost as if they were brothers, by the chains of faith."[19] But the moment passed.

The popes in those decades which were so crucial to the future of Italy did not seem to draw from events the conclusion that seemed inescapable, that is, about the necessity to make a definitive break with Byzantium. With respect for tradition and, in a certain sense, a sort of intimidation in the face of the empire—an intimidation that dated back to the time of Constantine the Great, even though the prestige and the authority of the throne of Peter had grown to an extraordinary degree—those popes remained unwaveringly faithful to the empire, in spite of everything, to the point that they provided diplomatic support to the Byzantine revival when in 732 King Liutprand occupied Ravenna. In a letter to Antoninus, patriarch of Grado, Gregory II's successor Gregory III (731–741) wrote that Ravenna, "capital of one and all"—inasmuch as it was the headquarters of the unified supreme command to which were answerable all the "duchies" (including the Duchy of Rome) that made up Byzantine Italy—should be reintegrated into the *respublica*—that is, the empire—in the service of emperors Leo and Constantine (Leo's son), "in order that, with our fervent efforts on behalf of the holy faith, and with our love for that faith, we may be permitted to persist firmly, with God's help, in the stability of the *respublica* and in service to the empire."[20]

It is pointless to wonder how the much-touted *zelus et amor fidei* could be reconciled with a *servitium* due to emperors whom the pope himself had solemnly excommunicated the year before in a council that the recipient of the letter of commendation had attended. A determined loyalty to the Christian empire demanded such leaps in logic.

The force of inertia exerted by tradition, which tends to favor the old and the familiar (however serious the shortcomings), as opposed to the new with all its unknown factors, was unable over the long term, however, to counter the push exerted in the opposite direction by the ineluctable necessities of politics. Thus, to defend themselves from the increasingly imminent threat of an attack brought by the Longobards against Rome itself, the popes of those decades, clearly

aware that they could no longer rely on the empire, took repeated
steps, in a daring political and diplomatic campaign, to win the alliance of the adjoining central and southern Longobard duchies of
Spoleto and Benevento, which always stood ready, for their part, to
establish their de facto independence from the kingdom of Pavia.
This triggered a predictable reaction from Liutprand. He went so far
as to lay siege to Rome not once but twice, the very same king
who—according to Paul the Deacon—put more stock "in prayers
than arms."

One decisive factor affecting the behavior of the popes in the intricate circumstances in which they found themselves, during the middle decades of the eighth century, was the unprecedented status that
they were acquiring during that span of time as the territorial masters of what has been called the Republic of Saint Peter (the designation of *Patrimonium san Petri* for the papal "temporal dominion" of
the early years, even though it is documented only as far back as
the second half of the twelfth century, is, however, preferable).[21]
This status would take increasingly distinct form beginning around
the year 680, following a long series of forerunners that can be dated
back to the time of Gregory the Great, at least as far as the exercise by the Roman Church of an increasingly extensive "temporal
power" is concerned (quite distinct from "dominion" over a territory). It was unmistakably established following the definitive conquest of Ravenna, accomplished by King Aistulf at the beginning
of 750.

The Duchy of Rome, like the other Byzantine duchies on the peninsula, remained at this point cut off from the decision-making center to which, at least in theory, it answered. It ceased to exist as a political entity, but it survived as a territorial entity, corresponding
roughly to present-day Lazio, or Latium. In contrast with what happened in Venice or Naples, where dukes with local roots were
elected, in Rome it was the pope himself who replaced, in practice
and without much notice, the duke named by Constantinople. From
that point onward, Rome was no longer merely the seat of the

"chief of the churches and priests of the whole world" and an increasingly popular destination for pilgrimages to the tombs of Peter and Paul, but rather the center—we hesitate to say the capital—of a full-fledged territorial dominion. Moreover—not to mention the contacts, established or reactivated and strengthened, with the Western churches, whose representatives traveled more frequently to Rome—it was precisely during the papacies of Gregory II and Gregory III that the Anglo-Saxon monk Wynfrith (680–754), rebaptized Boniface by Gregory II, traveled to Rome three times. There he received comfort and reassurance concerning the missionary work that he had undertaken with great success, on his own initiative but in the name of Peter and his terrestrial vicar, in Frisia, Hesse, and Thuringia, where Roman legions had never ventured.

The correspondence between the creation of the "temporal dominion" of the Church of Rome and the transformation of the primacy of morality and reputation, which the Church had attained by the second and third centuries, into a practical primacy of a jurisdictional nature—at least over the churches of the West (for Eastern churches, of course, the question is quite different)—changed over time from something informal, because chronological, as it actually was, into the foundation for the thesis that justified the existence of the church state, a thesis that was propounded as late as 1929 in a speech to the parish priests of Rome by Pope Pius XI. According to this view, the exercise of the Roman Church's jurisdictional sovereignty over the universal church necessarily presupposed some degree of political and territorial sovereignty, even though it was, and still is, limited to the modest dimensions of a trapezoidal enclave covering .44 sq. km. carved out of the urban fabric of Rome—the state of Vatican City.

This supposed connection was not perceived at the time, nor was it even glimpsed by those who were directly involved. And yet that did not change matters. It is possible to venture to hypothesize that had it been possible to overcome their inveterate anti-Longobard prejudice, they would have been able to accept a Rome that was the seat of the "chief of the churches and priests of the entire world," forming part of a Longobard Catholic kingdom that extended from the Alps to Reggium. But it is unimaginable that they would have seriously nourished the illusion that the former Byzantine duchy of Rome, entrusted by now to the leadership of the pope, would survive between certain and respected boundaries in an entirely Longobard Italy, protected by a high, and by this point merely theoretical, imperial sovereignty, which had not been formally rejected in 750, considering that as late as 781 papal documents continued to be dated according to the years of the reign of the *basileus*. One thing that might have prevented them from cherishing this hope, and it should have sufficed, was that already on 1 March 750, in the prologue to the laws of his first year of rule, King Aistulf proclaimed that the entire "people of the Romans" on the peninsula—including, therefore, the quota of the Romans and the Latians—had been "assigned to him by the Lord." And yet the biographer of Pope Zachary (741–752) had been able to write that under his rule the "people that God had entrusted to him"—that is, the Romans of Rome and of what was by now the former Roman duchy—had lived "in great security and cheer."[22]

Zachary was the first pope since the times of Justinian to be consecrated without waiting for confirmation from Ravenna or Constantinople. Deploying the techniques of persuasion of which the popes were past masters, he had in fact succeeded, by personally and repeatedly challenging first Liutprand and later Ratchis, and not only in inducing them to restore to Byzantine sovereignty the territories that they had seized for themselves over time. He had also managed, in setting himself up as a representative in Italy of the empire's interests, to negotiate a twenty-year truce with Liutprand in 742 between the Longobard kingdom and the Roman duchy, as it would still be known for only a short while—over which he clearly already at this point exercised a governmental role.

These necessarily precarious equilibriums were brought to an end, with radically differing outcomes for their respective causes, by

Aistulf on the one hand, and Zachary's successor Stephen II (752–757) on the other. According to the biography of Stephen in the *Liber pontificalis*, which is practically the only source of information available to us, and very close to the facts even if partisan by the very nature of things, at first Aistulf seemed to hesitate before undertaking armed action. In June 752 (Stephen had been elected in March), in fact, he extended the period of the truce that Liutprand had conceded to Zachary from twenty years to forty, even though only ten years had passed. Then, however, just four months later, he ordered all Romans to pay one golden *solidus* every year as a gesture of recognition of his "jurisdiction" over the city and the castles of the territory, unless they wished to be invaded. Tied to a cross borne in procession during the night between 14 and 15 August 753, when, as happened every year, the image of the Redeemer, said to be "not made by human hand" [*acheropita* is the Italian transliteration of the Greek—Trans.], was moved from the basilica of St. John Lateran to Santa Maria *ad praesepe* (St. Mary Major), the parchment bearing the agreement that Aistulf had signed in June of the year before was displayed to the Romans who had gathered in great numbers, as proof of his broken faith. It may be that things actually went slightly differently, and that Aistulf should be allowed the benefit of certain attenuating circumstances, even if that term is out of place, since we are not holding a posthumous trial here.[23] It is true that Stephen, in the meantime, had requested that the empire make a return to its old territories in Italy, even as he continued to negotiate with the Longobard king, though Steven placed no reliance on his true intentions. He was fully aware in his heart of hearts that he could not count on that card either. And so he restored a diplomatic channel that had been first opened by a predecessor. That channel had been shown by the course of events to have been the most successful option. Stephen called on the Franks for help.

A horror of new things and a propensity to invent precedents for them, in order to keep them from appearing to be new, seems to be part of the genetic code of the Roman Church. And so the biogra-

pher of Stephen II felt an obligation to point out, in bringing up the
topic of the pope's appeal to Pippin, king of the Franks (751–768)—
lest it be thought that Stephen had been the first to do such a
thing—that up to that point, Gregory II, Gregory III, and Zachary
had made similar appeals to Charles Martel, Pippin's father, mayor
of the palace (716–741) and the de facto ruler of the Merovingian
Frankish kingdom.[24] In fact, however, the only one who had actually
done so was the second of the three. About the third pope mentioned, he might have said (and who can say why he didn't?) that
aside from his close relations with Saint Boniface, who had become
in the meantime not only the "apostle of the Germans," but also a
reformer (less successfully) of the Frankish Church, Zachary had
played a role of primary importance in the accession to the Frankish
throne of the Carolingian dynasty of former palace ministers. Pippin had, in fact, sent to Zachary to ask whether he felt it was more
appropriate for the title of king to be assigned to someone who exercised power in the Frankish kingdom (that is, to himself, Pippin),
or whether it should remain with one who had no power (that is,
Childeric III). Zachary replied that he was in favor of the first alternative, and indeed in November 751 Pippin was anointed king by
Boniface at Soissons.

If we have dwelt at length on these intricate political, diplomatic,
and dynastic events, it is because they played—as we shall see—a
role of considerable importance in laying the groundwork for and
shaping one of the fundamental turning points in the history of Italy: the years that between 774 and 800 witnessed the end of the
Longobard kingdom and the restoration in Rome of the Western
empire.

In the course of the voyage that Stephen II undertook to the
Frankish kingdom in October 753 at the repeated invitation of King
Pippin, the two men came to an understanding, thanks to a series
of meetings that took place in various locations, since that kingdom lacked a capital. On his trip back home, the pope traveled with
the military expedition that Pippin led against Aistulf right up to

the walls of Pavia. When Pippin crossed the Alps, Pope Stephen cautiously remained behind, waiting to cross until the Franks had crushed the resistance of the Longobards at the Chiuse di San Michele. Although it was victorious in military terms, this first expedition failed to solve the problem for which Stephen had requested it. A second expedition was required, which assured him at least on paper, and only in part, of the territorial expansion that he had hoped to obtain. This takes us from October 753 to the summer of 756. In that period of twenty months or so, that "way of proceeding" was tested which was destined to become the typical method of the papacy, and which was to contribute in a decisive way in Niccolò Machiavelli's view to keeping "Italy disunited and weak."[25]

Concerning the negotiations that went on between the pope, the Frankish king, the Longobard king, and the emperor, we have scanty information, and—most important—only from one side: "There are few documents; none of them are of Byzantine or Longobard origin. . . . We cannot listen to the voices of those among the rivals whose rights or whose hopes were sacrificed; only the winners have a say. For the sake of justice, we must keep this circumstance in mind."[26]

Pippin's second campaign ended, like the first, without a capitulation from the Longobards. Apart from the clauses in the treaty of Pavia that directly concerned the Franks (handing over a third of the treasury, depositing a contribution to the war effort, and so forth), the one that required the greatest delicacy in its implementation had none other than Saint Peter as its beneficiary and, serving as Peter's proxy, of course, the pope. It reiterated the commitment, undertaken and then left unfulfilled at the end of the first expedition, in which Aistulf ordered that Ravenna and several other cities in the Ravenna area and in the Marches region (Pentapolis, as it was known at the time), which he had conquered after taking the throne, be handed over to the prince of the apostles. The difference was that this time there was a circumstantial description of the procedure whereby those cities would actually be ceded. It stated that the cities in question should first be delivered to the plenipotentiaries of the Frankish king and then, in a second phase, transferred to the possession of Saint Peter and, in the name of that saint, to the reigning pontiff and his successors. This would take the form of the delivery to Stephen in Rome of an act of donation, signed at Pavia by Pippin. And so it happened, even if this, a genuine donation, and not merely a "promise of donation"—like the incomparably more generous one that Pippin appears to have made to Stephen at Quierzy-sur-Oise during his voyage through the Frankish kingdom (though some doubt that the promise of donation actually took place)—remained incomplete for various reasons, all the way up to the thirteenth century. Likewise, there are a number of points that remain unclear about why this was held forth as a "restitution" to Saint Peter, given that the church had never possessed those cities. If there was to be genuine restitution, then the proper recipient would have been served by handing over the cities *ad partem reipublicae*—in other words, to the empire, which had held them until the recent Longobard conquest.

After 756 a Longobard king still ruled in Pavia. Nonetheless, Pippin's two expeditions into Italy, which Stephen had requested, could always serve as precedents. If necessary, should Rome or Latium be threatened, the Frankish king might well intervene to guarantee its safety. In this connection, one may wonder why the popes, who still feared—much like Gregory the Great, as if time had passed to no good purpose—being reduced to the condition of bishops of the Longobards, and no longer of the Romans, were willing to run the risk of becoming the first bishops of the Frankish territorial church.[27] Their prejudice in favor of the Franks was based essentially on two considerations. First, the decision of King Clovis, first among the Germanic kings to convert, not to Arian Christianity, but directly to Catholicism. Second, the Roman Catholic imprint that Wynfrith-Boniface had impressed on his missionary apostolate beyond the Rhine, with the support of Charles Martel and his son Pippin. A third reason, which is often called into play, has to do with the victory achieved one Saturday in October 733 by Charles Martel over an army of Islamized Berbers from Spain who, at the beginning of the march that would have taken them via Poitiers to Tours, after crossing the Pyrenees at Roncesvalles, had headed across Gascony toward Bordeaux, without the duke of Acquitaine's being able to stop them. One factor that helped Charles in the view of modern readers was the fateful term *europeenses*, used in a Latin text by a cleric of the church of Toledo, thought to have been a native of Cordoba, to describe the Christian warriors of Poitiers. The author lived under Muslim rule and was greatly cheered by the defeat dealt to these invaders of his homeland. From his peninsular and Mediterranean point of view, the victors of Poitiers were described, with no distinctions, as "people from the north," "people from Austrasia" (the northeastern section of the kingdom of the Franks) and . . . "Europeans." And yet only vague and confused reports—if any at all— reached Rome about this victory of Christian Europe over the infidels.[28]

⬤

MUCH AS IN the foundation of the temporal dominion of the popes, the Longobards indirectly and inadvertently played a role in another major event in the history of Italy during the seventh and eighth centuries: the birth of Venice. Following the invasion of 569 from mainland Venetia (which with Histria constituted the ancient *X regio,* the first region to be invaded) the local populace, led by the bishops, began an exodus to the adjoining lagoons. In a famous letter, Cassiodorus described them at length, indulging in a dramatic portrait, as if of some surreal landscape where, seen from a distance, the boats appear to travel through the fields, and then to be tied to the walls of the houses, as if they were domestic animals.[29] Much like aquatic birds, the inhabitants of the lagoon lived between the dry and the wet. Salt was the only resource in an economy characterized by equal poverty for one and all. . . . In the absence of other written sources, archaeologists have taken care to correct Cassiodorus's vision, but not to the point of establishing for certain that the settlements of the period preceding the migrations from the terra firma had the status of cities, or even of ancient villages.

From Alboin to their last king, Desiderius, the Longobards seem not only never to have threatened the islands of the lagoon—in all likelihood in part because they had no fleet—but also, with Aistulf, to have confirmed the right of the lagoon dwellers to preserve ancient rights held by custom and landholdings on terra firma. When Oderzo fell to the Longobards led by King Rothari, the presence of the Byzantines in mainland Venetia was reduced to a bare minimum. That presence also failed to reestablish itself in the lagoon. As a consequence, the spate of refugees from the cities of Venetia—either already occupied by the Longobards or more directly vulnerable to their menace—toward the more remote lagoon islands, and their initial settlements in new locations, seem to have possessed, at least for the first seventy years or so, qualities of spontaneity and self-sufficiency for the most immediate collective needs. One factor that was decisive in the development of the "lagoon identity" was the transfer—at first provisional (immediately following the invasion), then, shortly thereafter, definitive—of the patriarchal see of Aquileia to Grado, its farthest-flung port, at the northeasternmost edge of the lagoon zone, and especially the ordination between 606 and 607, with the support of King Agilulf, of a second patriarch in the old see of Aquileia, in response to the rejection of the schism of the Three Chapters and the vow of loyalty to the Church of Rome made by the patriarch ordained in the new see of Grado. Finally, confirming the fully attained "lagoon identity," in 775–776, the first bishopric originally based on the islands was appointed at Olivolo.

Once Ravenna fell to the Longobards, the various Byzantine duchies found themselves in a condition of fundamental independence, as we have indicated, and at the same time of formal dependency on Constantinople, without the awkward and long-standing intermediary of Ravenna. In the case of the duchy on the lagoon,

Venice, its progressive maritime expansion into the Adriatic and, over time, well beyond that stretch of sea, its most immediate watery domain, constituted a justification of considerable weight and importance for preserving and even intensifying relations with the empire, whose influence over trade in the Mediterranean Sea, even in a time of consolidated Arab Muslim maritime presence, should not be underestimated. Moreover, at least two Byzantine duchies, admittedly in new conditions, continued to exist as such within their traditional borders, and it matters little with what degree of precise definition. And so it is fair to say, however paradoxical it may seem, that Napoleon in 1797 and Victor Emmanuel II in 1870, by putting an end, respectively, to the Republic of Venice and the State of the Church, actually put an end to the historical existence of two formerly Byzantine duchies.[30]

In the time of the doge (at this point we should use the Venetian terminology, and no longer call him duke) Maurizio Galbaio (764–797), a number of indicators allow us to foresee that the entire lagoon area was about to establish a common center of gravity, focused on Rialto and Olivolo. For now this development took the form of increased demographic density and an intensification in the manifestations of civil and religious life. There was not yet a seat of political power; for now, that remained at Malamocco. If in those decades it had been possible to enjoy a panoramic view from on high, as it is in the present day, it would have been possible to see that, among the various settlements scattered across the lands emerging from the waters of the lagoon, one was beginning to differentiate itself from the others. This settlement was taking on the first features of a primarily urban center—a city, unquestionably a city of unusual appearance (though not entirely unprecedented, as was once wrongly thought), and in any case a new city, founded by no one, emerging spontaneously: Venice.

4

IN THE EMPIRE OF CHARLEMAGNE
AND WITHIN THE SHELTER
OF THE CITY WALLS

POPE ADRIAN I (772–795) had managed to prevent Desiderius from marching on Rome in the winter of 772–773 only by threatening to excommunicate him. Adrian then summoned Charles, king of the Franks (768–814), to come to his aid. Charles, after fruitless attempts to persuade Desiderius through diplomatic channels to abandon his ambitions to control the Patrimony of Saint Peter, marched on Italy with his army in the summer of 773. He crossed the Alps via the pass of Mont Cenis, and he shattered the resistance of the Longobards on the valley floor, at the Chiuse di San Michele. He then went on to lay siege to Pavia, capital of the kingdom since the turn of the century. Pavia surrendered in June 774. Instead of annexing the vanquished kingdom to the realm of the Franks, as had been the custom till then, he styled himself king of the Franks and the Longobards. This marked the first time in the Middle Ages that two crowns were united in the hands of the same person.[1]

The warrior tradition of the Longobard kingdom made it the only one, at least in theory, that would have been able to stand its ground against the kingdom of the Franks. Its effective liquidation, despite the continued appearance of life that Charles hoped to give it in 781 by creating a Longobard king, in the person of his second-born son, Pippin, marked a watershed in the history of Italy. Certainly, the course of Italian history would have been quite different if the kingdom of Pavia had not melted away like snow in bright sunshine. This was the lament of Niccolò Machiavelli, who laid all blame at the door of the papacy. He seems, however, to have failed to take into account—Machiavelli, who certainly never overlooked power relations—that the Longobards themselves played a considerable role in events, by failing to live up to their reputation for military prowess at the very moment that destiny had reserved for them, as if the effort they had made to civilize themselves had undermined their age-old superiority as a warrior people.

Having achieved the result that he had set out for, Charles crossed back over the Alps with his people and returned home. The Franks, then, cannot be considered invaders in the same sense that the Longobards had been two centuries earlier.

Between 1820 and 1822, when people began to speak seriously, though still in hushed tones, about independence, unity, and liberty, Alessandro Manzoni wrote a tragedy, *Adelchis,* whose protagonist was the son of the dethroned king of the Longobards, a self-renouncing antihero who rejected the logic of power.

Manzoni, a Catholic, was eager to portray the pope, who had urged Charlemagne to intervene, as the defender of the civil and national rights of the Italians, held in slavery by the Longobards to the very end. He did not wish to use this point, however, to validate the notion that liberation for the Italians could once again come from the intervention of other foreign powers. And so he took care to point out that even back then, precisely because the Longobard question had been resolved by the Franks, intervening as an outside force, the solution had proved to be far from painless. It would have been naive to expect them to be satisfied, as a reward for the good deed that they had come to perform in Italy at the behest of Pope Adrian I, with "turn[ing] back fate," that is, with changing a hostile destiny, and with "put[ting] an end to the suffering" of a foreign people, which the Italians were to them. Far different was the "hoped-for prize," and they did not hesitate to claim it:

> Hear! Those strong men who hold the field,
> And who block the escape of your tyrants,

Have come from afar, over a harsh trail. . . .
They have weighed their heads with battered helmets,
They have saddled their dark chargers,
And rode over the bridge which resounded somberly! . . . .
And the hoped-for prize promised to those brave men,
Would it be, O deluded ones, to turn back fate,
And put an end to the suffering of a foreign folk? . . . .
The powerful mingle with the vanquished enemy,
The former master remains with the new;
Both peoples stand on your necks.
They divide the slaves, they divide the flocks;
They settle together on the bloody fields
Of a scattered folk who have no name.[2]

Were the Franks also full-fledged invaders, then, despite all that
we have said? They certainly were, in the sense that their expedition
provoked, at the time, all the devastation and suffering that normally accompany invasions. Later, moreover, Charlemagne himself
repressed the revolt of the Longobards of the northeast in 776, after
first issuing a decree that restitution be made for the losses suffered.
There is more, however. If not in the immediate retinue of Charlemagne, certainly in the years following his expedition in 773 many
Frankish, Bavarian, Aleman, and Burgundian aristocrats, clerics, and
monks went to seek, and gained, their fortunes in the Carolingian
kingdom of Italy, winning counties, bishoprics, and abbeys, with
their accompanying appanages of substantial sources of territorial
revenue. These individuals entered into competition with their
counterparts, whether of Longobard or Roman descent, thus usher-
ing in the multiethnic ruling class that would come to govern the
country in the centuries that followed. The new arrivals, in any case,
never lost touch with the members, or branches, of their families
back in their respective lands of origin. These émigrés thus had so
many points of reference and support back home. It is unlikely, however, that when Antonius, the bishop of Brescia, who was of East

Frankish origin, wrote in 878 in a letter to Solomon II, bishop of Constance, "We, inhabitants of Italy, or rather, tenants," he was actually describing the feeling of all his peers.[3]

Moreover, the new arrivals facilitated or even promoted the diffusion throughout the lands of the Cisalpine kingdom of a type of agrarian regime, the *curtis,* or rural lordship, which was dominant north of the Alps. It entailed the division into two not necessarily equal areas of the landholding. One of the areas *(pars dominica)* directly cultivated was farmed in part by *servi* housed and fed by the master. Another part was cultivated thanks to the days of work (the *corvées*) due either in a specific number or else at the discretion of the master himself, from the *servi* (because *servi,* or servants, is still what they were!) housed on parcels of land *(mansi)* made available to them for open-ended periods of time. These parcels of land provided them with sustenance and constituted the other section of the landholding, called the *massaricium.* Although greater restrictions were imposed on the *servi dominici* (or *non casati*), they also enjoyed greater security. The *servi casati,* or servants of the glebe, lived with the constant risk of suffering from poor harvests, but by contrast they enjoyed a certain degree of independence.

This is one of those forms of rationalization of the processes of production whereby the advantages obtained by the master in economic terms are often counterbalanced by a worsening in the condition of the subjects. Even if the term *servus,* which in antiquity had meant "slave," continued to be used to designate their condition, that does not mean that we can automatically equate a medieval *servus* with an ancient *servus.* In fact, to designate the medieval equivalent of the latter, a neologism had already been coined: *sclavus* (from "Slav," since many of the new slaves were of that ethnic origin). By contrast, the condition of the medieval *servus* is even still often defined through the ambiguous notions of semi-liberty and semi-enslavement, in a reflection of the extreme difficulty of establishing a precise definition.

The type of agrarian regime that we have described briefly here is one of the precapitalist "modes of production" envisioned in Marxist analysis, which classes it as a "feudal mode of production." If, however, it is true that the rural seigniory was the agrarian regime most typical of the feudal age, it is equally true that we find evidence of it as early as late antiquity and, most important, that it survived until well after the end of the feudal period itself. In fact, on 11 August 1789, the French National Assembly, confirming in a definitive decree a deliberation that it had adopted on the night of 4 August, "entirely destroyed the feudal regime," making a careful distinction between rights over persons, which were abolished, and rights over property, which were declared valid. In so doing, the National Assembly was abolishing not the "feudal regime," which had died out as such long before, but rather the "rural seigniory." This is made clear by the very distinction, introduced in the decree of abolition, between rights over persons (servants of the glebe) and property rights (the revenue from landholdings). In contrast, then, with what the French revolutionaries of 1789 and later Marx and Engels believed, the rural seigniory was quite a different matter from the feudal institutions, even if, so to speak, it coexisted with them for many centuries.[4] If we have indulged in this digression, it is only because when Charlemagne marched into Italy, he carried with him in his baggage not only the model of the rural seigniory, but also the original model of feudal institutions, which were unknown to the Longobards, with the possible exception of minor factors tending in the same direction.

To be very clear, we should immediately point out that the extension to the Carolingian Kingdom of Italy of the custom whereby a *senior* (a lord, or seigneur, if not the sovereign himself) ceded to one of his followers a land in benefice—that is, without any compensation in cash, but with the commitment to provide that lord with highly expert services, services that usually entailed counsel, and especially mounted military service—did not mark the beginning of the feudal age. That took place (and in Italy with traits that were atypical compared with the rest of formerly Carolingian Europe) only two centuries later, at the earliest. It occurred when—with the collapse of public order at the end of the Carolingian empire, which had survived the decline of the ancient world, even with all the turmoil and disruption that had supervened in the meantime—the spread of feudal institutions became not the only, but the most distinctive and characteristic, of the various developments that allowed the reorganization of society on entirely new foundations.

With the Carolingian mayors of the palace while the Merovingian dynasty still ruled, and later under the kings of the new dynasty, the Frankish kingdom was the forum for the increasingly frequent coupling of two practices that had become broadly established during the preceding period: the practice of the *commendatio*—the passage of one freeman under the protection of another freeman, wealthier and more powerful than he and therefore capable of offering him that protection, in exchange for a service, usually military in nature—and the practice of the *beneficium*—that is, the lifetime concession of a plot of land, at very favorable terms for the lessee, if not actually free of charge. Merging these two traditional practices, up until then quite distinct, into a single practice, the Carolingian mayors of the palace of the Merovingian kings ensured their ability to call on the support of armed clients, which made possible their ascent to the throne. Subsequently, the Carolingian kings chose to establish similar personal bonds with their public officials, beginning with the holders of counties, who were already regularly remunerated. Also, and especially, the Carolingian kings recruited individual mounted soldiers, who were endowed with a greater degree of professionalism than their fellows the foot soldiers, who were mobilized instead through mass levies. These mounted soldiers would accompany the Carolingian kings on their seasonal war expeditions.[5]

Twenty-seven years after his first expedition into Italy, on Christmas Day 800, Charlemagne (at this point, the adjective *magne* [*magnus*], or "great," that was destined to be part of his name as recorded in history can no longer be withheld) was crowned emperor by Pope Leo III (795–816) in St. Peter's. The Roman people also acclaimed him Augustus.

Southern Italy was excluded from the Frankish conquest. Charlemagne and his successors, like the Longobard kings, never ruled over the entire peninsula. To the north of Rome there was no longer either a Longobard Italy or a Byzantine Italy, but only a Frankish Italy. Venice, in fact, which eluded conquest by the new arrivals, may perhaps be considered a Byzantine "frontier outpost" from the standpoint of its commercial traffic, and it was protective of its magnificent isolation.[6] In contrast, the "two Italys" from before 774 survived to the south of Rome, beyond the Patrimony of Saint Peter, which derived its best assurances of security precisely from that persistent division. The two Italys constituted the remains of three centuries of Italian history, resistant to assimilation until the arrival of the Normans, but also incapable of further expansion.

The genesis of a national Longobard script, interrupted in the north by the spread of the new script imported by the Franks ("Carolingian minuscule"), reached fruition in the territory of Benevento and is known, in fact, as Beneventan script. Salerno, the only point of access to the Tyrrhenian Sea for the Longobards of Benevento, who never managed to win out over Naples, was transformed by Prince Arechi II from the small fortified town that it had been into the second-largest city in the principality.[7] But beginning in 847, it split into two, and then three, different entities. Thus came into being the principality of Salerno and the county, or earldom (later it too became a principality), of Capua, frequently at war with each other. Even in those latitudes the seed of dissent continued to sprout in the Longobard tradition.

The cities of the Campanian coast were by now practically independent of Constantinople, even if they remained within its sphere of influence, to their obvious advantage when it came to trade. Benedetto Croce described their glory, which he believed hardly ephemeral, in the following words:

From the Longobards, our thoughts turn, perhaps by contrast, to the seaports, to the minor Venices of the southern Adriatic and Tyrrhenian, of which the most famous is Amalfi, an independent city with its own government, although it retained, to its advantage, a nominal dependence on the Byzantine Empire, with whose lands it traded. Amalfi invented or perfected the compass and spread its use, and kept records of its shipping in the famous *tavola amalfitana;* its citizens deployed their activities all over the Mediterranean shores . . . ; it played a part in such warlike enterprises as the siege of Acre and still speaks to us today through the noble monuments of its art, for instance the sculptured bronze doors which the Mauro family gave to the cathedral of their native town and to other religious shrines. . . . Along with the other ports of the South, Amalfi was a forerunner and inspiration of the free communes of the North; in all of them there flourished a very real political life, a spirit of conquest and defense, civic pride and patriotism.—The duchy of Naples cultivated the same qualities; the "militia of the Neapolitans," as it was called, was constantly in arms to defend itself against its threatening Longobard neighbors. The epitaphs of its dukes and consuls tell a tale quite different from that which we find on the tombs of the princes of Benevento. . . . The policy of Naples turned and twisted. Repeatedly and for considerable lengths of time it allied itself with the Saracens and did profitable business with them; the abundance of their faces and customs and tongues made the city seem like a "second Palermo." Moreover—as truth demands that we admit—it seconded their slave traffic, capturing Longobards and selling them overseas. At other times, alone or with the help of its sister cities, it lost patience with the arrogance of these troublesome allies, driving them away and slaughtering them, notably in a famous naval battle (the victory of Ostia, 849), which saved Rome and was recorded, seven centuries later, in Raphael's Vatican frescoes.[8]

Croce, in writing this fine description, may have been somewhat carried away by the evocative impulse, especially if we consider that his appreciation of southern Italy prior to the Norman invasion would turn in the pages that followed to a dismissal of the supposedly "admirable traits of the southern populations" under Norman and Swabian rule. In particular, we should, employing the arguments used by Giuseppe Galasso, reject that reference to the maritime cities of southern Italy as "precursors" to the "free communal formations of the north."[9]

In the rest of southern Italy, the Byzantine presence in the eighth century and the first half of the ninth century, continued to shrink almost to the vanishing point under Longobard pressure, and later partly Frankish pressure as well, until it was squeezed into the tip of the Italian boot (no longer Brutii, as in antiquity, but Calabria) and into the land of Otranto. Both those Byzantine outposts were exposed to the raids, which occasionally resulted in settlements of varying duration, of the Aghlabids of Ifriqiya (an Arabic dynasty that ruled over Tunisia and Algeria from 800 to 909). The Aghlabids later, beginning in 827, undertook the permanent conquest of Sicily, until then a Byzantine "theme" (or military and administrative territorial district). The situation changed in the last years of the reign of Basil I (867–886), the first monarch of the Macedonian dynasty, who recovered nearly all of Calabria, Taranto, and a considerable share of the principality of Benevento for the empire. In Apulia, the theme of Longobardia was established, with Bari as its capital. Also, Calabria, hitherto part of the theme of Sicily, was elevated, in turn, to the standing of full-fledged theme, with Reggium as capital. Later, perhaps in the first half of the tenth century, the theme of Lucania was established. Moreover, in the second half of the tenth century, the three themes (if they were already three in number) were reunited in the "*catepanato* of Italy," with Bari as the capital.

Even when, as early as the first few decades of the tenth century, the Byzantine reconquest had lost its initial impetus, the "efficacious hand of the State"[10] continued to make itself felt in these provinces, both in the form of an oppressive tax-levying presence and in the form of a concrete and effective protection exercised from afar on behalf of the local populace. The defensive walls built to protect many towns, and the castles erected to defend rural society—as lives and property were threatened by Saracen incursions—were in fact constructed at the expense and under the supervision of the public power, in a political and administrative setting that had no equivalents in post-Carolingian Europe.

By a singular stroke of destiny, several regions of Italy that beginning at the end of the eighth century BC had been the destination of the movement of colonization that had transformed them into a Hellenic land, to the point that all of southern Italy had been given the name of Magna Graecia, underwent, so many centuries later and—it is hardly necessary to specify—in a radically different cultural context, a second process of grecization. This process was particularly pronounced, as one might well expect, in both the ecclesiastical and the monastic sectors. This took place roughly a century after central and northern Italy had entered the orbit of the Romano-Germanic Continental West, the cradle of a new civilization in every area—political, social, ecclesiastical, cultural, and so on.

The accession of Basil I had come just before the death of Louis II, king of Italy and emperor (855–875), who "because he chose to live primarily in Italy, grew closer to Rome" (in comparison, of course, with his predecessors), and closer, beyond Rome, to southern Italy as well. Southern Italy had been, as we have seen, neglected until then by the Byzantines, and lay exposed to Saracen raids. It was especially ripe, then, for anyone from outside armed with the might necessary to impose order and ensure peace and tranquility. Louis II heeded the call, "first, because it was a province of Italy, and he wished to establish his power over the territories of all the kingdom; second, because the ferocious clan of the Saracens was already pressing at his borders."[11]

At first in concert with the Byzantines, and then—once the temporary collaboration had broken down—with his forces alone, he undertook a determined battle against the Saracens, which engaged his undivided attention in southern Italy from 866 until 871. Immediately following the great success represented by the reconquest of Bari (2 February 871), however, a town that as we shall see had been the center for the previous twenty-five years of an Arab Muslim emirate, Adelchis, the prince of Benevento, on 13 August of the same year, took the victorious emperor, who was a guest in that city, prisoner. Adelchis agreed to free Louis only on condition that he swear not to take vengeance for the outrage to his person. Louis died four years later, before he could restore the prestige of the imperial authority, which had been seriously undermined by this episode.

The efforts undertaken by the Frankish Carolingian emperor in southern Italy, in any case, had the effect of reawakening the interest of his Byzantine counterpart in those lands. We have already mentioned the political and territorial consequences of that reawakening. It also had a further effect, however, notable already in Louis's time. That effect became entirely evident only when (following an interlude of roughly one hundred years, during which there was a distinct lack of any strong and assertive Western presence on the political stage in southern Italy) the succession in 962 to the throne of the Western empire of the dynasty of the Ottonians marked the sharp reassertion of such a presence. This effect took the form of the transformation of the "problem of the two empires"[12] from merely an ideological clash between two abstract claims to universality to a conflict, at least in part, between two powers struggling for control, direct or indirect, of a certain territory.

Over the course of the ninth century, Sicily broke away—not only, and not so much—from Byzantine Italy, but just as much from the Christian world itself, in its twofold manifestation, Greek and Eastern on the one hand, and Latin and Western on the other. Indeed it entered into the orbit of the third of the three great politico-religious conglomerations with a presence on the shores of the Mediterranean: the Arab Muslim world. This was the most extensive of the three, even if it had recently lost its political unity. What it still possessed intact, however, was its drive for expansion. In contrast with what has been written and said in the past, this drive was not the product of "a groundswell of religious fanaticism," nor was its "immediate goal the conversion of the infidels." Instead, it should be attributed "to physical causes, specifically, the growing aridity of the Arab climate, so that nomadic tribes, deprived of their plentiful pasturage, were driven to seek out more fertile lands." It should be noted that "the religious factor played a decisive role in giving the Arab drive toward conquest a unified character, in sustaining the invaders' enthusiasm."[13]

In 827, Arab and Berber subjects of the Aghlabid emirate, by now practically independent of the caliph of Baghdad, invaded Sicily. They had been summoned, according to one of the many "stereotyped invitation legends," by the wealthy Euphemius, whose wife had supposedly been ravished by a high Byzantine official.[14] Palermo fell in 831. The last Greek stronghold to surrender was Taormina, in 902. Along with Spain, Sicily was the only province of the former Western Roman Empire where the Arab Muslim presence was not contained within the confines of a bridgehead or else consumed in the lightening-quick destructiveness of a raid. In Sicily, as in Spain, though for an incomparably shorter period of time, the Arab Muslims put down roots.

Many Sicilian words have Arabic origins. Some, such as *ammiraglio* (admiral) and *zàgara* (orange blossom) have entered into the Italian language proper. But most of the words of Arabic origin present in the Italian language came from the Middle East via the maritime republics, or from Spain.

The numerous rural place names of Arabic origin tell us that in Sicily during the Muslim domination small agricultural landholdings were common, at the expense of the large landholdings (Latin *latifundium*, Italian *latifondo*). Because they had mingled and merged with the local population, the invaders, abandoning their original customs as seminomads, had over the course of time become good farmers. They introduced the cultivation of citrus fruit, sugarcane, dates, mulberry trees, and even cotton to the island.

More perhaps than the few surviving buildings, with their unmistakable polychrome ornamentation, their stalactite ceilings, their bulging red cupolas set on flat roofs, it is the parks of the villas surrounding Palermo that still communicate a sense of the atmosphere of Muslim Sicily. Ibn Hamdis, "the greatest Arab-Sicilian poet," describes the island's orange groves in these words:

> Savor the oranges you have gathered. Their presence is the
> presence of happiness.
> Welcome the cheeks of the branches, welcome the stars of the
> trees!
> One would say the sky has rained down pure gold, and the
> earth has shaped it into gleaming globes.[15]

From Sicily, Africa, and Spain the Saracens—this is what medieval chroniclers called the Arab Muslims, using the name of an ancient tribe of robbers from the southern Sinai—staged numerous raids on the coasts of central and southern Italy. This is not to mention the frequent cases—and these in particular Pope John VIII (872–882) denounced relentlessly in his letters to the princes and dukes of southern Italy—in which the intervention of armed groups of Saracens was actually requested by leading local citizens to help solve conflicts with their peers. Thus we find confirmation of the fact that "every stereotype has roots in events," and so, therefore, do the "invitation legends."[16] If we leave aside the case of Sicily, in a class apart with regard to duration and territorial expanse, there were other relatively stable Saracen settlements, such as the emirate of Bari, which lasted from 847 until 871. Another was the fortified camp of Monte Argento, at the mouth of the Garigliano River, which, since Sicily was riven at the time by fighting between Berbers and Arabs, served for a certain period as the main base for the Saracen raids in central Italy. It was not destroyed until 915, by a vast coalition encouraged by Pope John X (914–928), in order to eject the raiders who were, as was emphatically noted once the dust had settled, plaguing *tota Ytalia*.[17]

But the best-known Saracen raid, given its very particular targets, culminated in the attack in August 846 on Ostia and Porto and, once the raiders had sailed up the Tiber River, the ensuing sack of the basilicas of St. Peter and St. Paul, both located outside the Aurelian walls. The event caused enormous consternation and led Pope Leo IV (844–857) to reinforce the existing walls. He further resumed work on a project that had been undertaken and then abandoned by Leo III (795–816). Leo IV built—with the help of the emperor Lothar I (840–855), who promised to take up a collection for this purpose in all his dominions—a new circuit of walls along the banks of the Tiber, to link St. Peter's, hitherto undefended, to the city's defensive system. But the Leonine City, as it was dubbed, was a "new city"—Leo IV reiterated this point three separate times on 27 June 852, when it was solemnly inaugurated—which "for many centuries remained a city apart, outside of and distinct from Rome."[18] In the same manner, as a new city, though not destined to be quite as long-lived, *Iohannipolis* was conceived, when John VIII some thirty years later arranged, in this case without the benefit of any imperial funding, to fortify the area outside the walls surrounding the basilica and monastery of St. Paul.

Along with the Saracens, the Normans (the "men of the north") and the Hungarians were the other protagonists in the great wave of invasions that swept down on Western Europe from the south, north, and east:

Forged several centuries earlier in the fiery crucible of the Germanic invasions, the new civilization of the West, in its turn, seemed like a citadel besieged—indeed, more than half overrun.

However much may be learnt from the study of the last invasions, we should nevertheless not allow their lessons to overshadow the still more important fact of their cessation. Till then these ravages by hordes from without and these great movements of peoples had in truth formed the main fabric of history in the West as the rest of the world. Thenceforward the West would almost alone be free from them. Neither the Mongols nor the Turks would later do more than to brush its frontiers. Western society would certainly have its clashes; but they would take place within a closed arena. This meant the possibility of a much more regular cultural and social evolution, uninterrupted by any attack from without or any influx of foreign settlers. . . . Consider above all, nearer home, eastern Europe, trampled underfoot until modern times by the peoples of the steppes and by the Turks.[19]

With his gaze on all of Western Europe, Bloch points out that the three invasions by "hordes from without" that it suffered between the ninth and tenth centuries were also the "last ones." This was also true for Italy, of course. This does not undercut the fact that Italy, more than other European nations, was to suffer the consequences of the "clashes . . . within a closed arena," to which Bloch likewise refers. They did not necessarily take the form of full-fledged "invasions," but rather of foreign "sway" or "domination," which is not the same thing. And if this had not been the case, the review of invaders of Italy that we have undertaken might very well have come to a halt at this point.

We have discussed the Saracens. In contrast with the Scandinavian raiders, for whom the Mediterranean coastline was difficult to reach (in fact, during the entire ninth century they landed there only once, in 859–860), the Hungarians, for whom Italy was within easy reach of Pannonia, their latest base of operations, visited the Po Valley on numerous occasions and, on the far side of the Tuscan-Emilian Apennines, peninsular Italy. There they carried out extremely destructive seasonal raids and then returned home, weighed down with what was usually a sizable haul of plunder. That was true, at any rate, until the intended victims learned to defend themselves, as they did in time, rendering the Hungarians' incursions less and less profitable, until they finally abandoned them entirely.

Until they learned to defend themselves *on their own*, we must hasten to add, for those who were institutionally obligated to see to their defense—that is, those holding public office—proved to be inadequate to what should have been their chief task. I am referring to the last kings and emperors of the Carolingian dynasty, the marquesses and counts who owed them allegiance, and the sovereigns of the so-called independent Italian kingdom, for the most part former titulars of border counties or earldoms (Friuli, Spoleto, Ivrea). In some cases it was actually one of the latter, or a rival interested in taking his place, that encouraged—in support of his cause—the devastating intervention of armies of Hungarian knights.

The age of the last invasions was—and not only in Italy, but in the rest of post-Carolingian Europe as well—a time of a breakdown in public order. This public order had in some sense held together, through the experience of the Romano-barbarian kingdoms, from the end of the ancient world until the restoration of the Western empire.[20] The power vacuum that came into being at this point was filled, in Italy as well, by a profusion of local undertakings. At first sight, it would seem that there was an endless series of repetitions on a lesser or minimal scale of what Pope Leo had accomplished in the middle of the previous century, when he did his best to protect St. Peter's Basilica from new attacks. Indeed, his biographer in the *Liber pontificalis* indulges in a depiction of a pope who, in defiance of bad weather, monitored day and night the progress on construction work on the defensive walls that were meant to surround, and especially protect, the new city that would be named after him. The difference between his undertaking and those which proliferated some fifty years later is not only quantitative but also and especially qualitative. It had been in fact undertaken by the pope, that is, the *dominus* of the Patrimony of Saint Peter, who for the occasion had mobilized the peasants (or *coloni*) who worked the large landholdings of the Roman Church situated all around the city of Rome; and he had largely made use of the help sent to him by the emperor Lothar I, his counterpart in the leadership of Western Christendom.[21]

The undertaking of building the fortifications in the post-

Carolingian era fell instead to new men, sometimes title holders of counties (though even they were acting in a new role), who acted without asking anyone's permission. Though there were indeed cases in which they received authorization from one king or another who happened to be present, for the most part after work had already been completed, in any case they used their own funds and resources, and that is what really counted. A separate case is that of the bishops, who can hardly be thought of as "new men." Still, the task they took on, of seeing to the safety of their cities by rebuilding the ruined walls—often because they had been delegated to do so by the monarchs themselves—lay outside the traditional responsibilities of the episcopate, and therefore fundamentally altered their role. When we speak of "new men," though, in the absolute sense, we are certainly referring to the *boni homines,* the men of goodwill, who volunteered or were asked to work with the local authorities in this undertaking for the common good. The "song of the watchmen of Modena" *(canto delle scolte modenesi)* renders, with an unmistakable literary emphasis, the actual tension of commune-governed cities, committed, alongside their bishops, to their own self-defense against invaders, in order to survive and to protect their possessions:

> I. You who bear arms to defend these walls, sleep not, mind
>   you, keep careful watch! So long as Hector watched over
>   Troy, the sly Greeks could not breach its walls. . . .
> IV. . . . . Gird, oh Christ, these fortifications of ours,
>   defend them with the strength of your spear. . . .
> VI. Stout youth, powerful and daring in war, your songs pour
>   over the city walls; and with weapons you take turns keeping
>   watch, lest the treacherous enemy take these walls by
>   surprise; let the cry echo: "Hey there, comrade, keep an eye
>   out!"; and across the walls the echo returns: "Hey there,
>   keep careful watch!"[22]

The fortifications built in the tenth century, which was also known as the age of castles or the age of castle building, were not comparable with the later full-fledged "medieval" castles equipped with battlements, towers, ramparts, and drawbridges. Instead, they tended to be terrepleins, or earthworks, topped by palisades and occasionally masonry structures, inside which people and livestock took shelter in times of danger. They might also be villages, many of which can still be seen in Sabina, built on natural high points at a healthy distance from the Roman consular roads. The houses of these villages, perched high atop towering cliffs, were built one adjoining the other, to ensure that there were no gaps through which outsiders could gain access to the settlement. The surrounding population, which had previously lived in isolated farmhouses scattered over the countryside, clustered within these villages on a permanent basis, with a resulting transformation of crops and farming practices.[23]

These defensive structures wound up taking on an importance that went well beyond their straightforward military function, though we should not underestimate that either. In particular, for the more vulnerable rural populations, they tended to become stable points of reference. Those who had arranged for their construction took on the status of great and immediate power. The instinctive willingness to obey them, then, outweighed the allegiance to any other holders of public power, who were often discredited by their malfeasance or nonfeasance with respect to the power they held. In place of the old order, a heterogeneous array of limited, and not always compact, territorial entities was forming, from the bottom up, and these claimed for themselves the future, at least the immediate future. In a patent oxymoron, or contradiction in terms— defined in the scholastic context as a *contradiction in the attribute,* "which occurs when one qualifies a subject with an attribute that is certainly excluded by the very nature of the subject (for example, 'cubic sphere,' 'inorganic animal,' and so on)"[24]—the process that was then under way was described, at least until about fifty years ago, as "feudal anarchy." Let us leave aside the fact that in reality, beyond the mere appearances that always seemed to impress the few

contemporary observers who put their impressions into writing, this
was not "anarchy," by any means, but rather the only path available,
tumultuous and disorderly though it might have been, given the
state of affairs then current. Still, this process in any case had nothing in common with "feudalism," whose ties of dependency, already
tested—as we have seen—during the Carolingian age, were if anything a guarantee of social order and cohesion. They would in fact
come into play, but only in a later phase, with the first hesitant signs
of a return of royal authority in territorial contexts that were at first
quite restricted. And when they came into play, they did so as a
mechanism that would allow the construction of a new order in
place of the ancient one, definitively shattered at the time of the
"last invasions."

———

IN 972, as he was crossing the Maritime Alps to return home,
Majolus (also known as Maieul, Mayeule), abbot (954–994) of the
monastery of Cluny, in Burgundy, was captured by Saracens. These
Saracens, from their lair in Fraxinetum (Garde-Fraînet) in Provence,
where they had settled at the turn of the century, were disrupt-
ing communications between Italy and southern France. A chronicler of the time described in his colorful style how and whence they
had arrived:

> By the will of God (unfathomable and just, nor could it be other-
> wise), a group of just twenty Saracens, who set sail from Spain
> aboard a small vessel, were carried here, drifting with the wind. The
> pirates land by night, they sneak into the town, and they slaughter—
> alas!—a number of Christians, they seize the town; they fortify
> Mount Moro, which stands behind the village, as a haven against the
> attacks of the neighboring people: their bulwark is that stand of
> thorns [Liutprand has already made reference to it in the previous
> chapter], which they enlarge and make even denser by ordering that
> anyone who cuts even a single branch be executed with a single
> blow from a sword; and in this way they eliminate all paths in, save

for a single very narrow way. Therefore, placing reliance on the harsh setting, they study from their hiding place the surrounding populations; they send messengers to Spain to summon many warriors, they enlarge their stronghold and ensure that there is no reason to be afraid of the people around them. They immediately bring back with them a group of about a hundred Saracens, so that these can confirm what they claim.[25]

This is just one of many episodes of the "final invasions," and it was concluded, amid the immense uproar prompted by the capture of the abbot of Cluny, one of the great men of the time, through the concerted actions of a number of local feudal lords.

Majolus was returning from a pilgrimage *ad limina apostolorum,* that is to say, to Rome. The apostles in question were, of course, Peter and Paul; "the term *limina* refers to the place and point toward which the faithful converged, the *threshold* of the martyr that they venerated, housed in his or her *sedes* . . . , which consisted of the tomb or mound in its most specific sense."[26]

The abbot of Cluny was an unusual pilgrim. It is certain that, after stopping to pray *ad limina apostolorum,* he had crossed other "thresholds" to engage in high-level negotiations concerning his monastery and therefore necessarily, since it was at the nexus of a very extensive network of priories, all of Christian Europe. A great many pilgrims, however, by far the majority of those who traveled to Rome—a pilgrim to Rome would later come to be known as a *romeo*—were going there not to deal with matters of state, but solely to pray over the tombs of the many martyrs who were buried there (many more than just the two apostles!), whose mortal remains, beginning in the second half of the seventh century, had been moved from the suburban catacombs into the numerous churches that were filling Rome, with the passage of time. There were some who returned from their journeys with the precious cargo of a relic, not always authentic—purchased or, for the nimble-fingered, pilfered. In the event that the pilgrim, on the way to Rome or on the way back home, might have met with a misadventure like that which befell

Majolus, one could rest assured that no one would learn of it, or even if someone knew, lift a finger on his behalf.

Peregrinus meant "foreigner" in classical Latin. Originally, a pilgrim "was a stranger wherever he went, known to no one, scorned by those who stayed in one place, deprived of the protection of a given collective."[27] At least at first. But as the practice of pilgrimages became increasingly widespread from the fourth century on, first to the Holy Land, and then toward other destinations (in the High Middle Ages, Rome beat them all!), "pilgrims," a term that by this point was used to indicate "travelers for religious reasons," came to constitute a category all its own of travelers distinct from those who traveled for trade and, later, went to study where, rumor had it, one could learn the most, that is, *in terra aliena*. This the master Bernard of Chartres (d. 1130) recommended doing, as long as those who left their father's house did not become overweening, as long as they managed to keep a *mens humilis,* as befitting a good Christian. Students, then, were in a certain sense themselves pilgrims—for the love of knowledge.

For everyone, the unknown factors of travel remained. Once they reached their destination, however, if nothing else, the pilgrims *ad limina apostolorum* could feel, in some sense, as if they were at home. Around St. Peter's, over the course of the ninth century, four *scholae peregrinorum,* that is, structures for the assistance and lodging of pilgrims, were already in operation; they were set up to welcome and house, respectively, Franks, Frisians, Longobards, and Saxons. On 29 November 799, on his return from Paderborn, where he had met with Charlemagne, Pope Leo III was greeted festively:

> The Romans, with the greatest joy, greeting their pastor all together on the eve of the day of the blessed apostle Andrew, both the heads of the clergy with all their clerks, the optimates, the Senate, and all the militia and the entire Roman people with the nuns, the deaconesses, the most noble matrons, and all the women, as well as all the *scholae* of the pilgrims—that is, of the Franks, Frisians, Saxons, and Longobards—all together they greeted the pope at the Milvian

Bridge, with insignia and banners and spiritual canticles, and they accompanied him to the church of the blessed apostle Peter, where he celebrated the Holy Mass and they all together devotedly had communion with the body and blood of our Lord Jesus Christ.[28]

Probably by *scholae* the papal biographer meant both the staff in charge of the structures in which the pilgrims from the respective countries were greeted and the pilgrims from the various countries who were being housed at the moment in the structures themselves. In one case or the other, these pilgrims, far from being the stateless people of a bygone time, foreigners by definition, seem to have been an integral part of the Roman citizenry gathered together on a feast day celebrating the return of the pope to his city, which was on the verge of becoming as cosmopolitan as it had once been, in a time long ago.

As they drew near Rome, the pilgrims were obliged to cross through malaria-ridden areas dominated by the ruins of ancient aqueducts. They sang:

Oh noble Rome, mistress of the world, most exalted of all cities, reddened by the purple blood of martyrs, gleaming with the white lilies of the virgins, we hail you, we bless you: flourish through all the ages.

Oh Peter, powerful gatekeeper of the heavens, always grant the prayers of your supplicants. When you sit as the judge of the twelve tribes, show clemency, judge with indulgence. And those who beg your mercy in this life, absolve them.

Accept our prayers, oh Paul, whose zeal conquered the philosophers. Having become administrator of the palace of the Lord, dole out our gifts of divine grace, so that the wisdom which you have in such abundance may, through your teachings, quench our thirst as well.[29]

Here Peter and Paul are still set on the same level in the pilgrims' scale of values. The day would come when the former would strongly outweigh the latter.

5

GERMANS AT LEGNANO, NORMANS
IN SOUTHERN ITALY AND SICILY

IN 1024, the Pavians revolted and burned the royal palace of Pavia, capital of the Kingdom of Italy—from the turn of the eighth century the only stable capital of the high Middle Ages, under first the Longobards, then the Franks, and finally the kings of the independent Italian kingdom. Everywhere else, the monarchs were itinerant. The palace of Pavia was never rebuilt. By now, the subalpine kingdom had become a sort of appendage to the kingdom of Germany. The Pavians, as well as the other Italians of the kingdom, saw it as a foreign body.

They had their good reasons. Once elected, the king of Germany acquired, with the office, the right to be crowned emperor by the pope, in Rome. It is no accident that from a certain point forward those kings came to hold the title "King of the Romans." On the way south, or on the road back home from Rome, sometimes though not always they would also have themselves crowned kings of Italy. It was just an extra touch.

An appropriate symbol for this imaginary kingdom is the "iron crown," preserved in Monza. It is not made of iron, and in Monza it never encircled the head of a king or an emperor. This is how things actually went. In Milan, at Epiphany in 1311, Henry VII of Luxembourg, who had been king of the Romans since 1308, was crowned king of Italy in the basilica of St. Ambrose—with the "iron crown," as we read, even in some authoritative places, even today. It is instead well established that the crown in question was searched for but not found. This should come as no surprise (at the time, however, some even thought it had been pawned), for the very simple reason that it never existed. A legend was told, however, that after being consecrated as king of Germany with a silver crown, the chosen monarch was to be crowned in Italy with an iron crown, and then go on to Rome to receive a golden crown from the pope. Therefore, a goldsmith in Siena was commissioned to make an iron crown, and it was placed on Henry's head in 1311. It was only in the fifteenth century, when the crown had become too rusty to be used, that the decision was made to use for the ceremony of coronation for the king of Italy that ancient diadem, with an iron hoop around it (mistaken for a nail from the Cross of Christ), that had been and still is preserved in the Church of San Giovanni in Monza. This new crown was used in the coronations of Charles V in Bologna in 1530, Napoleon I in Milan in 1805, and Ferdinand I of Austria, again in Milan, in 1838. In later years, it was carried in the funeral processions of the kings of Italy Victor Emmanuel II in 1878, and Humbert I in 1900.[1]

Upon the territory of the kingdom of Italy, now the appanage of the king of the Romans, and ignoring it as if it no longer existed (to the point of regularly usurping its natural prerogatives with impunity), in the meantime, the new Italy of the city-states, governed as "communes," was taking shape. In an initial phase of this process, the essential role was played by the bishops, first alongside and then later in place of the counts, the official representatives of the declining royal power. The counts were in general still able to wield their authority only in the countryside surrounding the urban nucleus, which was in fact known in Italian as the *contado* [count's land]. In the cities, however, as early as the turn of the tenth century, the bishops in many cases enjoyed an authority that went far beyond the strictly ecclesiastical realm, as we have already in part mentioned.

Often in league with them, though sometimes in opposition to them (because they were unwilling to sacrifice, or share with others, their personal prerogatives, which had grown progressively with the consent, or even in some cases at the directive, of the imperial and royal power), we find the politically more venturesome city dwellers, as well as the lesser feudal lords, who were attempting to win for themselves in the city the space that they lacked in the countryside. In contrast, wherever they were accepted they brought with them their experience in the use of weapons and especially their skill at mounted combat, which city dwellers tended to lack. Both groups began to establish in the course of time sworn voluntary associations, which spread like an epidemic: the "communes."

The former were the direct descendants of the informal groups of citizens of goodwill, the *boni homines,* who at the time of the raids by the Magyars and Saracens had banded together to restore the old Roman walls, by now completely dilapidated. Now, however, the citizens intended to found full-fledged local governments, extending their jurisdictions day by day, both to fill potential power vacuums and out of the perennial conflict with the established powers, which they hoped to replace.

With the clergy and especially with the bishops, things became exceedingly complex, however, once the city dwellers, and above all those city dwellers who in increasing numbers had learned to read, realized to their horror that their pastors were often leading a life that differed sharply from the ways that Christ, in the Gospels, had shown the apostles. It was one thing to hear matters explained from the pulpit, with the typical clerical tactic of shaving off the sharper points that stud Jesus's parables. It was quite another matter to read it for oneself, at home, or in one's workshop; quite another matter to engage in free commentary on those words in a small circle of friends. Christ had in fact said: "It is easier for a camel to pass through the eye of a needle" (Matthew 19:24), with what follows. And lo and behold, his unworthy followers had purchased a bishopric with one end in mind: to become even richer than they already were!

According to the biographer of Arialdus, the deacon who was

chief of the "Pataria" (this was the name given to a mass popular religious movement, Milanese—quite different from the usual little groups of solitary grumblers), the money coiner Nazarius supposedly invited him to come live at his house in the following words:

> Sir Arialdus, that the things you say are true and useful is evident not only to the wise, but even to fools. Who is so foolish that he cannot clearly see that the lives of those whom I summon to my own home so that they may bless that home, whom I feed according to my resources, and to whom, after kissing their hands, I make an offering [pay a tithe], and from whom I receive all the mysteries [sacraments], whereby I expect to receive eternal life, must necessarily be radically different from my own life? But as we all have had an opportunity to see, their lives are not only not manifestly cleaner, but indeed even filthier. All the same, you should understand that this wickedness is so deep-rooted and inveterate among us that it can only be eliminated either with great effort or with relatively limited efficacy.[2]

Paradoxically, the task of involving the papacy in the increasingly urgent task of undertaking a reformation of the Church—focusing on the fight against concubinage, or incontinence, and more generally the corruption of the clergy ("nicolaism") and the traffic in ecclesiastical offices ("simony")—was undertaken by a zealous German emperor, Henry III (1039–1056). In contrast with the canonical norm that stipulated that the naming of bishops, and therefore the bishop of Rome as well, was the exclusive task of clergy and populace, he set the tone for the changes to come by deposing, in 1046, the three popes who all laid claim to the papal tiara at the same time. He then imposed the election of four popes, Germans like him, who succeeded one another on the throne of Rome from 1047 to 1057, and all driven by the same reformist zeal that motivated him most of all. I said "paradoxically" because once the Roman aristocracy had been stripped of control over the making and unmaking at will of popes, control it had wielded for more than a century and a half, in 1059 a squadron of reformers, both Italian and foreign (especially from Lorraine) who had worked together in Rome, side by side with the four imperial popes (generally after time spent as monks in the monasteries that had been the breeding grounds for certain of the demands for reform), established revised regulations for the procedure of naming a new pope, restricting the active electorate to just the bishops of the seven dioceses surrounding Rome, the so-called suburbicarian bishops, the original nucleus of the future college of cardinals. And the result of this measure was to impede or if nothing more make it more difficult to meddle in things, not only for the Roman aristocracy but even, in future, for the emperor himself.

The direct intervention of Henry III in the election of no fewer than four excellent bishops of Rome, in fact, constituted only a fortunate exception. Neither exceptions nor particularly fortunate, at least in the context of what would shortly thereafter come to be known as the liberty of the Church—with respect, of course, to the imperial power—were, by contrast, the systematic cases of interference by the kings of the Romans, and in times to come the emperors, in the elections of bishops in the lands of the empire, and especially in Germany. Certainly, cases of the sort arose in other kingdoms of western Christendom as well.

The reasons this happened are easy to understand. From the time of the emperors of the house of Saxony (Otto I, Otto II, and so on) the tendency to prefer the great ecclesiastical imperial feudal lords over the great secular imperial feudal lords had been increasingly gaining a foothold. The secular lords, who had become the founders of noble dynasties, made their dominions hereditary possessions, thereby rendering their ties to the crown more and more fragile. The ecclesiastical lords, by contrast, although they often had mistresses and children, still offered the sovereign the opportunity when they died to regain the feudal estates that had been deeded to them. It was thus feasible to redistribute those estates, preferably to other bishops. It was therefore possible, within the realm, to prevent the consolidation of territorial seigniories that were independent in practical terms. All the more so because, by in turn subenfeoffing their own fiefs to their followers in exchange for the performance of military service, even when the ecclesiastical feudal lords did not themselves march at the head of armies, as was often the case, they were still capable of supplying the monarch with the forces mobilized by their vassals. Once this practice became widespread, it is understandable that the monarchs, no longer satisfied with assigning feudal landholdings to existing, regularly elected bishops, would tend to try to interfere in the selection of the bishops to be elected, whereupon they could endow them with fiefs and thus ensure candidates who would agree, from the very beginning, to remain loyal to them.

To force the kings of Germany to give up this practice, which from the standpoint of church law was an abuse, would, then, have triggered a crisis in the system of power upon which their reign rested. And that is precisely what the papacy, by now firmly in the hands of the reform party, was preparing to do. The papacy could not in fact accept the idea that the bishops of the land that formed the keystone of Christendom—a land that now systematically supplied the emperors of the Holy Roman Empire—were to be selected independently by those kings, who invested them not only with the scepter, symbol of temporal authority, but also with the ring and pastoral, symbols of spiritual authority. Even if the empire had long since lost the prestige that it had enjoyed in Charlemagne's time, the danger was above all that what happened in its dioceses would encourage the same behavior in the dioceses of the individual kingdoms. This was what was at stake in the "conflict of investitures," which in its most critical phase endowed Pope Gregory VII (1073–1085) and the emperor Henry IV (1056–1106), one facing off against the other, with a grim determination that led each to delegitimize the other.

In this struggle between the Roman Church and the German empire, an important role was played by the various popular religious movements that sprang up in support of the drive for ecclesiastical reform in many of the cities of the Kingdom of Italy, imperial domains likewise, but governed, as we have said, as communes. These movements openly advocated against the simoniac and nicolaist clergy, rejecting the sacraments administered by bishops and priests who were considered unworthy by vox populi. The re-awakening of the lay public provided a groundswell of support for the reforming papacy, which took unhesitating advantage of it in its campaign to improve the behavior of the clergy and combat the blight of simony, which battened off the growing stream of temporal benefices that came with the assignment of a bishopric or an abbot's throne.

In the long run, however, popular religious movements proved to be swimming against the current, and opposed to the underlying direction of the efforts at reform being undertaken at the summit of the hierarchy. The powerful push to dissolve the bonds that—from the times of the Christian Roman Empire, which had witnessed the birth of what may fairly be called an imperial Church, but also during the centuries of the High Middle Ages—tied ecclesiastical institutions (including the papacy) to temporal powers (whether rulers of Romano-barbarian kingdoms, emperors of the restored Western empire, local aristocracies, or sovereigns of the individual kingdoms)—the struggle undertaken by the papacy, in other words, to ensure the *libertas ecclesiae,* to use a formula that became popular during this period, entailed a sort of closure of the church within itself and therefore an increasingly distinct separation between the clergy and the lay faithful, including those who had supported it when the battle over reform was raging most fiercely. It was their disillusionment that broadly nourished the mass heresy of the twelfth century, a phenomenon unprecedented in the many centuries of the Church's history.[3]

The "conflict of investitures" concluded in a compromise, the Concordat of Worms in September 1122. One episode from that conflict has taken on in the history of the medieval empire the same emblematic value that the "Slap of Anagni" would have, 180 years later, in the history of the papacy: Henry IV, excommunicated by Gregory VII, the imperial subjects thus being authorized to refuse to obey Henry, was forced to appear before the pope in penitent's garb. He was still forced to wait three days to obtain an audience in the castle of Canossa, in the Emilian Apennines, where the pope was a guest of Matilda, countess of Tuscany (1046–1115). Since this took place in the heart of the winter (January 1077), the harsh weather clearly contributed to the burden of the humiliation suffered by Henry IV. For generation after generation of Germans, the memory of that wait in the snow imposed by the Roman pope upon their emperor remained deeply moving.

The conflict, which was settled at Worms, had been purely political and ecclesiastical in nature. When Henry, in 1076, before being excommunicated in his turn, had overthrown Pope Gregory at a synod of German bishops at Worms, for the offense of having harshly objected to the appointment of Henry's pawns as bishops, not only in Milan and in German dioceses, but also in Fermo and Spoleto, the bishops of Lombardy had expressed solidarity at Piacenza with their colleagues to the north of the Alps. All the same, that conflict laid the foundations for the new conflict that, over the course of the twelfth century, pitted Italian communes (supported by the papacy) against the German empire.

Even if it continued to call itself Holy until its demise in 1806, the Western empire emerged from the "conflict of investitures" desacralized, in the sense that it lost that aura of holiness that had surrounded the Christian Roman Empire ever since the times of Eusebius (ca. 260–339/340), a close collaborator of Constantine and the theorist of "imperial theology," who wrote that "just as there is only one God, and not two or three or even more—polytheism is nothing more than atheism—there is only one emperor; there is only one imperial law." Even though the emperors of the restored Western empire had never dared to describe themselves as simultaneously "kings and priests," as their counterparts in Constantinople chose to do, it is unquestionable that something of the same aura surrounded them as well,[4] if it is true that Charlemagne, the first and in some sense the inevitable model for them, was willing to be known as the bishop of the bishops. Moreover, at the time Constantius II (317–361), son of Constantine, was accused of doing the same thing. In the preface to a book that he is supposed to have written himself, we read that God had entrusted the Church to him "so that he might guide it through the stormy breakers of this time."[5] Now, and especially after Gregory VII, the popes claimed the right to "govern" the Church in the West, and they alone.

—————

IN THE second half of the twelfth century, the cities run as communes had attained institutional maturity. They oversaw every aspect of city life: from law and order to the collection of a levy on the wheat crop, from the administration of justice to the regulation of labor, oversight of markets, and protection of the environment. To perform these functions, they collected, in a fairly aggressive manner, tariffs, taxes, and tolls: the *regalia,* as they were known—so called because theoretically they could be collected only by the royal administration.

At the root of the struggle between the Italian communes joined together in the "Lombard League" and Emperor Frederick I (Barbarossa, 1152–1190) was the attempt of the latter to regain possession of his own property. Because he, much like his counterpart in Constantinople, believed that he was the direct successor of the Caesars of ancient Rome, he was first and foremost concerned with gathering accurate information on exactly what rights accrued to him, with the intention of reclaiming those rights, if necessary through the use of force, from those who had usurped them. In this research, Frederick was helped at the Diet of Roncaglia (11 November 1158) by four professors of the Studium of Bologna.[6] It was there that, beginning at the end of the previous century, a group of legal experts of a new sort, at least new to the centuries that followed the decline of the ancient world, had begun to study, on their own account, in order then to teach what they had learned, the corpus of Roman law—just as the emperor Justinian had intended in the sixth century—as a monumental whole, and no longer in the reduced compendiums with which the High Middle Ages had made do.

Aside from any short-term utility that Frederick saw in his campaign to recover what he considered stolen goods, the fact remains that in the Roman law reexhumed in Bologna the empire itself found a kind of renewed legitimacy. The episode of Roncaglia should not, however, be generalized in the direction of inducing us to believe that the Bolognese masters of law were so many "intellectuals in the employ" of the imperial power. The four masters of Roncaglia were in fact immediately condemned by certain of their colleagues who viewed matters differently, and who did not hesitate to speak up. And in the conflict that soon thereafter broke out between Barbarossa and many of the cities governed by communes in northern and central Italy, the Bolognese commune sided without hesitation and from the very first with its fellow cities. Last of all, it was in Bologna (where for that matter public law played an incomparably lesser role in legal teaching, in comparison with the emphasis devoted to civil law) that many of the leading figures of the ruling class of the commune cities were trained—in particular, future *podestà* and judges.

Alongside the destruction of Milan, ordered by Barbarossa as a reprisal in March 1162, the best-known episode from his conflict with the Italian communes was the battle of Legnano (29 May 1176), which ended in the victory of the communes of the League. In the wake of the victory, the Milanese wrote to the Bolognese:

We announce to you that we have triumphed over the enemies. Countless dead, drowned, prisoners. We have taken the emperor's shield, banner, cross, and lance. In his baggage we have found gold and silver. Impossible to calculate the value of the booty. Let it be clear that we do not consider this to be our possession, but the shared patrimony of the pope and the Italians. In combat, Duke Berthold was captured, a nephew of the empress and a brother of the archbishop of Cologne [in reality, Berthold IV of Zähringen was a third cousin of Beatrice of Burgundy and brother of Rudolph, archbishop *elect* of Mainz, unconfirmed, and then of Liège]. The other prisoners are so numerous that it is impossible to count them. They are all being held in Milan.[7]

For the losers, it was the world turned upside down. Scandalized at the outbreak of anarchy, a poet from Frederick's court wrote:

The emperor intends to restore the empire in opposition to overweening folk, among them the Lombards. The latter raise giant towers to the heavens, as if wishing to clash with God. They deserve the lightning bolt that struck down the cyclopes, because they break the laws of the princes with impunity. No one here even thinks about paying tribute to Caesar anymore. Everyone is a Caesar, and no one wishes to pay what is due. Like Troy, the city of St. Ambrose fears the gods little, and men not at all.[8]

Thus, one of the most creative periods in our history unfolded in a context of widespread civil disobedience. It was roughly the same as what was happening in other countries, with the difference, to our advantage, that here in Italy those who were usurping public power were not for the most part feudal lords, but rather city communities swept by a new spirit of associationism, which affected all social life, and not just the organization of local political and administrative power. If there was a negative factor in the Italian situation as compared with others (though this would only become clear in hindsight) it was that the counterpart of the communes was a sovereign who spoke a language very different from the language spoken in Italy and was thus seen as a foreigner. A foreigner who lived far away, marching into Italy from time to time at the head of his army on an expedition that often lasted only a season, and then marched back across the Alps to his home. Either one city-state would have to expand so powerfully that it could dominate all the others, or else there would never be an end to the anarchy of this realm.

At the same time, the struggle waged by Italy's communes against a foreign ruler certainly contributed to the formation of a common feeling of ethnic identity. This feeling was interpreted (with some considerable degree of contrivance, especially during the time of the Risorgimento, and in particular by the neo-Guelphs, who called for a united Italy under the auspices of the pope) as an indicator of a dawning Italian national identity. The passage from the letter written by the Milanese to the Bolognese after the battle of Legnano, quoted above, in which it is stated that the plunder won on the field of battle is "the shared patrimony of the pope and the Italians," would seem to be evidence supporting that thesis, as long as we recognize that when we speak of Italian communes battling the German emperor, we generalize to an inappropriate degree, because many of the communes, especially (but not necessarily) the smaller ones, took sides with the emperor, fearful as they were, and with considerable cause—as was already evident and as would become increasingly clear—that they might wind up falling prey to neighboring cities with expansionist aims. They knew that the putative Italian national feeling would do little to protect them. It was preferable, then, to rely on the emperor—to come to terms with him if possible, even at the cost of sacrificing some of the freedom that they enjoyed.

The importance that travel to and from Italy acquired for the German monarchs was reflected in the "policy of the mountain passes," which they pursued with tenacity and determination until the second half of the tenth century.[9] If their hopes of restraining Italian anarchy proved illusory over time, it became all the more vital to their interests to ensure that the Alpine passes remained accessible and open for use at any time.

The patriarchate of Aquileia and the principality of Trent constituted the linchpins of this policy, designed to encourage the infiltration of ethnic German elements along the mountain valleys.

Reinforced by the support of the emperors Henry II (1002–1024) and Conrad II (1024–1039), the patriarch of Aquileia, Poppo (d. 1042), of Bavarian heritage, claimed that his church was independent of Rome and had a sort of primacy over all the other churches on the peninsula. The inscription on his tomb refers to the bell tower that he had built: "a proud tower that reaches to touch the sky." The cathedral chapter comprised predominantly German clerics, who operated shops and storehouses for merchandise in transit, on the site of ancient Roman Aquileia. For a couple of centuries, the patriarchs acted as the chief representatives of the empire in Italy.

In 1002, Poppo led a section of Henry II's army on an expedition into southern Italy. In the midst of the fierce conflicts between Conrad II and Ariberto d'Intimiano (1018–1045), it was Poppo again who held prisoner the mutinous archbishop of Milan, builder of the *carroccio* [a cart of war and an emblem of the league, whose capture was tantamount to that of a banner or a Roman eagle—Trans.]. At its time of greatest expansion, the seigniory of the patriarch of Aquileia stretched from the river Isonzo to the river Piave. In terms of ecclesiastical jurisdiction, his most worrisome rival was the patriarch of Grado, who shifted his residence to Venice in 1112.

In the second half of the twelfth century, however, the situation began to change, in that the patriarchs tried to become independent of the empire. In view of this objective, they began to involve themselves in Italian politics. In the meantime, beneath the veneer of German political and cultural influence, the "fatherland of Friuli" had preserved intact its native traits, beginning with the language, which is a linguistic variant of Ladin. Finally, in the fifteenth century, it would be Venice that would leave its mark on the land.

To some extent, matters were different in the case of the ecclesiastical principality of Trent. It was founded in the first half of the eleventh century to ensure that the empire could control the road through Isarco and Adige, leading right up to the gates of Venice. This road was of vital importance to trade and communications with Italy. The principality was finally annexed by the house of Austria in 1363, in the person of Rudolph IV of Hapsburg.

A NEW KINGDOM had sprung up in the meantime in southern Italy and Sicily. Roger II of Hauteville (Hauteville-la-Guichard, in the present-day department of Manche), its first monarch (d. 1154), was crowned "king of Sicily and Italy" in Palermo on 25 December 1130. In 1138—at the insistence of the pope, and in order to keep from offending the sensibilities of the kings of Germany and the emperors, who, inasmuch as they were also kings of Italy, were unwilling to accept that Italy extended no farther south than Rome—he adopted the title, which better reflected reality, of "king of Sicily, the duchy of Apulia, and the principality of Capua." In the second half of the twelfth century the kingdom included the counties of Marsia and Abruzzo (in practical terms, present-day Abruzzo), which were actually autonomous, but which had once belonged to the Kingdom of Italy; the former Longobard principalities of Benevento (except for the capital city, which had been a papal holding since 1051), Capua, and Salerno; the former Byzantine "themes" of Longobardia (Apulia), Lucania, and Calabria; the former Tyrrhenian duchies of Naples, Amalfi, Gaeta, and Sorrento, which had originally been independent for all practical purposes, even if they were nominally subject to the Byzantine Empire; and the former Arab Muslim emirate of Sicily. In the multiplicity and diversity of the respective political and administrative structures, of ethnic origins, of languages and cultures, and—not last—of religious faiths and confessions, these powers, unified into the Kingdom of Sicily, constituted a mosaic as variegated as one could possibly imagine. The three contemporary civilizations, Romano-Germanic, Graeco-Byzantine, and Arab Muslim (the first Continental European, the other two European-Mediterranean and Asiatic), were all equally represented.

The incomplete conquest of the peninsula by the Longobards had led to the existence of "two Italys" for the first time. But it was the establishment of the Kingdom of Sicily, covering roughly a third of what is now Italy, that consolidated and clinched this initial duality over the centuries that followed. It was founded, in fact, at the very time when in northern Italy and part of central Italy the cities run as communes were with growing determination asserting their intention to govern themselves, usurping one by one the rights claimed over them by the ghost of a realm to which the Kingdom of Italy had by now been reduced.

The Kingdom of Sicily was not created by any of the local powers that we have cited, neither the Byzantine Empire nor the Western empire, even though they had indeed clashed repeatedly in the past for hegemony over southern Italy. Rather, it was a power extraneous to the peninsular context, much as the Longobards had been in their time, and more recently the Arabs and Berbers of Ifriqiya. It was a few hundred, or according to another calculation, a few thousand Norman knights who had landed a handful at a time in southern Italy during the previous century. They were following in the footsteps of forty of their countrymen, who had landed in Salerno in 999 on their way back from Jerusalem and had then been recruited by the prince of the city to repel a Saracen attack. According to another tradition, they had arrived in the footsteps of a group of Norman pilgrims, who at the sanctuary of San Michele al Gargano in 1016 supposedly met the leader of a Longobard revolt in Apulia against the Byzantine authorities and agreed to fight on his side.

These were the distant descendants of the reckless, ferocious sailing warriors known as the Vikings (a name that indicates not a nationality, but rather the profession of pirate), who, beginning at the end of the eighth century, setting out from the peninsulas of Jutland (present-day Denmark) and Scandinavia (Sweden and Norway) aboard long, slender ships with shallow drafts, just deep enough to navigate the high seas, had sown terror along the coasts and, sailing easily upriver, far into the interior of France and England as well. "Something that, in the past"—one contemporary observer noted—"had never been heard of, it was never written that this had happened." But they descended especially from that small group of Danes led by the Norwegian Rollo, who in 911 had obtained the peninsula of Cotentin from Charles the Simple, king of the West Frankish kingdom (898–922). They thus found a first fixed dwelling place in a Christian land in the region that extends along both banks of the river Seine, which was the seat from then on of the duchy that came to be known as Normandy, because they came from the north.

Normans, then, from Normandy, who promptly converted to Catholicism: they spoke French, and because their duke was a vassal (and, let us add, a troublesome vassal) of the man who was already, at the dawn of the eleventh century, the king of France, they were familiar with the inner workings of the feudal regime. They also knew how best to prevent the degenerations of that regime which—between the Rhine and the Loire, where it had been conceived and tested at length—tended to run counter to its fundamental nature. And indeed they imported the feudal model in its purest state into the Kingdom of Sicily or, perhaps we should say, into those provinces that proved best suited to ensure its acclimation because nothing like it had ever before been seen there (I am referring to the formerly Byzantine Calabria and the formerly Arab Muslim Sicily), and especially not in the kingdom of England, where the duke of Normandy, William (1035–1087), replaced the last Anglo-Saxon king sixty-four years before Roger II was crowned king of Sicily. In these two kingdoms, which contemporaries would have regarded, to a large degree precisely for this reason, as examples to be imitated, there thus took place "a considerable phenomenon of juridical emigration: the introduction of French feudal institutions into a land of conquest."[10]

It is possible to speak of a "conquest" followed by a full-fledged "invasion" of the territory of a state by the armed forces of another, and rendered stable by a substantial subsequent spontaneous immigration, not only from Normandy, but also from Anjou, Brittany, and Flanders, in reality, only as it applies to England. William, duke of Normandy, harbored claims to the crown of its kingdom, inasmuch as he was a cousin of its childless king, Edward the Confessor (1042–1066). He expected to make that claim count when the time came, by relying upon the formal promise of support he had extorted from the powerful duke of Wessex, Harold, when the latter had become his prisoner in 1056. Ten years later, when King Edward died, Harold instead wasted no time becoming his successor. William, at the head of a massive army, whose core strength lay in its mounted soldiers and its bowmen, crossed the Channel and landed on the island (29 September 1066). On 14 October, near Hastings, he defeated the Anglo-Saxon army, larger in number but made up mostly of poorly armed peasants on foot. And on Christmas Day William was crowned king in place of Harold, who had been killed in battle. The coronation took place in Westminster Abbey. And so the kingdom of England, in practical terms, was annexed to the duchy of Normandy. A lightning invasion, and William was known from then on as the Conqueror. It had been so spectacular that it became legendary, and Adolf Hitler, 874 years later, dreamed, fortunately without success, of imitating it.

In the footsteps of the Conqueror, many *juvenes* set out from the neighboring Continent, in search of glory and wealth; these were the younger sons ("cadets") of aristocratic families who had been deprived by the spread of the right of primogeniture of any hope of personal status if they remained in their homeland. To these cadets, William conceded feudal rights over lands confiscated from the Anglo-Saxon aristocrats who had rebelled against him on numerous occasions—a sort of scorched-earth policy at the expense of the rebels. In exchange, he demanded from the recipients an appropriate repayment in services, largely though not exclusively military in nature. The Anglo-Saxon ruling class was replaced by a new dominant class, which spoke French and saw itself as French.

The first Norman settlements in southern Italy were entirely different in nature. We have already seen that the vanguard of new arrivals was probably made up of groups of pilgrims who had no hesitation about placing their physical labor in the service of those who required it, turning themselves, from the transient pilgrims they had been, into resident mercenaries. The news that in far-off southern Italy plenty of lucrative work was available did not take long to filter back to Normandy, accompanied by the shipment of an alluring array of products of the local soil and industry ("lemons, almonds, stuffed walnuts, imperial fabrics, iron tools decorated with gold")[11] that induced many *juvenes*—who embraced adventure, as we have seen, out of necessity—to travel in that general direction, either in family groups or in scattered formation. Because the potential employers were numerous and constantly at war with one another, the expectations of the newcomers were not disappointed. It was inevitable, however, that Norman knights in the service of one seigneur should occasionally find themselves in combat with their compatriots in the service of another. These were the occupational hazards of the soldier's profession, easily outweighed by the proliferation of opportunities to plunder and loot. But "rapine is especially the business of the times of war that precede the true conquest. In fact, what the cadets of Normandy had come to find was first and foremost durable wealth, that is to say, land, which ensures respect and power."[12] And in fact, it also happened that a group led by an especially perceptive and enterprising chief would receive feudal rights to a town or a seigniory with a large landholding in exchange for a service already performed or still to perform, or else that the group would simply seize them by force. The first permanent Norman settlement was established in 1030 at Aversa, a fortified site that had recently been built by the duke of Naples, to ward off the threat posed by the Longobards of Capua; the second was established in 1042 at Melfi, a border town of Byzantine Apulia; the third was established in Capua, in 1058–1062, by the Norman duke of Aversa, who thus became a prince. The already variegated geopolitical map of mainland southern Italy was thus further enriched by the presence of Norman seigniories, small at first, but larger with the passage of time.

The course of history in southern Italy was shifted in the opposite direction, away from an even more marked fragmentation, the product of a hunger for land and power among the new arrivals, by the numerous sons of Tancred of Hauteville, who "by common accord, . . . having first abandoned their homeland, going in search of material gains in one place or another that could be won by force of arms, finally came, guided by God, to Apulia, a province of Italy";[13] or, perhaps we should say that two of them in particular—Robert Guiscard, duke of Apulia from 1057 on, and his younger brother, the great count Roger—left their mark on the course of Italian history. These two, after prevailing over their countrymen who had infiltrated through their settlements into the whole highly complex network of political society in southern Italy, enveloping it in an increasingly close-woven network, undertook by common consent the invasion of Byzantine Calabria and Arab and Berber Sicily. This was indeed a genuine invasion, followed by a stable conquest, enforced by the many castles built by the invaders. Reggium was occupied in 1060, Palermo in 1072; but the last city to fall to Roger was Noto, in 1091. This was all the work of a surprisingly small host of Normans, at least if we trust the word of the chroniclers of the time, a host that took on armies far more numerous, but apparently not particularly formidable. One item of interest: the Norman chronicler Goffredo Malaterra was impressed by the use that the Muslims of Sicily made of carrier pigeons for military communications.[14]

Upon the death of Robert Guiscard (1085), the attempt to preserve the unity of his territorial dominions proved futile—a hope concentrated in the person of Roger Borsa, the son borne to him through his marriage with the princess Sichelgaita of Salerno. This was one of the typical matrimonial alliances, unthinkable back home, upon which in part the Norman chiefs built their success. When instead another pretender to Robert's throne came forward, a period of anarchy ensued. This chaos was ended by the war, more than ten years long, for the (re)conquest of southern mainland Italy—in practical terms another full-fledged invasion—begun in 1127 by Roger II, son of the great Count Roger (d. 1101) and, as we have said, from 1130 on "king of Sicily, of the Duchy of Apulia, and of the principality of Capua":

Sicily's conquest of southern Italy took a good deal of time and created great hostility. In the regions outside Sicily and southern Italy, for the pope and to a lesser degree for the two emperors and for the nascent Italian maritime powers, the creation of a strong state in an area that had heretofore served primarily as a buffer zone was a cause for considerable concern.

In fact, in the interior the Sicilian conquest possessed the crucial importance of a profound institutional transformation. Although it was implemented by a Christian prince, originally from Normandy, who had pledged his loyalty to the pope, the conquest still clearly shows a military and political superiority that had resulted from the Arab-Norman fusion that had taken place in Sicily. It was thanks to a partly Arab administration and army that Roger II had been able to seize control of mainland southern Italy. The regime that he established there was radically different from that which had been introduced there by the Norman conquerors of the eleventh century. Certainly, the Sicilian monarchy was based on feudalism and allowed . . . counts and barons a number of prerogatives of public origin. But the second pillar of that monarchy was an eastern-style bureaucracy, run largely by easterners, which Roger II began to install in the 1130s in the land he had conquered. This administration had no equivalent in any western kingdom of the time. . . . There can be no doubt that he was an exceptional man, who succeeded in founding in the remote outposts of the West, the first solidly structured state of the High Middle Ages, many decades before Henry II Plantagenet and half a century before Philip Augustus.[15]

In religious terms, although the Latin church was favored, the Greek church was respected (and would survive until the seventeenth century), while Islam and Judaism continued to be practiced regularly. In Sicily, the cradle of the monarchy, Arab, Greek, and

Lombard high officials and technicians played a more important role in the court of the count and later king than did the Norman barons. Last, in contrast with what happened in England, Norman Italy and Sicily, although they continued to attract western Frenchmen and Anglo-Normans until the middle of the eleventh century, had no institutional tie to the duchy of Normandy or its dependencies. The chief traits of the Normans coexisted with the traits that distinguished the various peoples already present on the site. The very term "Norman Italy" is inadequate to describe an original construction.[16]

In the niches that adorn the facade of the royal palace of Naples we can see, lined up one after another, statues depicting the founding fathers of the various foreign and merely "outsider" *(forestiere)* dynasties—from the Normans to the Piedmontese—who ruled over the southern kingdom from the time of its founding to its annexation to the Kingdom of Italy.

Renowned under the Norman kings as an unrivaled example of good government, it won the reputation for itself under the last of the Bourbon kings of being the worst-governed state in Europe. Benedetto Croce wondered why the state,

where for the first time there [were] civilized legislation and well-ordered finances and administration, where the government was conducted by sovereigns who were statesmen as well, and by ministers and diplomats who served the interests of their country, where there was the first conception of an absolute secular and enlightened monarchy, . . . that this state should arise and assert itself in the southern strip of Italy, which, in the centuries to follow, was to appear excessively disorderly and ill-regulated, famous, or rather, infamous for its constitutional weakness, its dishonest administration, brigandage, and generally backward conditions, and is, even now, in circumstances inferior to those of the other parts of the Kingdom of Italy.[17]

The answer that Croce offered to the question that he himself was asking was that

the Norman-Swabian story is ours only in small part, practically not at all. Norman-Swabian politics and culture had no indigenous and national character. . . . Much theorizing has revolved around the question why the kingdoms of Roger and of William the Conqueror, founded by men of the same stock and governed in the same way, should have followed such divergent paths and met with such different fates. . . . The reason is self-evident. In England the barons quickly adopted the aims and defended the interests first of their own class and then of the entire population. . . . Thus, in spite of racial differences and the contrast between conquerors and conquered, an English nation was born. In the Norman-Swabian kingdom things did not go the same way. No people, no nation came to birth.[18]

Because of Croce's great authority, this thesis, which in any case had the advantage of constituting a reaction against the excesses of southern Italian patriotic historiography, long stood at the center of debates among historians of the Kingdom of Sicily. Nowadays, of course, it has been rendered obsolete by the undermining of its central point. Without in any way dismissing the well-established reputation of the Normans as state builders, it cannot be overlooked that the human material that they used in their Sicilian and southern creation, considering that they arrived here in tiny numbers and not as invaders, as would later be the case in England, was what they found on the site—and it could not have been otherwise:

The term "Norman" Sicily has conjured up an image of a kingdom analogous to the Norman state in England and France, conquered and held by a powerful aristocracy of Norse descent. As far as Sicily is concerned, the label "Norman" is really of use only as a dynastic label, with which to describe its ruling family, the Hautevilles, who established the Sicilian monarchy with the help of Norman, Italian, and other knights. It has been seen that these knights did not win great estates in Sicily proper, though they prospered in southern Italy where there were more Norman settlers, but also many Latin Christians of native origin. The Normans intermarried with the south Italian aristocracy and, personal names apart, lost most of their links with the duchy of Normandy. Memories of the Norman connection remained alive, but more in the minds of Anglo-Norman chroniclers, . . . than among the Italianized Normans of Apulia, Calabria, or Sicily.[19]

If we have referred to Croce's thesis, it is also because it offers us an excuse to note that in the same decades in which it held sway, in the Soviet Union, the author Andrei Amalrik—who wrote in a historical essay (going against the official party line that only Slavic tribes had founded the first Russian state, Kievan Rus') that the Swedish merchants and warriors known as Varegs had actually played a role—paid for his innocent bit of heresy with detention in the Gulag.

CERTAINLY far more numerous than the Norman knights who landed on the coasts of southern Italy at the turn of the eleventh century, and at least as numerous as the German knights who accompanied their rulers on expeditions into Italy, were the students who came from every corner of Europe—from Spain, Poland, and the kingdoms of England and Sicily—to Bologna, beginning at the turn of the twelfth century, as soon as word began to spread that a group of local legal experts, on their own initiative, as mentioned above—that is, without any established power's having invited them to do so—had begun to gloss the legislative anthologies of Justinian. These were the subject of regular courses of lectures, during which those famous creations of Roman juridical wisdom were dissected, analyzed, and commented upon, with the goal of refining the *ratio,* the logic that had inspired them. They produced a rich trove of valuable teachings for the technicians of the law who were obliged to do their work in a medieval society, so different from the societies of antiquity and late antiquity.

In contrast with the laws issued by monarchs of the time, the statutes established by cities and professional guilds, and the customs that still guided life in many territorial seigniories, the Roman law that was being reinterpreted in Bologna was presented as "common law"—the law to which all could turn when their own specific laws did not answer the case. It is clear, then, why a period of time spent studying in Bologna—even if the voyage was lengthy and full of risks and the long stay costly, even for the well-to-do—became the necessary passport for those who hoped to become members of the ruling class of their own nation and city.

In order to work together to overcome the difficulties of every sort posed by an extended stay in a foreign land, the students from a given country soon formed mutual-help associations (or *nationes*). When these organizations were joined together, in the early decades of the thirteenth century, they led to the creation of the *universitas ultramontanorum*, the association of law students from north of the Alps (literally, "ultramontanes"), which constituted, over the course of the centuries, the structure of the Studium of Bologna, to the point that the term *universitas* would in time come to replace that of *Studium*.

6

THE METEOR FREDERICK II AND
THE BITTER "CHICKPEAS" OF
THE FRENCH IN SICILY

FREDERICK BARBAROSSA had a hard time resigning himself to the idea of the existence of the Norman Kingdom of Sicily. Well run, prosperous, and sun-kissed, it constituted a clear refutation of his faith in the universal character of the office of ruler of the Holy Roman Empire. "In the 1160s, the armed conquest of the outlawed kingdom was a firm imperial intention. The very word was to be canceled, though it seems unlikely that Frederick meant to dismantle a bureaucracy that produced such vast wealth."[1] Later, however, the emperor softened his stance: in 1177 he recognized the Kingdom of Sicily; in 1186, his son Henry, whom he had named as his successor in 1167, was married in Milan, at the Basilica of St. Ambrose, to Constance of Hauteville (1154–1198), the youngest daughter of Roger II, the first ruler of that kingdom.

It is in fact reasonable to suppose that the goal of the marriage was nothing more than a quest for peaceful coexistence with the southern kingdom. If, for instance, when the marriage was stipulated, Constance was the presumptive heir to that kingdom because her uncle William II was childless, it should also be pointed out that he had been married only three years, and he might very well have had children in the years to come. In fact, the planned marriage was probably encouraged by none other than Pope Lucius III (1181–1185), and he would never have urged it if he had even suspected that one day it might lead to the "union of the kingdom with the empire," with the ensuing encirclement of the Patrimony of Saint Peter and, concomitantly, a serious threat to the existence of what rightly or wrongly was thought in Rome to be an indispensable guarantee of the free exercise of universal ecclesiastical jurisdiction.

But in one of those typically unpredictable developments in the diplomacy of dynastic marriages, William II's death (in 1189) without heirs gave rise to events that no one could have predicted in 1186. Before he could fulfill his father's former ambitions, Henry VI would have to wait as well for the death (in February 1194) of Tancred of Lecce, the illegitimate son of Roger of Apulia, the eldest son of Roger II, who had been crowned king of Sicily in 1190, thanks to the support of what Benedetto Croce ventured to call "the mere hint of a national party among the barons," hostile to Henry as a foreign sovereign.[2] Their resistance, however, was in no way comparable in either numbers or fierce determination, to what had been seen in northern Italy when the communes had united in a league to ward off the threat that the German emperor posed to their independence. On Christmas Day 1194, Henry VI was crowned in Palermo. The following day, the empress Constance, by now mature in years, gave birth to a son in the town of Jesi. She was just passing through Jesi, on her way to Sicily to reach her husband. She named the boy Constantine, perhaps to mark him as her own through the similarity of first names; later, the child was baptized Frederick-Roger, combining the names of its two grandfathers. The child was destined to go down in history, however, as Frederick II.

Left fatherless at the age of three and motherless at the age of four, Frederick, who had been crowned king of Sicily (17 May 1198) seven months before Constance's death, had been entrusted by his mother to a very unusual guardian: Pope Innocent III (1198–1216), who did everything within his power—unsuccessfully, as we shall see—to keep his ward from becoming anything more than the king of Sicily, to keep him from becoming also king of Germany and emperor (as well as, implicitly, king of Italy), and thus following in the footsteps of his father, Henry, who had held those titles from 1194 until his death in 1197. Henry, for his part, believed wrongly that he had established a *fait accompli* by arranging the election in Frankfurt, at the end of 1196, of Frederick as king of Germany, even before his mother arranged to make him king of Sicily. To nullify that election, Innocent III, in a document dating from 1200/1201, adduced the wisdom of *Ecclesiastes* (10:16): "Woe to thee, O land, when thy king [is] a child, and thy princes eat in the morning." Clearly, the warning was meant only for Germany, and not for Sicily, where Frederick was under the pope's own guardianship.

While Innocent III watched over him from afar and as European politics followed their course, largely ignoring the existence of the *puer Apuliae* (Apulia was the name used to designate all of southern Italy—that is, the mainland section of the Kingdom of Sicily) whose birth had awakened so many hopes and fears, Frederick set about obtaining an education on his own in the streets of the capital city of his realm, Palermo, in contact with a human environment that, in the extraordinary diversity of its religious, ethnic, and linguistic components, constituted a *unicum* that had no counterpart in the Europe of the time, with the exception of the cities of Muslim Spain. While we may guess that he taught himself smatterings of Provençal, French, German, Arabic, and Greek in the streets and marketplaces of Palermo, a proper *magister* must have taught him Latin. Someone, perhaps an Arab, must have inculcated in him, from when he was quite small, the taste for observing nature—animals, and birds in particular, plants, the stars, the human body itself—that would become one of the distinctive traits of Frederick II the adult. But the resistance that the ward of Innocent III put up, punching, scratching, and kicking—at the age of seven!—to the armed soldiers of Markward of Anweiler (a loyal German follower of Henry VI, whom Constance had sent away during her regency) when they attacked the royal castle in Palermo to seize him is already an indication of the rapid transformation that was to turn a child—till then the object of the ambitions and concerns of the adults of varying ethnic origins who surrounded him—into the active and determined protagonist of a story that still smacks of the incredible.

In the meantime, the struggle was under way for the succession to Henry VI's thrones in Germany and the empire between Philip of Swabia (1198–1208), brother of the late emperor, and Otto of Brunswick (1198–1218), the youngest son of Henry the Lion, duke of Saxony and Bavaria (d. 1195), who had been Barbarossa's most implacable foe in Germany, as well as the nephew of Richard I the Lion-Hearted, king of England (1189–1199), who with his support, especially financial, lavished with great largesse, gave Otto, as chief of the anti-Swabian party, the means with which to oppose Philip's candidacy. In this connection, we should remind the reader that it was from *Welfen,* as the members of the house of Bavaria were called, and *Weiblingen,* a term used to describe the members of the house of Swabia, taken from the name of a Hohenstaufen castle, that the words "Guelphs" and "Ghibellines" would later develop in Italy, a pair of names that became the indelible symbol of Italy's disunion, with the aggravating factor that, as we have just seen, they were above all a product of foreign importation. Still, it is also true that this "conflict and division," so typical of Italy, took the form of a division, true enough, but one that, like the *conflits et partages* which characterized even a history as traditionally unified as that of France (let us think of the Burgundians and the Armagnacs in the fifteenth century, or in more recent times *les bleus et les blancs* or *les rouges et les blancs*),[3] objectively served to organize under two opposing banners forces that were otherwise engaged in a welter of uncorrelated local conflicts: "It is a very remarkable fact and, if we like, paradoxical, that Guelphism and Ghibellinism, identified, scorned, and cursed in the jeremiads of generations as the chief misfortune, the incurable hereditary defect of Italian history, should later have constituted the path or one of the paths by which the political fragmentation of the communes was reduced and consolidated into regional entities."[4]

From Rome, Innocent III took care to play off one against the other the two claimants to Henry's crown, who would inevitably sooner or later have tried to succeed to his title in Sicily as well, shoving aside the child that Constance had entrusted to him. But the intrigues of the "Latin" pope did not pass unobserved:

Oh how the Pope laughs now, so like a Christian,
as he tells his Italians: "I've got it all arranged. Listen!"
The things he says down there he never even should have
  thought.
"Two *tedeschi* beneath one crown," he says: "That's what I
  have wrought.
Let them lay waste the Empire, burn it, bring it under—
we rummage in their chests while all that's going on there.
I've goaded them to my big pole there, all their goods are
  mine,
their German silver emigrates to my Italian shrine.
Eat chicken, churchmen—all you priests, drink wine,
and let the Germans fast up yonder."[5]

In 1208 the pope put an end to the regency, and Frederick took
possession of the Kingdom of Sicily. He had just turned fourteen.
The following year, he married Constance of Aragon (1181–1222),
who was the daughter of King Alphonse II (1152–1196) and the sister
of King Peter II (1174–1213), respectively. To rule in Palermo, restoring the authority of the central power after years of domestic dis-
cord between Sicilian Normans and Sicilian Germans, would have
been no easy task for anyone. While Frederick was preparing to take
up the challenge, a sudden change in the situation in Germany
opened an unexpected field of action for him. Otto IV of Brunswick
became Holy Roman Emperor in 1209, and in November of the following year he invaded the Kingdom of Sicily, to which he laid claim
as the husband of Beatrice, the daughter of Philip of Swabia, the
other pretender to the succession of Henry VI, who had been murdered in June 1208. In the face of the threat that Germany, Italy, and
Sicily might wind up once again in the hands of a single monarch,
Innocent III excommunicated Otto and then promptly instigated
against him Frederick's candidacy in Germany, with the support of
Philip Augustus, king of France, as well. In September 1211, by which
point Otto was master of the mainland provinces and ready to set
sail for the island and Frederick was on the verge of seeking safety in

Africa, the princes of Germany assembled in Nuremberg invited Frederick to travel to Germany to be crowned king of the Romans, a title which, as explained earlier, entailed sovereignty over Germany and also designation as the Holy Roman Emperor.

After winning out over the resistance of many in his circle, beginning with his wife Constance, who had warned the seventeen-year-old ruler of Sicily about the risks involved in the undertaking for which he was girding himself, and after providing the pope with the necessary guarantees (Frederick himself would not be king of Sicily; instead, his son Henry, born the year before, would hold that title; in any case it was understood that the kingdom was a feudal holding of the Church), Frederick boarded a ship at Messina in March 1212 with a few comrades and sailed to Gaeta. Then, after a month's stay in Rome without an army, where he struggled to learn a little German, encouraged only by the support of the king of France and the pope—to many, grounds for ridicule—he set sail for Genoa and then continued through northern Italy and over the Alps toward Germany. On 5 December, still in 1212, he was formally elected king of the Romans in Frankfurt. On the ninth of the same month he was crowned in Mainz by the archbishop. Up to this point, things had gone according to Innocent III's plans.

On 22 November 1220, Frederick was crowned emperor in St. Peter's by Innocent III's successor Honorius III (1216–1227). But as he was, practically speaking, about to abandon Germany to its fate (he did not set foot there for another fifteen years), after having spent seven years there, during which time he had done everything possible to win the favor of princes and bishops through the continual concession of privileges, which further diminished the already badly undermined prestige of the royal institution in that land, Frederick brought his son Henry to Germany, with the intention of having him elected king of the Romans and therefore his successor as emperor (the election took place as planned in April of that same year), ignoring the promise he had made to Innocent III in 1212. Despite this precedent, Honorius relied on the assurances that Frederick gladly offered him: never would the crown of Sicily be joined to the

crown of the empire; the southern kingdom would remain subordi-
nate to the Apostolic See; the empire and the kingdom of Sicily
were two distinct entities, joined only in his person. As if the union
of the two (or three) crowns that were intended to be merely temporary even for him had not already been established in advance for
the person of his son as well!

All these royal titles and the constant appeals to the imperial ide-
ology, however, never corresponded to the reality of power actually
exercised, with equal intensity, on either side of the Alps, much less
on either side of the Apennines. The son of a Swabian-German father and a Sicilian-Norman mother, Frederick considered himself a
Sicilian. He would always speak of Sicily and the other provinces of
the kingdom as "his land," and of Italy as "his heritage." He was ap-
palled by Germany, with its "shadowy forests" and its "long win-
ters," with its "muddy cities" and its "crude castles." It was on the
Kingdom of Sicily that Frederick focused all his energy and passion
as a statesman.

The code of laws promulgated at Melfi in 1231; the coins that issued from the royal mints, and from those mints only (among the
other varieties, we should mention the gold *augustalis* coin, minted
as a "prestige issue . . . its propaganda function perhaps surpassed its
monetary function," and not for economic logic);[6] the documents
that describe the activity carried out on a daily basis by the tribunals
and public offices to protect the rights of subjects against the abuses
of the powerful: all these are so many elements that help character-
ize Frederick, even more than his astonishing intellectual curiosity.
Still, they are not enough to justify the description of him as the first
modern ruler that historians have attributed to him in the past. This
even though the very historian who more than any other has helped
restore to the "first modern ruler" the garb of a "medieval emperor," more appropriate to the time when he lived and the chief
rank that he held, was able to write:

Thus the reign of Frederick II marks a major stage in the transformation of Europe from a community of Latin Christians under the

headship of two competing universal powers, pope and emperor, to a Europe of nation-states, in which the Roman Emperor counted for much less. In some respects Frederick's other major territory [other than Germany, that is], the smaller but better-controlled kingdom of Sicily (often called the *regno,* the kingdom), is the place to begin any study of the emergence of the nation-state; its inhabitants were far from being a "nation" in any sense of the term, but the centralized methods of government adopted in Sicily were as important in the development of the nation-state as were the gradually evolving notions of ethnic, cultural or linguistic unity that Sicily acquired more slowly than most other European kingdoms. Frederick ruled both a universal empire and a territorial monarchy, and he ruled them in very different ways, with no intention (contrary to frequent assumption) of integrating them into a monolithic Roman autocracy stretching from the borders of Denmark through Italy to Sicily.[7]

In a chapel in the cathedral of Palermo, in sarcophagi made of porphyry, the imperial marble of ancient Rome, are preserved his remains and those of his father, Henry VI; his mother, Constance; his grandfather Roger II; and his first wife, Constance of Aragon—monarchs of the two foreign dynasties, Norman and Swabian, that together contributed to make the Kingdom of Sicily, along with the English realm, the most advanced state in Europe for a century and a half. They had come speaking French and German. They would end up sinking roots here, in southern Italy and Sicily. In contrast with Henry VI, who wrote poetry easily in Middle High German, Frederick was an unexceptional poet writing in vernacular Italian. Poets from other regions of Italy came to his court. Dante hailed the role that court played as a national Italian linguistic and literary forum, with the result that "whatever our predecessors wrote in the vulgar tongue was called Sicilian"; and he noted:

But those illustrious heroes Frederick Caesar and his happy-born son Manfred, displaying the nobility and righteousness of their character, as long as fortune remained favourable, followed what is human, disdaining what is bestial; wherefore those who were of noble heart and endowed with graces strove to attach themselves to the majesty of such great princes; so that in their time, whatever the best Italians attempted first appeared at the court of these mighty sovereigns.[8]

Alongside the poets writing in vernacular, other honored guests of Frederick's court were Jewish and Arab Muslim scholars. In Sicily, the latter still felt quite at home. In a science like astronomy, abstruse and still viewed with a degree of suspicion because there was no distinction at the time between it and astrology, or in the difficult art of raising and training falcons to hunt, the learned Arab Muslims were unrivaled.

The attention that Frederick devoted to falcons, and to birds in general, went well beyond what one might expect from an impassioned hunter. His interest was rather that of a naturalist, an ethologist, observant of the arrangements of flocks, the behavior of birds during storms that catch them by surprise over the open sea, the shape of nests. All these subjects, together with material more specifically regarding falconry, are discussed in a treatise that the emperor drew up on the basis of information and texts given to him by his Muslim friends. In *De arte venandi cum avibus* Frederick did not hesitate to question, on the basis of his own direct observations, a number of passages from the treatise on animals by Aristotle, an author whose work in that period had only recently been translated from the Arabic and enjoyed an authority second only to that of the Scriptures.[9]

The translations of philosophical, medical, and astrological texts from the Greek, Hebrew, and Arabic won Sicily during the Swabian period a place of some importance, though not comparable with that accorded the work being done in Spain to recover the classics of ancient thinking and science and to popularize in the West the most recent achievements of Arabic and Jewish thought and science.

And yet despite his extraordinary openness to new ideas, Frederick, in a contradiction that is only an apparent one, if we stop to consider the array of demands with which he was faced, fought the

Muslims of Sicily. Even before his time, around 1190, the urban Arab presence had experienced a final and definitive decline on the island. But having taken refuge in the mountainous regions of the Sicilian interior, the Muslims constituted at the beginning of the second decade of the thirteenth century a very serious problem of law and order, a problem that Frederick took on with relentless energy. The hero of the Arab resistance in Sicily was Ibn Abbad, known as Mirabetto. He was sentenced to death, along with his two sons. It was not a full-fledged war; rather, it was a series of guerrilla actions on one side, and on the other a vast police operation. The stronghold of the Muslims was Girgenti (Agrigento). From there, they were in regular contact with their fellow Muslims in Africa. The struggle was long and harsh, but it culminated in victory for Frederick's troops. Frederick arranged to settle the survivors of the repression in Apulia. The refugees were allowed to live at Lucera in a sort of obligatory colony, despite the complaints of the local clergy and even the Curia in Rome. Pope Innocent IV (1243–1254) could not think of the colony "without the sensation," as he had occasion to say, "of a thorn thrust into the eye of the Church." Normally assigned to farmwork, the survivors constituted in case of necessity a select army corps, exceedingly loyal to Frederick, it goes without saying. In February 1237, when he took possession of Padua in his own name and the name of the emperor, Ezzelino (III) da Romano (1194–1259) commanded a detachment made up of German knights and Saracen bowmen from Lucera.

NEWLY ELECTED emperor in 1220, Frederick had tried to oblige the communes to respect the terms of the treaty established with Barbarossa at Constance in 1183. The conflict, which seemed on the point of turning into a full-blown war in 1226, was defused for a decade. At first, Frederick was triumphant. At Cortenuova in 1237, he captured several parts of the Milanese *carroccio*, which he saw fit to send as a gift to the Romans with a solemn accompanying letter, in all likelihood composed by Pier delle Vigne, one of the emperor's closest collaborators:

> Our intentions would diverge reprehensibly from observance of just conduct if we who receive such an abundance of light from our standing as the Roman Caesar were to allow the Romans themselves to be deprived of the manifestations of joy for what *is* a Roman victory.
>
> Having defeated Milan, the city at the head of the Italian conspiracy, we send you its *carroccio,* as booty and plunder from the conquered enemies. Please accept joyfully, then, O Quirites, the victory of your emperor.
>
> According to a rumor that has reached our ears, those who suffer in the depth of their hearts at the sight of such a perpetual commemoration of Caesar's triumph are preparing to destroy the *carroccio* by arson. Take care, lest those envious of your glory be enabled to boast of their ill will. Let the Roman Senate and people by law sanction capital punishment against any who might make such an attack.[10]

Nonetheless, despite the opposition of the pope (it is to him that the letter alludes)—a chronicler records that when Gregory IX learned of the undertaking, he wept—the relics of the Milanese *carroccio* were placed in a specially built edicule in the Campidoglio, or Capitol. Of that structure, two pillars made of *verde antico* (Thessalian marble), reused after the edicule was dismantled and destroyed, still exist. The inscription was also preserved (and is now visible in a recently restored hall), likewise dictated by Pier delle Vigne, and recalling the humiliation of Milan and the victory of Frederick and the Romans.[11] Skillfully, the emperor and his spokesman took advantage of the battle of Cortenuova to try to place a wedge between the idea of Rome and the incipient national feeling of the Italians, which could never have survived without that idea.

In 1248 came the first triumph of the communes: the failure of the siege of Parma, with the destruction of the imperial camp. Frederick had solemnly "founded" the camp, as if it were a new city, christening it imprudently with the name Victoria (victory).

In 1249, a second and more serious check for Frederick: during the course of a battle between the Bolognese and the Modenese near Fossalta, Enzo, king of Sardinia, his favorite son—Falconello (or little falcon), as he called him—was captured by the Bolognese, who refused the offer of ransom. In vain, Frederick reminded them that fortune is fickle, that it often raises someone up, only to ensure that he will tumble all the more disastrously to the earth below. The arrogance of the Bolognese and the Lombards would in any case be punished, their present joy transmuted into grief tomorrow. If instead they agreed to free Enzo, Bologna would be exalted above all the other cities of Italy. The Bolognese replied by quoting David: "Let the wicked perish at the presence of God" (Psalms 68:2). It was pointless to try to frighten them with empty words: they were not marsh reeds that could be shaken by a breath of wind. In short: "We have taken King Enzo prisoner, and we shall hold him, we shall keep him forever."[12] And they refused to yield. King Enzo would in fact die, still imprisoned, in Bologna in 1272. Only then did the Bolognese show any generosity: his corpse, embalmed, was buried in the church of San Domenico. Enzo, the Italian version of Heinz, a shortened form of the German Heinrich, was by this point so emphatically not a foreigner that he took advantage of his many years in prison to encourage the transplanting to Bologna of the Sicilian poetic style, thus earning for himself a position of some importance in the history of early Italian literature.

———

AFTER FREDERICK II's death in 1250, the popes worked successfully to prevent any kings of Germany and Italy from ever ruling in Sicily as well. Just as in the distant past his predecessors had turned to Pippin and to Charlemagne to save them from the Longobards, so also Clement IV (1265–1268), a French pope—French, just as his predecessor, Urban IV (1261–1264), the first to have the idea, had been

French—in 1265 urged Charles of Anjou (1226–1285) to come to Rome. Charles was the brother of Louis IX, king of France (1226–1270), who had rejected the invitation, which had initially been extended to him with a view to making him—as opposed to Manfred (1232–1266), Frederick II's illegitimate son—king of Sicily, thus nipping in the bud any hopes of a Hohenstaufen revival in Italy.

On 28 June 1265, at the behest of Clement IV, four cardinals invested the count of Anjou with the kingdom of Sicily, which the Church considered to be its own feudal possession, on the basis of a remote and questionable precedent. On 6 June 1266 Charles was elected king of that realm. In the meanwhile, the pope had taken steps to secure the necessary financing for the expedition against Manfred that his protégé would need to undertake in order to gain possession of the kingdom that was already his, on paper at least. With that goal, he placed the indulgence ordered for the Crusade in the service of anti-Swabian recruitment in France and northern Italy and ordered that the tax revenues raised in France and Provence to finance the Crusade should be diverted to underwrite the expedition. Moreover, since time was of the essence, when he learned of Louis IX's refusal to advance the necessary cash or to offer to act as guarantor with the Italian bankers who he hoped would lend him the money, Clement did not hesitate to negotiate the loan with the Roman and Tuscan bankers himself, committing as collateral "not only the revenues of the tithe for the Crusade, but also the other revenues of the Apostolic Chamber and finally also the treasury of the Church and the possessions of many Roman churches."[13]

As early as February 1266, Charles defeated Manfred at Benevento and became the ruler of the kingdom. Thereafter, he experienced little difficulty in overcoming as well the opposition of Conradin (1252–1268), the son of Conrad IV (1228–1254), who was another one of Frederick II's sons. Conradin had come to Italy from Germany in the foolish hope that he would be able to win back his grandfather's entire bequest. Defeated by the Angevin monarch at Tagliacozzo on 23 August 1268, he was beheaded in Naples in what is now the Piazza del Mercato (market square), as a disturber of the peace. The victor of Tagliacozzo was by now, with the pope's blessing, the supreme guardian of that peace.

Dante, in the *Divine Comedy* (*Purgatorio,* III, verses 103–145), would mention the *orribili peccati* (horrible sins) of Manfred, who remained obstinate until the very moment before his death (but seizing that moment, he saved himself) in his stubborn determination not to submit to the authority of the Church. He paid him military honors: *biondo era e bello e di gentile aspetto* ("fair he was, and handsome and kind in appearance"). It was meanwhile for Charles, who had been summoned by the pope, that Dante (a Guelph, though a Guelph *sui generis*) reserved his bitterest sarcasm. That was what the butcher of Conradin and (as a common rumor had it) the poisoner of St. Thomas Aquinas deserved.

WITH THE ANGEVINS, the capital of the Kingdom of Sicily was moved from Palermo to Naples, even though no official document exists proclaiming it the capital.[14] For Charles, who was also count of Anjou, of Maine, and of Provence, as well as, and especially, acknowledged chief of the Guelphs in central and northern Italy, Palermo was too remote a capital. This decision marked for all time the "Parisian" destiny of Naples. Frederick II had founded the Studium there, accessible at first only to citizens of the kingdom, but from 1239 on also to *ultramontani* (ultramontanes—literally, those from over the mountains) and *italici* (or Italic people), though the latter only with the appropriate exceptions (no Milanese, Brescians, Piacentines, Bolognese, and so on), consisting of his enemies. Now the transferal of the court and the central administration accelerated the city's development, on the economic and urbanistic plane as well. Under the new dynasty, Naples became one of the leading centers for the spread in Italy of Gothic art, which had originated on French soil. The churches of San Lorenzo and Santa Chiara, containing the tombs of the Angevin rulers, still stand, testimony to the first historic phase of Naples as the capital of southern Italy.[15]

Charles was an energetic and ambitious man. "King Charles"— wrote a troubadour in his court—"will be the lord of most of the world. It belongs to him and suits him."[16] He meted out harsh punishment to all those in the kingdom who had sided with Conradin of Swabia in 1268. He confiscated their lands and redistributed them to some seven hundred Frenchmen and Provençals, who were required in return not to leave the kingdom for more than a year at a time. The cities were stripped of what little autonomy they still enjoyed. By contrast, the administration of justice was improved. But the king's ambitions in the sphere of foreign policy entailed taxes, taxes, and more taxes. Like the other sovereigns of southern Italy, Charles too considered southern Italy and Sicily a bottomless well, from which he could draw as much and as often as he liked.

It did not all go on military spending, however. The roads were improved, and harbors were enlarged; agriculture and sheepherding benefited. The forests, which provided the lumber for shipbuilding, were protected. But the benefits of this development tended to be pocketed by entrepreneurs from outside the kingdom, merchants and bankers from Tuscany for the most part, upon whom privileges were heaped. As a result, local initiative was discouraged and the financial and commercial inferiority of southern Italy began to solidify, marking the beginning of what would become over the centuries one of the main traits of the less advanced of the "two Italys."

In Lucera, if the cathedral offers evidence of the spread of Gothic art to the provinces as well, the castle looming over the town represented the oppressive face of Angevin power. Here in August 1269 the surviving followers of the Swabians and the Saracens of Frederick's colony fought their last battle against the French dynasty. Charles spared the lives of the Muslims alone. A Provençal troubadour criticized the king for this disparity in treatment. An end was put to the scandalous existence of the name of *Lucera Saracenorum* under the rule of Charles I's son and successor, Charles II (1289–

1309), in August 1300. The following year, he expressed "his fervent hope that 'Holy Mother Church would be venerated and that the Christian faith would be cultivated to the praise of God in that place where once the profane rite of the Synagogue [*sic!*] of the condemned prince Mohammed took place,' in Città Santa Maria (City of Saint Mary), formerly known by the name Lucera."[17]

———

ON THE AFTERNOON of Easter 1282, in the square before the Church of the Holy Spirit, just outside Palermo, a great crowd stood waiting for the ceremony of vespers to begin. A few French soldiers arrived, slightly drunk. One of them, a Sergeant Frouet (or Droetto), importuned a young Sicilian bride. The husband drew a knife, attacked Droetto, and killed him. The other French soldiers tried to respond to the attack. But the enraged crowd surrounded them and killed them all. Just then, the church bells rang for vespers.

From Palermo the cry of "Death to the French" ("*Mora, mora!*" as Dante put it: *Paradiso*, VIII, verse 75) spread to the rest of Sicily. The Angevin strongholds (forty-two castles scattered across the island) melted away. To root out the French who were trying to save themselves by passing for Sicilians, the rebels devised the test of asking them to pronounce the word *ciceri* (Sicilian for "chickpeas"), which was unpronounceable for a Frenchman. Even Sicilian women who had married Frenchmen were slaughtered without mercy. In a certain sense, it seemed fair to think that Sicily was preparing to take the path that the cities of northern Italy had already followed several centuries earlier.

But the revolutionary euphoria soon dwindled. Charles of Anjou immediately launched a counterattack from the mainland. Pope Martin IV (1281–1285) rejected the plan to transform Sicily into a federation of communes under the sovereignty of the Holy See. At that point, the Sicilians, who were determined at all costs not to return to French rule, had only one remaining option: to ask for the intervention of another foreign monarch, Peter III of Aragon (1276–

1285). Peter had married Constance, daughter of the dethroned king Manfred, and could therefore lay a specific claim to the crown of Sicily. He ruled over the island until his death, as Peter I.

In the collective memory of the Sicilians, the Revolt of the Vespers has remained an important point of reference. That event was viewed as a moment of consecration for the Sicilian people's long struggle for the independence of its island homeland, which constituted from that time on the dominant note in Sicilian history. In order to mobilize Sicilian resistance against the Anglo-American forces that landed in Sicily on 10 July 1943, the Fascist government availed itself—unsuccessfully, as we shall see—of the device of forming "Volunteer Centuries of the Vespers." After the war, the "Sicilian separatist movement" harked back, as well, to that distant memory.

In the nineteenth century, a great Sicilian Arabist, Michele Amari, supported the idea that the Vespers was a spontaneous popular uprising.[18] Others, looking at the final outcome, have focused attention on the Mediterranean politics of the period and raised the question whether the long arm of agents of the king of Aragon might not have been behind the "spontaneity" of the rebels. More recently, emphasis has been placed on the fragility of the equilibrium between Sicily and the mainland provinces, in the context of the kingdom. With Frederick II a certain degree of equilibrium in favor of the latter was reestablished, but under Charles of Anjou the center of the monarchy shifted too sharply toward the mainland for the Sicilians to refrain from reacting. The Aragonese, who wound up establishing themselves here, were if nothing else a power with primarily Mediterranean interests, as the Normans had been in their day.

For the papacy it meant going back to square one. How to return Sicily under the Angevins and therefore under the eminent dominion of the Church, was the problem that almost wholly occupied the papacy of Boniface VIII, elected in December 1294 (d. 1303). In the end, he was forced to resign himself to the inevitability of the Aragonese presence on the island, in part because in the meantime his dispute with the king of France, Philip IV (the Fair, 1285–1314), had intensified. Philip was grimly opposed to the idea that the clergy of France should contribute, as Boniface wished, to financing the various attempts undertaken to win back Sicily while Philip needed those resources to fund his war against England, to eject the English from the Atlantic provinces of France, which they still held.

Peter III was succeeded in Aragon only by his first-born son, Alphonse (1285–1291), the third of that name, while in Sicily he was succeeded by another son, James (1285–1295), the first to bear that name. And so Sicily came to have a king of its very own. When Alphonse III died, James had however also become king of Aragon (1291–1327), the second by that name, holding on to Sicily until 1296, when another son of Peter III, Frederick (1296–1337), the second to bear the name, was elected king of the island. Because when James II died, his son Alphonse (IV) became king of Aragon, and when Frederick II died, his son Peter (II) became king of Sicily, the two kingdoms once again separated, and remained separate until 1409. In 1302, with the Peace of Caltabellotta, Boniface VIII had been obliged to give Frederick II sovereignty over the island. In order to reaffirm the right of his beloved Angevins to rule over the entire Kingdom of Sicily, however, he forced him to adopt the bookish and archaic title "King of Trinacria," which Frederick later abandoned. As a result, until 1372, when Joanna I of Anjou (1343–1381) formally renounced possession of the island, titling herself Queen of Naples, there were two kingdoms of Sicily. So great was the renown that still surrounded the memory of the ancient Norman and Swabian kingdom!

On 7 September 1303, the "Slap of Anagni" occurred. In symbolic terms, it was a sort of reverse Canossa, because this time it was a pope who suffered the humiliation. The most important aspect was that, in contrast with Canossa, facing Boniface VIII was not an emperor, with his claims to a universal government, antithetical and yet in some sense analogous to those held by the pope himself. Rather, it was the ruler of a specific kingdom. He too, however, was in his way an emperor, because—much as Innocent III had once incautiously proclaimed in his day, when he saw no other adversary than the emperor—he recognized no power greater than his own.

In the second half of August, word spread that on 8 September Boniface planned to post a papal bull on the main door of the cathedral of Anagni, one of the towns in which the popes had for roughly the past century been spending their summer months, to escape the oppressive heat of Rome. This bull would state that Philip the Fair, with his uncompromising attitude, had been excommunicated and that the pope would soon arrange to absolve Philip's subjects of their vows of loyalty and annul the alliances that the French king had established. The group of soldiers that forced its way into the papal palace of Anagni on Sunday the seventh was a composite formation. It included Guillaume de Nogaret, Philip's chancellor, with a small group of knights who bore the insignia of the king of France, along with a number of local lords who had been harmed economically by Pope Caetani and who were taking advantage of the opportunity to settle the score. Leading the latter and their henchmen, and setting the tone of the entire episode, was Sciarra Colonna, a member of a family of cardinals with landed interests in southern Latium that conflicted with the interests of the increasingly and aggressively wealthy Caetani family.

The sources agree that Boniface, practically alone and with an astylar cross in his hand, rejected with great dignity the order to abdicate. He supposedly replied, in the vernacular, "Ec le col, ec le cape" (here is the neck, here is the head). Apparently, his captors derided him by wrapping a donkey hide around his shoulders as a cape. The famous "slap," however, is just the product of a misreading of *manus inicere* (lay hands on), the phrase used in the Gospels to describe the capture of Jesus in the garden of Gethsemane (Matthew 26:50), which was cited at the time to describe what happened to Boniface. For that matter, did Dante—who so detested Boniface that even though he could not, for reasons of timing, place him in the Inferno (Boniface had not yet died in 1300, the year of Dante's journey to the world beyond), he included him without hesitation on a sort of waiting list for admittance (*Inferno*, XIX, verses 52–63)—not see in the victim of the assault of Anagni the figure of Christ himself, for whom the pontiff was considered to be the earthly vicar as well (*Purgatorio*, XX, verses 85–90)?

The kidnapping of Boniface VIII lasted for three days. Then the inhabitants of Anagni, who had acted as passive observers until that point, rose up and freed the pope. The banner of the king of France was tossed into the mud. Boniface was escorted safely back to Rome, and he died a month later.

THE THREE DAYS during which a Roman pontiff was actually held prisoner in Anagni by the chancellor of the king of France were followed by, and in some sense corresponded to, the seventy years of the so-called Babylonian captivity—that is to say, the period in which seven popes, all seven of them French, resided almost uninterruptedly in a location that was geographically French, even if Avignon, the city where the Curia was established, actually formed part not of the kingdom of France, but rather of the county of Provence (one of the dominions of the Angevin kings of Naples). Avignon, which possessed easy access to the sea along the course of the Rhône, moreover, constituted an enclave in the Comtat Venaissin—the only portion of the Church's temporal dominion situated to the north of the Alps (and so it would remain until the French Revolution)—to which it would be annexed in 1348 when Queen Joanna I of Naples sold it to Pope Clement VI.

The legend of the "Babylonian captivity"—Avignon as a latter-day Babylon, the city to which the Jews had been deported at the orders of Nebuchadnezzar II in the sixth century BC—had long been discredited. And yet the fact remains that many Italians saw the transfer of the seat of the papacy as an affront to Rome, and therefore to Italy. And so the dispute about the popes' residence in Avignon contributed to the creation of an Italian national sentiment—or resentment. And yet it also risked verging on excess, owing to the excessive emphasis placed on concerns of an ecclesiastical and religious nature, and the nostalgia for the grandeur and glories of ancient Rome.[19]

In response, Avignon launched the slogan: "Ubi papa, ibi Roma," or "Where the pope is, there is Rome."[20] And Francesco Petrarch, lost as he was in the dream of restoring the Roman past conceived by *his* Cola di Rienzo, the tribune of the people who had seized control of the city on May 1347 without spilling a drop of blood, shot back that Rome was not only the natural, necessary seat of the papacy, but also the *domina provinciarum,* the "mistress of provinces":

> Woe betide you [here Petrarch was speaking to Avignon, not to Cola di Rienzo, to whom the letter was addressed], wretch, if she [Rome] begins to awaken; what am I saying, to raise her head and recognize the damage and injuries done to her as she slept. . . . Perhaps you fail to realize who you are, where you are, to whom you are subject? Perhaps you do not know that the name Provence derives from *provincia* [note the lower-case 'p']? . . . Is this how you revere the mistress of provinces? She was in a slumber; you thought that she was dead. . . . You would like to appear to be something, to have some power. For a certain period of time, in delirium, we have allowed you to cherish this desire of yours; the time has come for our warning to cause you to regain your senses. . . .
>
> You, meanwhile [here Petrarch addresses Cola again], you who have taken pity upon our plight, O noble man, raise up the nascent fatherland and show the unbelieving peoples what Rome can still do today! As far as the rest of Italy is concerned, who can doubt that Rome has the power she once had and that she lacks neither wisdom nor strength nor material resources nor courage, but only harmony?[21]

From Avignon, the response came back that Provence was located in the heart of Europe and not on its outskirts, as Rome was. The pope could not return to Rome because the Italians were cowardly, riotous, dishonest, ignorant, and violent. In Italy, the food and drink was far inferior to the food and drink in France. The pope would certainly be poisoned there. . . . But St. Catherine of Siena shot back that "poison is found at the tables of Avignon and other cities, just as at the tables of Rome." She added that Italy was, yes, poisoned, but with a poison of mistrust, contempt, rancor, and bitterness, a poison that would continue to increase in intensity the longer the pope stayed away.

—————

IN RESPONSE to those who adduced, as an argument in favor of Avignon, the difficulty in obtaining adequate provisions, which the Curia would have to face once it returned to Italy (this emphasis on the quality and quantity of food at Avignon and Rome clearly demonstrates what we already knew, that the sin of gluttony was considered venial), Petrarch pointed out how many foreigners had come to Rome for the jubilee of 1350, the second in the series, and that none of them had starved.

Fifty years before, the jubilee of 1300 had been the finest hour of Boniface VIII.[22] Cardinal Stefaneschi tells us of the uncertainty on the eve of the holiday:

An ambiguous and almost incredible rumor concerning the centennial year about to begin had reached the ears of the Roman pontiff—the year 1300, which we were awaiting, was just around the corner—a rumor that announced that the power of salvation of that year would be so enormous that all those who came to Rome to the basilica of the prince of the apostles, Peter, in that year would attain full and complete purification from all sins. As a result of this, the merciful Father decreed that research be done into the recollections recorded in the ancient volumes. Since even these investigations failed to bring to light that which was being sought—perhaps because those books had been lost as a result of the negligence of the fathers . . . , that is, as a result of the schisms and wars, about which we might reasonably be more saddened than surprised that Rome is so often riven, or else because this was based more on opinion than truth—while the same pontiff resided in the patriarchal palace of the Lateran, the centennial year arrived.[23]

The first of January 1300 passed without events of any particular importance. But as the sun set, the Romans, as if by prearrangement, began to gather in St. Peter's. As the days passed, larger and larger crowds of pilgrims from outside Rome—from everywhere—began to join the faithful of Rome. It was the end of one of the centuries since the birth of Christ, which had signified a promise of salvation for one and all. And so there were many who believed that the passage of another century signified a new reconciliation, in the form of the remission of temporal penalties.

Until, on 22 February, Boniface VIII decided to proclaim a plenary indulgence for all those who came to Rome in that year, to pray in the basilicas of the Apostles Peter and Paul. The measure even applied retroactively for the nearly two months preceding. Thus, a movement that had originated spontaneously, from below, was skillfully guided, organized, and channeled into the streambed of ecclesiastical discipline. Through what would be known only later as a jubilee and would be held at fifty-year intervals (the name and the interval were both borrowed from the Old Testament, which in fact mentions the jubilee of the Hebrews), the *plenitudo potestatis* (fullness of the power) of the bishop of Rome, the ultimate administrator of the "treasury of merits" stored up by Christ and the saints, was exalted as the source of the value offered in a broad and easily accessible indulgence, unprecedented, considering that in the past such an indulgence had been accorded only to those who had gone to fight in Palestine for the liberation of the sepulchre of Christ.

At this point, the problem shifted from one of theology to one of logistics. Never before had a river of humanity been seen like the one that poured into Rome in those twelve months. There were also a great number of female pilgrims, in contrast with the custom of the time, which called for women to stay at home, close to children, spinning wheel, and hearth. And certainly it was inconceivable that the women might ever become Crusaders. According to Dante (*Inferno*, XVIII, verses 28–33), who, without having been there himself, probably quoted "information he received from others," to regulate the flow of pilgrims across the Ponte Sant'Angelo, a traffic divider was set up: on one side, those who were going to St. Peter's, on the other side, those returning from there.[24] The Florentine chronicler and merchant Giovanni Villani estimated that each day two hundred thousand outsiders came to the city, a figure that seems to have eluded the skepticism of someone who must have had some notions of accounting.[25] Matteo, his brother, reports that all Romans had become amateur hoteliers: such and such a sum of money for a bed (and a bad one), so much for the horse; board and oats extra.

Along the consular roads, which were hardly as broad and grand as they once had been (but all the pilgrims needed was a muddy track), bands of the faithful flocked from every region in Italy and every country in Europe toward Rome, with departures that were staggered across seasons:

> Apulians, Sardinians, and Corsicans, who had taken advantage of the hot summer, made way for others in fall and winter. By contrast, some from Spain, many from Provence, great numbers also from France, and a very few from England because of the wars, and all the other Westerners waited for cold weather similar to that in their own countries, and then, in a thoughtful and devoted crowd, went on pilgrimages to Rome at the end of fall or the beginning of winter. Nor were they the only ones who found these climatic conditions favorable; indeed, in the same season the arrival of Germans and Hungarians—peoples from the northern regions—resumed, and for the whole of the centennial year their numbers continued to increase.[26]

7

THE CHALK OF CHARLES VIII
AND THE LANCE OF FIERAMOSCA

In 1443, Alphonse V the Magnanimous, king of both Aragon and Sicily, became the king of Naples as well. In 1435 the Angevin dynasty of Naples had come to an end. This meant the reestablishment of a unified Kingdom of Sicily, as in bygone centuries. The name, however, was changed to the Kingdom of Naples. After the house of Anjou had given up possession of the island once and for all, that term was used to indicate the only part of the kingdom, first Norman and later Swabian, that they had held on to—that is, the mainland.

Political and territorial fragmentation had characterized the preceding centuries everywhere in Europe. In Italy it had been especially marked, owing to the absence of any native royal power and the great autonomy attained by the cities run as communes—and not only the larger cities, but also many of the medium- and smaller-size cities, to the detriment of a foreign royal power exercised discontinuously and therefore perceived as all the more alien to those dominated by that power. In Italy, furthermore, the process of recomposition of power did not coincide, as it did elsewhere, with the inauguration of a national state under the auspices of a sovereign. Instead, it stopped with the establishment of five regional states: the Duchy of Milan, the Republic of Venice, the Republic of Florence, the Papal States, and the Kingdom of Naples, which were surrounded by a series of lesser powers. Each of these five major powers attempted at different times, and with different methods, to expand its territories at the expense of its neighbor or neighbors, even revealing in some cases ambitions for hegemony over the entire peninsula. None of them were successful, however, because even if one moved in concert with another of the five, the others would hasten to block their moves to keep them from attaining their goals.

Suggested by the deadlock that followed on the heels of these failed efforts, which had for that matter entailed considerable cost, a plan took shape to render permanent the equilibrium existing among the forces at play. It was thought that this equilibrium could be assured through use of a consummate art of diplomacy. It was through separate, successive steps, then, that the "policy of equilibrium" was established. First (on 9 April 1454), with the peace of Lodi stipulated between Venice and Milan with the approval of Florence, then (on 30 August of that same year) with the establishment of the Italian League, promoted, again, by Venice and Milan. Their belief was that the assurances they had exchanged a few months earlier that they would no longer harbor ambitions of expansion or aggrandizement would have very little value unless they were accepted by all the rulers of the peninsula. In short, it was necessary for the five big powers and several of the smaller powers to feel that they were bound to respect shared principles and norms. Once this goal had been attained, and once the preservation of the territorial status quo among the states belonging to the league had been assured, it was thought that what was then pompously termed the "liberty of Italy" would be guaranteed against the appetites and the armies of the powers to the north of the Alps.

In this connection, the Italian political career of a non-Italian prince like Alphonse the Magnanimous is exemplary. From his father, Ferdinand I, he had inherited in 1416 not only Aragon, but also the kingdoms of Majorca, Sicily, and Sardinia, principal pillars of the Catalonian-Aragonese system of security in the western Mediterranean, which served as a support and a base of operations for the undertakings of Catalonian merchants in the Levant. The "island route" led to the spice ports. Alphonse, with his conquest of the Kingdom of Naples (his entry into the city, on 2 June 1442, was immortalized in the frieze with a magnificent portrayal of the triumph that was held in his honor, in the arch erected next to the portal of Castelnuovo, better known as the Maschio Angioino—literally, the Angevin Keep), consolidated the position of the Catalonians in the Mediterranean with respect to their most dangerous rivals—the Genoans. The king himself was a shrewd and enterprising businessman, but he tended to look beyond goals of short-term profit. He pursued dreams of Crusades, the destruction of the Turkish empire, the conquest of the Balkans, perhaps even empire.

An anonymous poet from his court described him as he watched the comings and goings during the siege of Naples of Catalonian vessels, both warships and cargo ships:

> The king of Aragon one day
> was watching from Campovecchio,
> watching the Spanish sea
> as it rose and fell;
> some ships left, others arrived;
> some were armed,
> others carried goods;
> some were sailing for Flanders,
> others to Lombardy.
> The ships that were returning from the war,
> oh, what a handsome effect they made!
> He looked at the great city
> that was called Naples;
> he looked at the three castles
> that were in the great city:
> Castelnuovo and Castelcapuano,
> Castel Sant'Elmo that glittered
> like the sun at midday.
> Tears poured from his eyes;
> his mouth said:
> "Oh city, how much you cost me

to my great disgrace!
You cost me dukes and counts,
men of enormous worth."[1]

Following the death in 1447 of Filippo Maria Visconti, duke of Milan, Alphonse attempted to accede to his throne. He failed however, and in the last years of his life this setback established a limit to his ambitions. However belatedly, he joined the Italian League, and when he died (1458), he left his hereditary kingdoms to his brother John II, and the Kingdom of Naples to an illegitimate son, Ferrando (d. 1494). With the southern kingdom under the rule of an Aragonese monarch, but independent and free of the demands of Catalonian maritime expansionism, the Italian balance of power was preserved, at least for the nonce.

The formula of the "policy of equilibrium," undertaken with precariously positive results by the regional states of Italy, would in time be adopted, with the necessary adaptations, by the nation-states of Europe. But by a tragic twist of fate this acceptance took place only after those states had massacred that original Italian "equilibrium"—which, when exposed to the test of reality, proved far more fragile than expected—and along with it, the "liberty of Italy," which it had been invoked to protect. They clashed violently in the *guerres d'Italie,* the wars, that is, fought by foreigners and for the most part among foreigners on Italian soil, which over the course of fifty years or more would lead to the establishment of a "foreign domination" over the peninsula: the "dark centuries" of Italy's history, as the period that begin in those years has sometimes been called, in a dramatic expression that is, however, accurate at least in part.

The years that preceded and witnessed the "wars of Italy" were a time in which, by a coincidence that constitutes perhaps the greatest peculiarity of the history of Italy, our country gave its greatest gifts to the world. These were in fact the years of the mature Renaissance. Naples, too, established itself during the reigns of Alphonse and Ferrando as one of the leading centers in the development and diffusion of humanistic culture and Renaissance art. They were the final, magnificent manifestations of the vitality of Italy's traditional particularism. Without the multiplicity of capitals and princely courts of the regional states, and even smaller courts and states, and without its background of political and cultural polycentrism, the Italian Renaissance would have been absolutely unimaginable. That is at least what Francesco Guicciardini believed, leaning toward the first alternative in the dilemma that he formulated himself, whether "Italy's not coming under a monarchy has been fortunate or unfortunate for this land," and concluding with an explicit statement that it was true that Italy, divided as it was, had experienced many calamities and that those calamities might well have been averted if the country had been united; it was also true, however, that "during every one of these periods Italy has had so many flourishing cities that she would not have had under one republic [a few lines earlier, Guicciardini wrote, "under a single dominion," meaning the same thing] that I deem a monarchy would have been more unfortunate than fortunate for her."[2]

But all these flourishing cities were soon to be ravaged by a veritable storm of foreign armies, the French first among them. Guicciardini emphasized this coincidence at the beginning of his *Storia d'Italia (The History of Italy)*, though without wondering why it could have happened and whether perchance Italy's lack of unity might not be a factor worth taking into consideration in any account of the things that happened, such as the one he was about to undertake:

> I have determined to write about those events which have occurred in Italy within our memory, ever since French troops, summoned by our own princes, began to stir up very great dissensions here: a most memorable subject in view of its scope and variety [that is, of occurrences], and full of the most terrible happenings; since for so many years Italy suffered all those calamities with which miserable mortals

are usually afflicted, sometimes because of the just anger of God, and sometimes because of the impiety and wickedness of other men. . . . But the misfortunes of Italy . . . tended to stir up men's minds with all the more displeasure and dread inasmuch as things in general were at that time most favorable and felicitous. It is obvious that ever since the Roman Empire, more than a thousand years ago, weakened mainly by the corruption of ancient customs, began to decline . . . , Italy had never enjoyed such prosperity, or known so favorable a situation as that in which it found itself so securely at rest in the year of our Christian salvation, 1490, and the years immediately before and after. The greatest peace and tranquillity reigned everywhere; the land under cultivation no less in the most mountainous and arid regions than in the most fertile plains and areas; dominated by no power other than her own, not only did Italy abound in inhabitants, merchandise and riches, but she was also highly renowned for the magnificence of many princes, for the splendor of so many most noble and beautiful cities, as the seat and majesty of religion, and flourishing with men most skillful in the administration of public affairs and most nobly talented in all disciplines and distinguished and industrious in all the arts.[3]

On this page there is of course no explicit mention, nor could it have been otherwise, of the word "Renaissance," which was not adopted to describe that period until 1860, in *Civilization of the Renaissance in Italy* by Jacob Burckhardt. But in Francesco De Sanctis's *Storia della letteratura italiana (History of Italian Literature)*, the contradiction between that prodigious flowering (or reflowering) in Italy of art and culture, accompanied by an unprecedented exaltation of the creative gifts of man, and the intrinsic political and military weakness of the Italian regional states, beginning with the Kingdom of Naples, is openly denounced:

One fine day, towards the end of the [fifteenth] century, when Pontano was frolicking in Latin verses and Sannazaro was playing the flageolet, suddenly into the middle of that society of balls and festivals and songs and idylls and romances came the foreigners and shook it awake. And at the first clash with the foreigner the monarchy [the Kingdom of Naples] collapsed, like a thing that was rotten at the core. Charles VIII rode into Italy and conquered it "with chalk." He found a people who called him a barbarian; a people in the full vigour of its intellectual forces, but empty of soul and weak of fibre. And Italy was bled by Frenchmen and Spaniards and Swiss and Landknechts until, with the fall of heroic Florence, the whole of the country was in the hands of the foreigner. The resistance had lasted for half a century, and these were the fifty years of struggle in which Italy developed the full sum of her forces and attained the ideal that the *Quattrocento* had bequeathed her. . . . On the threshold of the *Cinquecento* we are met by Machiavelli and Ariosto.[4]

De Sanctis, who was writing in 1870 and who had been educated and shaped in the atmosphere of Romanticism, strongly believed in the link between literature and civil life. The explanation that he offers for the Italian crisis of the late fifteenth and early sixteenth centuries has the enormous advantage of attempting to take matters together, aside from any purely aesthetic or intellectual appreciation of the civilization of the Renaissance in Italy:

> That the century was corrupt and that it was great was not the fault nor the merit of the literati or the princes, but the reason lay in the very nature of the movement that had produced it, and which now was showing itself clearly. It was not the result of intellectual struggles and of new beliefs, as in other countries, but was born from a profound indifference as to religion and morals, an indifference accompanied by diffusion of culture, growth of intellect, and the development of the feeling for art. Here was the germ of life, and here also the germ of death: the greatness of the century and its weakness.[5]

The Italians were proud to consider themselves heirs to the ancient Romans and were always ready to boast of their ancestry in front of others: the "barbarians." In reality, however, to take the words of as sharp-eyed an observer as Niccolò Machiavelli, they had ignored the lessons of their ancestors on a point that he considered essential. After listing the "principal states" and the most important of the secondary states that made up the polycentric landscape of the Italy of his time, so divergent from the unity with which Italy had won its prosperity in Roman times, and which it had never regained since, Machiavelli addressed a question that was of special importance to him. He laid out this question in considerable detail, setting forth the terms that made it up in 1434, which—since that was the year "in which . . . the de' Medici family, owing to the merits of Cosimo and his father Giovanni, seized greater authority than any other family in Florence"—was when he had at first planned to begin his *Istorie Fiorentine (Florentine Histories).*[6] It was only later that he decided to preface the work with a sort of "universal treatise," specifically the first book, dedicated to the consequences that an event as catastrophic in his view as the fall of the Western empire had for Italy:[7]

> None of the principal states were armed with their own proper forces. Duke [of Milan] Filippo [Filippo Maria Visconti] kept himself shut up in his apartments, and would not allow himself to be seen; his wars were managed by commissaries. The Venetians, when they directed their attention to terra firma [the Venetian Lombard mainland], threw off those arms which had made them terrible upon the seas, and falling into the customs of Italy, submitted their forces to the direction of others. The practice of arms being unsuitable to priests or women, the pope and Queen Joan [II of Naples] were compelled by necessity to submit to the same system which others practiced from defect of judgment. The Florentines also adopted the same custom, for having, by their frequent divisions, destroyed the nobility, and their republic being wholly in the hands of men brought up to trade, they followed the usages and example of others. Thus the arms of Italy were either in the hands of the lesser

princes, or of men who possessed no state; for the minor princes did not adopt the practice of arms from any desire of glory, but for the acquisition of either property or safety. The others (those who possessed no state) being bred to arms from their infancy, were acquainted with no other art, and pursued war for emolument, or to confer honor upon themselves. The most noticed among the latter were Carmignola, Francesco Sforza, Niccolo Piccinino the pupil of Braccio, etc.[8]

and, twisting the knife in the wound, he added:

Who [that is, the lesser princes and the stateless men], being constantly in arms, had such an understanding among themselves, and so contrived to accommodate things to their own convenience, that of those who were at war, most commonly both sides were losers; and they had made the practice of arms so totally ridiculous, that the most ordinary leader, possessed of true valor, would have covered these men with disgrace, whom, with so little prudence, Italy honored.[9]

The cowardice of the mercenary captains and their troops on the battlefields of fifteenth-century Italy, the selfish pettiness of their behavior, the inclination to betrayal common to both leaders and soldiers—these are some of the dominant elements in Machiavelli's explanation of the crisis of the end of the century. But the use of professional soldiers, whether Italians or foreigners, that had become increasingly common since the end of the previous century (in place of the citizen-soldiers that had been fielded by the communes) was the rule in the major European states of the time that were preparing to come and fight their wars on Italian soil. In Spain, as in France or Germany, the national militias served only as territorial militias for the defense of individual "lands," not as an army capable of maneuver. The kings of France, for instance, "continued to maintain on their payrolls Swiss, lansquenets, Gascons, and Picards, and with these mercenaries they won the battles that ensured the

greatness of their country." One distinctive trait of the Italian situation, by contrast, was the phenomenon the Italians called *condottierismo*. A mercenary commander—a "condottiere"—by shifting
nonchalantly from the service of one lord to that of another, balanc-
ing factions one against the other with acrobatic agility within a
given state, or else taking advantage of one of the recurring dynastic
crises (a prince dying without male heirs), would sometimes manage
to elbow his way forward and win power for himself—an enterprise
that was beyond the grasp of a mercenary captain fighting in the service of the king of France. Instead, here in Italy Francesco Sforza,
mentioned by Machiavelli in the passage that we quoted, became the
duke of Milan in 1450.[10]

Stated in these terms, the problem of the militias of the Italian
states of the fifteenth century no longer appeared as a matter of
more or less appropriate military practices. Instead, it seems to be an
indicator, as significant as one wishes, of the conditions of weakness
and political and social instability into which those states were falling
on the eve of a period that would be decisive to their very survival.

AFTER THE DEATH (1492) of Lorenzo the Magnificent, ruler of
Florence, the "liberty of Italy" could be seen in all its fragility. Eager
to seize territory at the expense of their direct rivals or to prevent
those rivals from doing the same thing at their expense, all the
princes of Italy, flying in the face of the logic that guided the "policy
of equilibrium," were ready and willing to solicit the intervention of
a foreign monarch.

For the kings north of the Alps, by now relatively well consolidated within their borders, possessing plenty of arms, subjects, and
money to mobilize at the appropriate time, Italy with its hundred
cities was the promised land, an opportunity well within reach for
competing among themselves in what amounted to a sort of no-
man's-land that each hoped to claim. To make things all the easier
for them, behind the backs of the rulers of Milan, Venice, Florence,

Rome, and Naples, who still fooled themselves into believing that they were pulling the strings, their subject cities, often heirs to a great past (let us consider Pisa with respect to Florence, Pavia with respect to Milan, Padua with respect to Venice, and Palermo with respect to Naples), waited—if not anxiously at least with no great enthusiasm to fight against a danger that they hardly considered such: that a foreign sovereign might restore to them the autonomy that they had lost years before.

The first foreign ruler to step forward was Charles VIII, king of France (1483–1498), weak, sickly, but confident. He advanced the claims of the house of Anjou to the kingdom of Naples, which had fallen into the possession of his father, Louis XI. Charles crossed the Alps in September 1494; by February of the next year he was in Naples. Shortly thereafter, Machiavelli would write that Charles had conquered Italy only with the chalk that he used to mark the lodgings of his soldiers at each stage of the march.[11] In Pisa, he himself was lodged in the house of Piero de' Medici:

> The Pisans were treated with great cruelty by the Florentines and held as slaves, since they had been conquered a century before, in the same year in which the Venetians had taken Padua, which was their first step onto the mainland *(terraferma)*. These two cities were in practically the same circumstances, because they were the old enemies of those who possessed them, difficult to conquer and nearly equal in strength. For this reason, these Pisans took council and, seeing that so powerful a man encouraged them and desiring their liberty, they went in a great crowd of men and women to shout to the king, who was going to attend Mass: "Liberty, liberty!" and to supplicate him, with tears in their eyes, to restore their liberty. A *referendarius* named Rabot, counselor in the *parlement* of the Dauphiné, who was walking before the king in accordance with his office, told the king, either because he had promised to do so or because he did not clearly understand what the people were asking for, that it was a pity, that never had people been treated so harshly, and

that he should give them their liberty. The king, who did not understand the meaning of the word and who by law could not give them their liberty (since the city was not his, but was merely offering him hospitality, out of friendship and on account of his great need), and who was only beginning to become aware of the piteous conditions of Italy and the treatment that the princes and communes meted out to their subjects, answered that their request met with his pleasure; and the counselor told them as much. Immediately, the people began to cry, "Bravo, hurrah!" Then they ran to the end of the bridge that extends over the river Arno and which is a handsome bridge, and they overturned a great lion called the Marzocco, which stood on a great marble column and represented the seigniory of Florence; this they dragged into the river. And on that column they had a king of France carved, with a sword in his fist who was trampling beneath the hooves of his horse that Marzocco, which is a lion. But then, when the king of Germany entered the city [in 1496], they treated their king as they had that lion. This quality of complying with the powerful is the nature of the peoples of Italy; but they were, and are, treated so badly that we must pardon them.[12]

We have a similar account for Vicenza, which at the time of the war of the League of Cambrai—urged against Venice in 1508 by Pope Julius II (1503–1513) and involving Louis XII, king of France (1498–1515), Emperor Maximilian I (1486–1519), Ferdinand II of Aragon (1479–1516), and the dukes of Ferrara and Mantua—opened the gates to Maximilian, out of hatred toward the ruling power:

And so a great array of provisions, laden on mules and carts, entered the city, a good while before his own person; and these were followed by a band of foot soldiers called lansquenets, experienced men, his particular favorites; then came a platoon of German men-at-arms (almost a light cavalry), each holding a lance and seated on a low saddle, all without armor on any part of their legs other than their knees and with foxtails tied to their armor. . . . Behind them came in order all the renegades, I believe, in the world; for they

came from various nations, and many were Italian and German gen-
tlefolk, as well others as from other places. They were followed by a
large and magnificent host of halbardiers, in the midst of which was
the person of Maximilian himself, mounted on a great steed, black
as a piece of burnt charcoal, armed, and likewise covered in black
velvet. . . .

Our city, appearing like a temple bedecked with garlands and
other adornments, with all the honors, human and divine, ventured
just outside the walls toward him. Here, his person having been
shaded beneath a magnificent baldachin carried by gentlemen of
Vicenza, he was led in great pomp to our episcopal palace, which
had been readied to receive so great a personage. . . . But while the
royal banquet was being prepared, he mounted his horse just a short
time after night had fallen, and rode away from Vicenza for four
miles in the direction of Verona. . . . So little, and without reason,
did he trust in our city, so deeply loyal to him; and the city was
greatly saddened to see so little reliance placed in it by its lord, after
its having sworn loyalty to him and having been heretofore obedient
to every envoy he had sent, as well as to His Majesty—and yet he did
not dare stay a full night there.[13]

The Republic of Venice, at that moment standing alone against
everyone, had inscribed its banners with the phrase *Defensio Italiae;*
and the Venetian troops faced the armies of the league with the cry
of "Italy, Italy," which was the war cry of the Italian infantry when
facing soldiers from another country. But all this had evidently failed
to resonate in the hearts of the people of Vicenza, who did not hesitate to throw themselves into the arms of the foreign ruler. He, in
turn, took care to break his word to them.

THE PERIOD of the "wars of Italy" witnessed the spread of a new
disease that was destined to cause widespread death: syphilis. The
first cases were reported among the troops of Charles VIII laying

siege to Naples. That was why the Italians hastened to dub the new disease *mal francese,* the French disease. Meanwhile, the French, paying more attention to the place where the disease made its first appearance, called it the *mal napolitain,* or Neapolitan disease. The name that is still used to indicate this disease was the creation of the Veronese physician and humanist Girolamo Fracastoro. In his little Latin poem set in hexameter, *Syphilis sive de morbo gallico* (1530), after reporting the results of his observations concerning the nature and the treatment of the disease, he told the story of a shepherd named Syphilus, a native of one of the lands discovered by Christopher Columbus. Syphilus angered the gods by neglecting the worship of the Sun God, preferring to worship his own king, Alcitous. Indignant, the gods cursed him with a terrible disease that spread rapidly, and which the peasants named after him, calling it syphilis. The spirochete *Treponema pallidum* is thought to have been the first living creature from the New World to reach Italy.

IN THE PERIOD of the "wars of Italy," during which the Italians often clashed with the armies of the great national monarchies of Europe, then forming or being consolidated, they earned a reputation as poor soldiers. They were never able to rid themselves of that reputation.

Many arguments have been offered to disprove the humiliating myth that the Italians are unwilling to fight. First of all, it is not true that the armies of the Italian states made a specialty of mass surrenders in the wake of feigned battles, which were more like tournaments waged for sport, in which the combatants take care not to risk their skins, than like genuine battles. For the most part, the wars were hard-fought and bloody. In the second place, Italian military art was in no way inferior. Quite the contrary, for instance, in the area of fortifications: it was actually superior to that of the states north of the Alps. Last, it is safe to say that no great foreign victory was won in Italy during this period that was not tied to the name of some Italian "condottiere." "No fewer Italians fought to ensure the ruin of Italy than fought to prevent it!"[14] It is upon this aspect, which certainly does no credit to our honor as Italians, that we must rather reflect.

The judgment that we have just examined will lead us from the field of military history to the domain of ethical and political history, and to the underlying causes of the particularism that is, for worse (according to Machiavelli) and for better (according to Guicciardini), the overriding feature of our national history.[15]

Still on the topic of war and militias, there can be no doubt that, in the crisis of the late fifteenth century, Italians paid the price for the type of social development that had characterized the preceding centuries. The early departure Italy's social structure had made from feudal organization led not only to the adoption of new techniques of production and trade and new forms of social organization, but also to the very early abandonment of those values which typify that feudal organization and the class that had dominated it: the aristocracy. These values can be listed briefly: courage in war and a highly developed regard for loyalty and honor. The literary genre of epic poetry, which elsewhere served as a forum for the expression of the feudal and chivalrous ideas of life, did not sink deep roots in Italy. The characteristic expression of the new emotional structure that established itself in Italian society, especially in central and northern Italy, as a result of the political and economic consolidation of the mercantile and artisanal classes of the city-states was instead the *novella*. Now, we can hardly claim that wars, heroes clad in heavy armor, fine questions of chivalry and feudal law, and military valor are dominant themes in the episodes of Giovanni Boccaccio's *Decameron*.

Even if it had been defeated politically by the monarchy, a feudal aristocracy with the grand traditions of the French nobility continued to offer a model of behavior that served as a positive example for the armies that the king of France fielded for the "wars of Italy." The nobles who frequented the Italian courts of the time, courts both great and small from Ferrara to Mantua, had learned to smile at the warlike deeds of the paladins of Charlemagne as portrayed by Matteo Maria Boiardo and Lodovico Ariosto.

Although they were in the service of Spain, the thirteen knights who on 13 February 1503 took the field at Barletta against an equal number of French knights, in a prearranged challenge, were Italian, hailing from various regions of the peninsula. Their victory, which would be celebrated in *Ettore Fieramosca*, a novel by Massimo d'Azeglio (1833), immediately took on the value of a limited but effective challenge to the rumor that Italians did not fight:

> In order to recover certain [French] soldiers who had been seized at Rubos [Ruvo di Puglia], a trumpeter went to Barletta to attempt to redeem them [rescue them], whereupon certain words were uttered against the French by several Italian men-at-arms, and when those words were reported by the trumpeter to the French camp, and once the French had responded to the Italians, both sides were so aroused and angered that in order to uphold the honor of their own nations, they agreed that a battle to the finish should be fought together on a safe field of combat by thirteen French men-at-arms and thirteen Italian men-at-arms; and the place of combat was established in the countryside between Barletta, Andria, and Quadrato [Corato], to which they were led with an entourage of a certain number of people; all the same, to guard against treachery, each of the captains with the bulk of his armies accompanied his party halfway to the site—encouraging the men by saying that since they had been selected out of the entire army, they should bring their soul and all their strength to bear on the expectations that had been engendered, which were such that all had by common accord placed in their hands and in their valor the honor of so noble a pair of nations. The French viceroy [Louis d'Armagnac] reminded his men that these were the selfsame Italians who, not daring to uphold the name of the French, had, without ever putting their valor to the test, always yielded to them every time they had crossed the Alps and had al-

lowed them to march unimpeded to the very tip of Italy; nor would they now find a renewed generosity of spirit or new vigor but, finding themselves in the pay of the Spanish and subject to their command, [the Italians] would not be able to defy their will, and, accustomed to fight not with valor but with treachery and fraud, [the Italians] were often the idle spectators of the dangers of others; but as soon as the Italians were led onto the field and confronted the arms and the ferocity of those who had always beaten them, they would return to their customary cowardice, and either they would not dare fight or, if they did fight, they would fight so timidly that they would easily fall prey to them, as the empty words and bravado of the Spaniards would not serve as adequate shields against the iron of the victors. On the other side Consalvo [Gonzalo Fernández y Aguilar de Córdoba, known as Consalvo; also called the Great Captain] incited the Italians with equally pointed reminders, telling them of the ancient honors of that nation and the glory of their arms, with which they had already conquered the whole world, and that it was now in the power of those few, in no way inferior to the valor of their masters, to show one and all that if Italy, victor over all the others, had for the past few years been dominated by foreign armies, this was the result only of the fecklessness of her princes, who, had themselves, because of their rivalrous ambitions, summoned foreign armies to fight one another; that the French had never won a victory in Italy by true valor but had won either thanks to the advice or the weapons of the Italians or because they had yielded to their artillery—out of fear of which—as this was a new thing in Italy— and not fear of their arms they had yielded before the French; that this was an opportunity to fight man to man, with iron and valor, for the leading nations of Christendom were present at so glorious a spectacle, and so many nobles from those nations, who fervently wished for victory on either side. That they should remember that they had all been pupils of the most famous captains of Italy, continually trained at arms, and that each of them had in various places made honorable employment of his valor; and therefore either they were destined to earn laurels for restoring to the Italian name the glory that it had possessed not only at the time of their forebears but in times that they themselves had witnessed, or else, if such honor were not to be earned at their hands, they could despair of Italy's ever enjoying another state than that of ignominious and perpetual servitude.

Desiring that the names of the thirteen of Barletta, beginning with the name of Ettore Fieramosca, the Capuan, should be "handed down to posterity through the instrument of letters," Guicciardini cites them one by one, though only after describing their triumph in the wake of the victory:

And they were greeted with enormous joy by their people, and when they met Consalvo, who was awaiting them on the way back, they were received with incredible festivities and acclaim, each of them being praised as a reviver of Italian glory, and they entered Barletta as if in triumph, leading their prisoners before them; the air echoed with the sound of trumpets and drums, the thunder of cannons and applause, and soldierly shouts.[16]

It is obvious that much, far too much, was made of the import of this episode, and it continued to echo down the centuries. This is a clear indication of Italy's need to restore faith in itself, especially in the area of military valor, a need that was agonizingly present for many Italians. It was not until the end of the nineteenth century that a Neapolitan scholar could write, as N. Faraglia did, that

the challenge of Barletta, one of the last and most splendid exploits of chivalry, already moribund, was esteemed and celebrated as a great national event, because matters in Italy had come to such a sorry pass that the Italians considered themselves satisfied and vindicated by the happy events of a single day, while two foreign kings competed to be lord of Italy. Nor did those thirteen knights fight for the fatherland; indeed, their valor served only to hasten the conquest of the kingdom [that is, of the Kingdom of Naples by the Spaniards] and the harsh servitude of two centuries.

As early as 1629, as evidence of the fact that "we all know from experience that the quality of being official and monumental in the long run tends to corrode and consume the individuals or events that are subject to it, and in some cases exposes them to satire and derision," the poet of Nursia Gian Battista Lalli had shown no restraint in ridiculing the episode. He set forth the matter as if the motive of the dispute had been the discussion mentioned above as to whether the origin of syphilis was French or Italian. It was the victory of the thirteen Italian knights on the field of Barletta that ensured

> . . . that so foul a disease should be called
> under the grave pain of a *tournois* [originally a coin from
>   Tours]
> not the mal italiano, but mal francese.[17]

Toward the end of 1510, the German Augustinian monk Martin Luther arrived in Rome to take care of certain affairs pertaining to his order. He returned home disgusted by the latter-day Babylon that he had seen on the banks of the Tiber, by its simoniac clergy, by its cardinals devoid of faith and morality, by the "bravos," ruffians, and courtesans who crowded the city's streets. He was not the first nor would he be the last to have this experience. But this has little to do with the reformulation of the message of Christ that was ripening within him. With respect to that message, even the trade in indulgences—which, authorized by Leo X (1513–1521), was being carried on in Germany before his eyes in 1517 (the proceeds, with a payment of one thousand florins for the emperor Maximilian I, was split evenly between the pope and Albert von Hohenzollern, who held the titles to the archdioceses of Mainz and Magdeburg and the diocese of Halberstadt)—was only the straw that broke the camel's back, prompting him to go public with what he had in mind—that is,

> to substitute for a religion that placed the faithful, carefully circum-scribed and placed in context, within a great and magnificent con-struction, . . . an entirely personal religion that would place a crea-ture, directly and without intermediaries, before his God, alone, without a retinue of merits and good works, without the parasitic mediation of priests or interceding saints or indulgence acquired in this world and valid in the next or absolutions freeing him from the demands of God himself.[18]

Ten years later, his voice resounded from one end of Germany to the other. And the lansquenets (literally, "servants of the land") were Lutherans, after their fashion, a mercenary militia that under the command of Georg von Frundsberg had an opportunity to express its feelings during the Sack of Rome in May 1527. One of them re-corded his participation in that memorable event in an inscription scratched into a fresco in Villa Farnesina: "Why shouldn't I laugh: the lansquenets have put the pope to flight."

The pope at the time was Clement VII (1523–1534), a member of the Medici family, elected as the successor to Adrian VI (1522–1523, the last non-Italian pope until Karol Wojtyla), with the support of the emperor Charles V (1519–1556). Dragged into the conflict be-tween Charles V and Francis I, king of France (1515–1547), at first he worked to resolve it, but in 1526 he joined the League of Cognac with France, Milan, Florence, and Venice to oppose the growing power of the emperor. This was a fairly incautious decision, which triggered the invasion of Italy by an imperial army, formed of lans-quenets and Italian and Spanish mercenaries and commanded by the former constable of France, Charles de Bourbon-Montpensier, who passed over to the opposing side—as well as the ensuing Sack of Rome, during which Charles de Bourbon-Montpensier died:

The year 1527 will be full of atrocities and events unheard of for many centuries: overthrow of governments, wickedness of princes, most frightful sacks of cities, great famines, a most terrible plague almost everywhere in Italy; everything full of death, flight, and rapine.[19]

On the fifth of May, Bourbon and his army took up quarters in Prati near Rome. . . . The following morning at daybreak, he determined either to conquer or die . . . , and [as he was] approaching the Borgo on the side toward the hills and Santo Spirito, a bitter battle began. . . . At the beginning of this battle, Bourbon, goaded by ultimate desperation, was at the forefront of his troops . . . because he saw how the German footsoldiers were marching coldly into battle . . . wounded . . . by a shot from an arquebus and fell dead to the ground. But his death did not chill his soldiers' ardor, but rather caused them to fight with the greatest fury so that after two hours they finally broke into the Borgo, aided not only by the great weakness of the fortifications but also by the poor resistance put up against them. The battle demonstrated—as has been demonstrated many other times to those who have not yet learned to evaluate present situations from examples of antiquity—how much the virtues of men trained in warfare [that is, mercenaries—professional soldiers, as they are] differ [are greater] from [those of] new armies picked up here and there at random, and from a popular multitude [clearly a slap at Machiavelli, already as of this writing]. . . . Nevertheless, because it is difficult to capture a town without artillery, about a thousand footsoldiers of the attacking forces were killed. As soon as the assailants had broken in, the defenders took to their heels, many running to the Castello [Castel Sant'Angelo], and the outskirts were totally abandoned as prey to the victors; and the Pope, who was waiting at the Vatican palace to learn what had happened, as soon as he heard that the enemy had broken into the city, fled immediately with many cardinals into the Castello. . . . Therefore, the same day, the Spaniards meeting with no resistance whatever and encountering neither order nor planned defense, entered Trastevere; and from there without any difficulty, on the same afternoon at twenty-three hours [an hour before sunset] broke into the city of Rome by the Ponte Sisto. . . . As soon as they had entered the city, the imperials began to run about tumultuously in search of booty, respecting neither friends [the Roman Ghibellines] nor the authority and dignity of prelates, nor even churches, monasteries, and relics, honored by pilgrims from all over the world, nor sacred things. Therefore it would be impossible not only to narrate but even to imagine the calamity of that city, destined by heaven's orders to consummate greatness, but also to drastic shifts of fortune; having been sacked by the Goths 980 years before.[20]

The comparison between one Sack of Rome and the other was borne in upon the liberal, Protestant German from eastern Prussia Ferdinand Gregorovius, who, just after the middle of the nineteenth century, decided that he was qualified to write the *History of the City of Rome in the Middle Ages*—even though in principle this task would more naturally have fallen to a Roman or Italian historian—because he was convinced that this history had a *national* character for the Germans as well, especially because of the emperors, but also because the Germans had been involved in the history of Rome during the Middle Ages by their distant forebears, Goths and lansquenets, both of whom had sacked the city in 410 and 1527. Significantly, he selected these two sackings of the city as the chronological boundaries of his work:

The Sack of Rome committed during the barbarian era of Alaric and Genseric could be considered humane in comparison with the horrors with which the army of Charles V stained itself. Perhaps the reader will recall the triumphal procession of the Christian religion in the heart of Rome despoiled by the Goths; in vain will one seek a similar act of piety in 1527. This time, all that was seen was a Bacchic procession of lansquenets on horseback, riding toward the Vatican surrounded by half-naked courtesans to drink toasts to the death or capture of the pope. Lutherans, Spaniards, and Italians amused themselves by aping the sacred rites. Lansquenets were seen riding here and there on the backs of asses, posing as cardinals, and in their midst a soldier would walk, dressed as the pope; and they would often advance in this guise as far as Castel Sant'Angelo, and there they would cry that from then on, they would name only popes and cardinals who were pious and devoted to the emperor, people who would cause no more wars, and they would conclude by proclaiming Luther pope. Drunken soldiers dressed an ass in sacred vestments and forced a priest to administer the holy sacraments to it, as the animal kneeled before him; the unhappy priest swallowed the host each time; then his tormenters tortured him to death.[21]

The year 1527 marked a watershed for Rome. Clement VII's successor, Paul III (1534–1549), gave the first signal of the change. Rome had in recent years been the seat of one of the most magnificent courts of the Italian Renaissance and, most important, the capital of a state engaged, like the other states of the peninsula, in the grueling experience of wars, leagues, and peace treaties, constantly seeking a balance between the imperative of fighting for survival and the temptations of expansion into the holdings of its rivals, in order to win sufficient territorial appanages for the *nepotes* of the reigning pope. It had in fact been the age of "grand nepotism," now in its final years. Renaissance popes had been determined to ensure that their relatives would enjoy not only a jump in social standing, but even a leap into the realms of princedom, as had been the case with Cesare Borgia (ca. 1475–1507), the illegitimate son of Pope Alexander VI (1492–1503), who became the master of Romagna, part of the Marches, and other areas in the state of the Church. Now, after 1527, although this nepotism did not disappear entirely and moreover actually took new forms, Rome began to be the driving force behind the initiatives for the revival and even the reform of the Church, in opposition to the reformers of the various confessions.

―――

IN FLORENCE during the siege of 1529–1530, it had been as if the old Italy of the city-states had shot off its last stocks of gunpowder. Clement VII had made peace in June 1529 with Charles V. Charles, in exchange, had agreed to restore the Medici to power. Clement assigned to Philibert de Chalon, prince of Orange, who was the secular instrument placed at his disposal by the emperor, the task of overthrowing the republic, which had been established only two years before, thereby clearly taking advantage of the situation in which the Medici pope had found himself at the time of the Sack of Rome. In the uprising, the Florentine Republic was harking back to the tradition, never fully extinguished in the city, of the rigorist preaching of the Dominican monk Girolamo Savonarola, who had been tried for heresy in 1498 at the behest of Alexander VI and then hanged and burnt at the stake. The struggle thus took on a religious aspect as well. According to the Venetian ambassador to Florence, "it is not easy to say which is greater, the stoutness of the souls in their defense, or the reliance they place upon the divine majesty of most certain salvation."

When the Spaniards reached the hill, or Colle dell'Apparita, within sight of Florence, on 22 October 1529, they cried: "Apareja brocatos, señora Florencia, que venimos a mercarlos a medida de pica" ("Prepare your brocades, Madame Florence, for we are coming to purchase cloth by the lance-length").

Thus begun the memorable defense with which this people, known for the greatness of its civilization, showed the world another, unexpected greatness. Suited to the arts of peace, it mobilized for war; famous for its refined politics, it redeemed itself in the wake of a politics of madness with impulses of a Romantic generosity. Those thoughtless, hopelessly stubborn people were worthy to be placed among those whom Guicciardini, in his *Ricordi* (Memoirs), often called madmen. But there is a point, difficult to discern through mere reason, at which "madmen" become heroes.[22]

The eponymous hero of the Florentine resistance (in which Michelangelo Buonarroti also fought) was the merchant-soldier Francesco Ferrucci (his twofold profession is already quite eloquent), who had been assigned to attempt a diversion toward Volterra to lighten the pressure of the siege. He was killed at Gavinana, on the Pistoian Apennines, on 3 August 1530.

> The Florentines were singing:
> O pope, to dream of ruling Florence
> Is nothing but presumption
> You will rule only a dying city,
> To give it extreme unction.[23]

Florence surrendered on 12 August. Six months before, the curtain had been rung down in Bologna on the first act of the "wars of Italy." On 20 February 1530, Clement VII, the pontiff who had suffered the humiliation of the Sack of Rome, had crowned Charles V king of Italy with the "iron crown" of Monza in the royal chapel of the city hall, and immediately afterward he had crowned him emperor in a chapel of the church of San Petronio.

The leading states of Italy, from Milan to Venice, had taken part in the Congress of Bologna, along with a great many smaller states, from Mantua to Savoy and Monferrato. They were all resigned to the new equilibrium, which differed from the old one that had been overthrown in 1494 in that it was an equilibrium imposed from without. This meant peace for Italy, after more than thirty years of unremitting wars.

In the church of San Petronio, that day, the setting was a medieval tableau of the Holy Roman Empire, with the pope and the emperor united and in agreement, for once, as they had been in the time of

Otto III and Sylvester II. Actually, deceptive appearances aside, this was what was happening: Spain, at least for the time being, had managed to prevail over France in the struggle for hegemony in Italy. As for the Holy Roman Empire and all that it could still ideally represent, the Reformation, which was by this point victorious in Germany, was hollowing it out from within, and for all time.

8

MILAN AND NAPLES
IN THE CASTILIAN EMPIRE

BY SANCTIONING the presence of the Spanish in Milan and Naples, the treaty of Cateau-Cambrésis (1559) marked the beginning of the period of Spanish dominance in Italy: roughly a century and a half. With respect to the entire era of foreign domination, this century and a half appears to have been the low point of decadence and insular rejection of the outside world. In fact, it was during this period that many Italians chose to employ their artistic, literary, religious, and even military talents in other lands, places that offered greater opportunities for personal affirmation.

Even during this period, some individuals took positions—one example is the Modenese writer Alessandro Tassoni, author of a well-known heroicomic poem—that clearly showed an awareness of the common interests of the Italians. But the policies of the states on the peninsula that still retained their independence (to name one, the Duchy of Savoy) were almost exclusively oriented toward the protection of their own private interests. People still and inevitably thought of foreign intervention as the only possible solution to every local problem. Three or four centuries before, in the central and northern cities governed by communes, a custom had been established that has no parallels outside Italy: when the struggle among municipal factions was no longer amenable to settlement through a sharing out of spoils among those factions, a *podestà forestiero,* or "outside" magistrate, on being summoned to restore order, would often require the banishment of one of the two quarreling parties. It almost seems that this practice was etched deeply into the collective mentality. The distinction between *forestiero* (roughly equivalent to "outsider," and according to the Italian definition of the dictionary of the Istituto dell'Enciclopedia italiana, "a person who is not native to the place in which he finds himself; he does not live there on a permanent basis, either, but has come there from another city or nation to stay for a relatively short time") and *straniero* (roughly equivalent to "foreigner," "referring to a person who belongs to a foreign state") is subtle, and is typical of the Italian language.

The political crisis and the concomitant failure of what Benedetto Croce aptly described as "moral enthusiasm," did not necessarily, for instance, mean that there was a corresponding crisis in the arts.[1] From this point of view, the Renaissance continued, though gradually evolving toward forms that were in some cases radically different. The presumption that we Italians were more civilized than the others—the "barbarians," who did not enjoy our privilege of being direct descendants of the ancient Romans—still guided the hearts of Italians. In architecture, for instance, the first decades of this period were dominated by Andrea Palladio, second to none in his worship at the altar of antiquity, combined with his skill at adapting the ancient compositional schemes to the types of buildings that his clients most wanted: the city palazzo and the country villa, which aristocrats, or rich people who were striving to become aristocrats, considered indispensable to their sense of dignity.

Italy and Spain were also the two countries that made the greatest contribution to the Counter-Reformation—that is, the counterattack that Roman Catholicism launched against Protestantism in the various forms that it was assuming. The central episode of this counterattack was the Council of Trent. Charles V imposed this city as the site of the council, which he wished to have take place on German soil, in the belief that he could thus facilitate the vainly hoped-for participation of the Protestants in the work of the assembly. It was a reflection of the so-called policy of mountain passes pursued by the German emperors during the Middle Ages.

Meeting for the first time in December 1545, the council held twenty-five sessions over three different periods of time, concluding its work in December 1563. On the one hand, in contrast with what is remembered by definition as the Reformation, later articulated in a number of confessions, the council identified within the context of the abundant baggage of traditions of the ancient and medieval Church a single tradition, authoritatively enshrined as "catholic," on all the controversial points that had emerged in the preceding decades and even centuries. On the other hand, it issued a long series of decrees with which it proposed to put an end to a series of problems and abuses of varying degrees of seriousness, present in the Church at every level. While those problems and abuses may have played only a relative role in the formulation of the theological and ecclesiological theses of the reformers, who focused instead on the essential points of the evangelical message, they had certainly encouraged rapid and extensive diffusion of the theses among the masses of the faithful. Many of the underlying problems that emerged at the time of the Council of Constance (1414–1418) and the Council of Basel (1431–1449) regarding the way that ecclesiastical institutions functioned (at the time demands had been advanced from numerous sectors of the Church for a reformation of the Church "in its head and limbs") had remained unsolved. And they also remained unsolved after the Council of Trent, even if the issues related to the care of souls, the training of priests, and the encouragement of active forms of charity did receive attention, laying the foundations for later practical measures that only an obstinate anti-Roman prejudice might lead one to overlook.

Erasmus of Rotterdam once wrote: "Wherever Lutheranism reigns, there you will find the death of fine literature." If we take a further step and carry out a contextual inversion of the value judgment in question, the opposition between Reformation and Renaissance became the opposition between Germany and Italy, between the German inner life of the mind and the Italian cult of beautiful forms and fine living. Still, such an author as Voltaire, who could certainly not be suspected of having hidden sympathies for the clergy, chose quickly and surely: in contrast with the rest of Europe, bloodied by the wars of religion, Italy, which remained almost universally Catholic, with its religious rites that captured the imagination of the simple folk, with its Baroque architecture, its gardens, its music, had been the most prosperous land in seventeenth-century Europe, the only place where it had still been possible to cultivate the pleasures of the spirit.

Diametrically opposed to Voltaire is an entire tradition of typically Italian thought, scarcely negligible in its influence, which emerges especially when the future of our country is most called into doubt, comprehends the Counter-Reformation and the Council of Trent, and at the same time the failure to institute religious reform, as the root of all the ills that plague us. Because we failed to take the inner life of the Protestants into consideration at the appropriate time, the mental structure of the Italians is said to have been irremediably imprinted with a form of extroversion, which is nothing more than a facile approach to things and a willingness to compromise, first of all with one's own conscience, too easily pacified in the shadow of the confessional. Since we obviously cannot offer any remedy for that failure, we would therefore be condemned without possibility of appeal to a condition of inferiority with respect to almost all the other peoples of Europe, who, having passed through the experience of the Reformation and the Wars of Religion, are made of sterner stuff than we are.

But as usual, matters were much more complicated. In the meantime, Italy itself had its own reformers, even though most of them were obliged to emigrate elsewhere. Through the portals of Milan and Venice, which were closely tied to northern Germany and Switzerland on account of their commercial relations, the new doctrines had eventually irrupted into Italy as well. The Italian heretics distinguished themselves from the others because they attempted to reconcile moral austerity with the love of study and the humanistic tradition, and because they were the first supporters of the idea of religious tolerance, which would struggle to make itself heard through the din of intolerance that reigned on all sides.

As far as the counterpart was concerned—the Catholic Church, which was the winning side in Italy—there can be no question that its behavior was first and foremost all that could be expected from an institution that, wounded to the quick, defends itself fiercely, availing itself of all the means at its disposal. Concerning the use of these means, an entire body of blood-curdling literature exists, from which we can expect everything but objectivity. But there is no doubt that the tools of torture and burning at the stake were actually used. Those who point to the recent opening to scholars of the archives of the Roman Inquisition, founded by Pope Paul III in 1542 and reorganized by Pope Sixtus in 1588, in the expectation that those archives will lead to a rehabilitation of the institution on the basis of the adherence to formal procedures that accompanied the trials—or more regrettably, in an appeal to a generic understanding of the spirit of the time—are sadly in error. What should not be overlooked, however, is the impact that the Spanish Inquisition had on the origin of the Roman Inquisition. The Spanish Inquisition had already been founded in 1478. Gian Pietro Cardinal Carafa, the future Pope Paul IV (1555–1559), had direct exposure to it during his nunciature in Spain.[2] Here too, law was dictated by the hegemonic power in Italy.

Let one episode serve as a confirmation of this. Guardia Piemontese, in the province of Cosenza, was founded as a colony at the turn of the sixteenth century by "Waldensians," that is, followers of Waldo, a merchant from Lyon who lived in the second half of the twelfth century. Waldo had preached evangelical poverty, much as Francis of Assisi had a few decades later. But unlike Francis, who meant to do so by example, Waldo claimed for laypeople the task of preaching the Gospel, which the Church had very clearly reserved for priests alone. His teachings led him into heresy. The Waldensians who took refuge in Calabria to escape the persecution to which they had been exposed in their home territories—the valleys of the Angrogna and Pellice rivers, between Piedmont and France—spoke langue d'oc, that is, Provençal. In the first half of the sixteenth century all the Waldensians, and therefore those in Calabria as well, voiced allegiance to the Reformation, specifically leaning toward the teachings of Calvin. In 1561, while their fellow Waldensians who had remained behind in the valleys of Piedmont survived under the rule of the dukes of Savoy, the Waldensians of Calabria were brutally persecuted by a Spanish viceroy of the Kingdom of Naples. In Guardia Piemontese, the Porta del Sangue, or "bloody gate," commemorates the massacre. The survivors converted to Catholicism.

In the long run, the most positive result then achieved was the preservation of our country's religious unity. As disunited as Italy was politically, it would certainly not have helped to introduce a new element of division—a division, as Benedetto Croce points out, between a Protestant north and a Catholic south. But the price that it exacted was a sort of hibernation of Italy. The country, under the protection of Spanish arms, remained detached from the political and religious turmoil and the development of ideas of the Europe of its time, in lockstep with "the fate of the monarchy of which it was a province, a fate that deteriorated throughout the century, worsening in social, economic, and cultural terms." This was very cold comfort: "Italy (as is often said), then, was tired, and it rested; and it is a beautiful and optimistic metaphor to avoid saying that it was finished and dead."[3]

But if Italy slept, it was not a peaceful sleep. Even though it was "under the *amparo* [Spanish for "protection"] of our lord the Catholic king, who is the sun that never sets" (a reference to the Spanish empire, spanning the New World and the Old World), the subjects of the state of Milan, especially the poor and the defenseless, such as Renzo and Lucia in *The Betrothed (I Promessi sposi)*, were continually vulnerable to the malfeasance of the powerful and their "bravos," who "engage themselves . . . to some cavalier or nobleman, officer or merchant . . . to render him aid and service, or, verily, as there is cause to presume, to plot against others."[4]

"Edicts" of this sort, issued by the governors against the squadrons of bravos, clearly had little if any effect, if it was necessary to repeat them every other day.

When Alessandro Manzoni wrote his masterpiece, Italy had

finally awoken from its slumber. The author proposed to portray "by means of invented events" the "true and authentic ways" of those times, and in so doing he inevitably tended to highlight and emphasize to some degree. It was a way of exorcising the past, in view of a future that he hoped would be different and brighter. But his overall judgment on Spanish Italy should be considered substantially valid, aside from the necessary considerations of the art of fiction.

Having arrived in a cart at the monastery where they were to be given shelter, Agnese and Lucia showed their letter of recommendation from Fra Cristoforo to the father superior, who, "when he had finished reading . . . , said: 'The only thing for it is the Signora; if the Signora will undertake this charge.'" Because the father superior was walking several steps ahead of them, the two women asked the carter "who the Signora was":

> "The Signora," replied the other, "is a nun; but she's not the same as other nuns. Not that she's the abbess, or the prioress—in fact, from what they say, she's one of the youngest there—but she's sprung from one of Adam's ribs; and her people were great folk in the olden days, and came from Spain, where the people who give the orders are; and that's why they call her the Signora, meaning she's a great lady; and the whole town calls her that, for they say they've never had a personage like her in that convent; and her folk count a lot down in Milan now. They're the kind who always have their own way in everything; and they count for even more here in Monza, for her father's the chief person in the town, although he's not here now; so she can order everyone about in the convent if she's a mind to."[5]

The young man to whom, as we all know, "the wretched woman replied," was a "professional rogue, one of the many who were able, at that period, with the help of their minions and of the alliance of other rogues, to defy justice and the forces of the law up to a point."[6]

The story of Gertrude, who was "not the same as other nuns," and Egidio, a "professional rogue," is a story of moral decay told against a backdrop of political and social disarray, impermeable both to the "edicts" of the Spanish governors and to the "decrees" of the Council of Trent, applied only reluctantly even in the dioceses of Italy.

—————

"I WAS WHAT I AM NOT—I am what I was not—You will be what I am—Spain gave me birth—Italy gave me good fortune—Here is my sepulchre": these words were engraved on the tomb of a certain Roderigo Nuñez de Palma, who died in Naples in 1597 and was buried in the church of Santa Maria la Nuova. It is quoted by Benedetto Croce in an essay entitled *Una passeggiata per Napoli spagnuola (A Stroll through Spanish Naples):* "For me, who often and happily go strolling around Naples, daydreaming and looking at the old alleys and streets and entering the churches to read the engravings on the tombs and looking at all the other countless monuments of this city, it is a special pleasure to find traces, marks left here and there, of the foreign people who lived so many years alongside us."[7]

This is an instance of that special *pietas* that no historian can do without. But it was from their Spanish rulers—as Croce himself points out—that the Neapolitans learned, among other things, the custom of resorting regularly to duels to settle supposed questions of honor that arose among gentlemen; the habit of showing off the things one owns (and even things that one does not own); as well as more innocent customs, such as a stylish way of removing one's hat, which gave rise to the expression "sberrettarsi alla spagnuola" (to tip one's hat in the Spanish fashion), or the specific rules governing who should be the first to enter or leave through a door; and a sport that had never been practiced in Naples before, known as the *caccia al toro*—the Spanish *corrida*. *Lazzaro* (beggar), *guappo* (swaggering tough), and *camorrista* (member of the *camorra*) are three strategic words used in Neapolitan dialect that come from the Spanish.

It is not always the case, however, that the origin of a word corresponds to the origin of the things identified by that word. In contrast with what was once thought, no one now would dream of ascribing the present ills of Naples and the south of Italy in general to the harmful influence of the Spanish domination. Milan and Lombardy passed through the same experience.

After 1503, instead of being ruled by an Aragonese monarch residing in Naples, and ruler of this kingdom alone, as had been the case with Ferrando I (1458–1494) and his successors, the kingdom went back to being ruled, as in the time of Alphonse the Magnanimous, by a nephew of Alphonse, Ferdinand the Catholic, who was also king of Aragon (1479–1516). But his marriage to Isabella of Castile (1469) led to the de facto unification of Spain and then, following Ferdinand's death (1516), the accession of his nephew Charles to the Spanish throne. Since Charles was also nephew of Emperor Maximilian I of Hapsburg, he inherited the Low Countries and managed to succeed his uncle as Holy Roman Emperor (1519). As a result, the Kingdom of Naples found itself in a setting that was much different from the one in which Alphonse had been obliged to operate. Its position in the broader context of Italian and European politics was thus radically changed.

Under Alphonse the kingdom balanced precariously between the demands of Catalonian maritime expansionism and those of the "policy of equilibrium" among Italy's regional states. With Ferdinand, however, who accepted "the inheritance of Aragonese policy in the Mediterranean, endowing it with a broader scope than it . . . had had in the preceding period,"[8] the kingdom was fully involved in the "wars of Italy." And with the accession of Charles the Catalonian and Aragonese tradition, which aspired to control of the central and western Mediterranean and which therefore required first and foremost absolute dominion over Italy, once again clashed with a conception primarily of Castilian origin, "ideologically . . . still bound up with the idea of the universal Christian empire, over which still hovered the myth of 'Christendom,' of dominion over all of Christian Europe, the *corpus christianum* for which Caesar was still meant to be the ultimate temporal chief."⁹ As a consequentce, therefore, the Kingdom of Naples was called upon to share fully in the fortunes of a great continental and extracontinental empire, which in consideration of the special relationship that was established between Castile and the ruling dynasty modern historians understandably dubbed the Castilian empire by.

From a juridical and institutional point of view, certainly, the difference was not too great from the times of Alphonse the Magnanimous. The fact that the Kingdom of Naples should be governed by a monarch who lived in Flanders or Madrid and was represented on the site by a "viceroy" did not mean that it had been downgraded to the rank of a "viceroyalty," comparable to the *virreynados* into which the Spanish dominions of the New World were broken down. In theory, at least, it continued to be a proper kingdom, on a par with Aragon and Castile: "Charles V did not even try to organize his dominions in a uniform manner, and each of them preserved its original institutions, its practices, its autonomy. The link between the various realms consisted in the person of the sovereign."¹⁰

A turning point, in the sense of an accentuated "hispanization" of the Kingdom of Naples and especially of the former Duchy of Milan, however, came after Charles V, "slowly and gradually" between 1554 and 1556, rid himself of his governmental responsibilities, assigning to his son Philip II (1527–1598) the Spanish crown, his Italian dominions, his American colonies, and the Low Countries, and assigning to his brother Ferdinand I (1503–1564) the hereditary dominions of the house of Austria and the imperial crown.¹¹

Within this more limited context, the Kingdom of Naples carried considerable weight, which only increased in the wake of the national and religious revolt of the wealthy and very advanced Low Countries. Second only to Castile, the center of power, with the might of its infantry and its extensive holdings in the New World, the Kingdom of Naples, like Castile, paid a high price for its relative primacy in service to the cause of the Catholic king, becoming a sort of major point of assembly from which a constant flow of men and financial resources were drawn to sustain the requirements of the war under way in Flanders. This may not have been genuine exploitation on the colonial model, but it was a forced participation in an undertaking that was determined to be, a priori and without possibility of appeal, a joint operation.

At the same time, the question remains open whether Spain can truly claim credit for having undertaken the construction of a modern state in southern Italy, in laying the foundations of a centralized power similar to what was developing all over. It was precisely in the Norman and Swabian Kingdom of Sicily that this structure made its very first appearance between the twelfth century and the first half of the thirteenth century.[12] After the accession of the Angevin sovereigns to the throne of Sicily, however, the island's secession from the mainland of southern Italy in the wake of the Revolt of the Vespers (1282) had had the pernicious effect of encouraging those monarchs to be especially generous in their concessions to the barons, in hopes of winning their favor in view of their numerous attempts, all unsuccessful, to regain possession of the island.[13] Replacing the Angevins, the Aragonese monarchs, after Sicily had been reunited with the rest of the kingdom, did everything within their power to reinforce their royal authority, though they failed to take the battle to the barons, who held power in the provinces, with anything like the degree of determination that would have been required to solve the problem once and for all. Further tying the hands of Alphonse the Magnanimous was his concern to ensure the succession to the throne of Naples for Ferrando I, his illegitimate son. His choice would provide an excellent pretext for the barons to support another claimant, unmarred by the stigma of illegitimacy. Ferrando did succeed in claiming the throne when the time came, but he was then faced with the great conspiracy among the barons. The conflict culminated in the monarch's victory (1487), but a victory that was tarnished and destabilized by the deception Ferrando used to lure the defeated conspirators to Castelnuovo, supposedly to negotiate a peace treaty, but actually to slaughter them all.

In the face of the Castilian giant that had superseded the heirs and successors of Ferrando, the barons, hitherto so relentlessly trouble-some, now prudently fell into line. Now that the monarch was able to instill respect and fear, they showed that they were actually capa-ble of a certain degree of loyalty. Although they had always been a pernicious element, they now actually began to cooperate with the central government. Gratified with the results they had obtained, however, the Spanish kings and viceroys failed to carry their actions against the barons to the logical conclusion. The natural alliance that had during this phase in the development of the modern state led the ruling dynasty and the new middle classes to make common cause in the struggle against the feudal aristocracy failed to develop in the Kingdom of Naples. The Spanish government, for which Na-ples was only a pawn on a much larger chessboard, had no interest in pressing the modernization of the state past a certain point. The Spanish authorities preferred to make use of the domesticated bar-ons (well, domesticated to a certain point) as so many guarantors of public order in the countryside deep in southern Italy, allowing them the political elbow room—within their feudal landholdings and terri-torial seigniories—of which they had deprived them at the level of the kingdom. The cost of this operation, of course, was paid by the peasants, who saw their ancient bonds of servitude strengthened and harshened. As would happen to some degree also in the wake of 1860, when for the second time the Kingdom of Naples was dragged forcibly from its isolation, the external push for reformation of soci-ety and state soon dwindled into a sterile compromise between the *forestieri* ("outsiders"), concerned primarily with preserving order, and the most prominent local citizens, determined at all costs to safeguard their privileges.

The first century of Spanish rule in Naples, "the sixteenth century was unquestionably the decisive century in the history of Naples that is still, to a very great degree, our own [Italian] history."[14] The extraordinary concentration of all the most important tribunals in Castelcapuano made this building a curiosity for foreigners pass-ing through.[15] From the hill, the Colle di San Elmo, the castle, which had been expanded and strengthened by the viceroy Don Pedro de Toledo (1484–1553), overlooked the new quarters, which were being constructed along the course of the road that he had ordered built. It was here that the Spanish soldiers of the garrison lived, between five and six thousand in number. The other two castles, Castel dell'Ovo and Castelnuovo, gradually lost their military functions, as the inhabited area expanded at dizzying speed past the boundaries of the medieval city. The viceregal court and the offices of the central administration for the kingdom attracted more and more people to the city: aristocrats who had come to show off their wealth; miserable paupers willing to do any and all odd jobs, who had been uprooted from the countryside and the smaller cities, only to wind up as servants in the homes of the wealthy. In order to respond to the critical shortage of housing, builders began to erect houses that were four, five, or even six stories tall, unheard of elsewhere.[16] In a short time, Naples grew until it was second only to Paris in population. The advantages of housing the administration of a state in the process of modernizing, although in a very specific way, were just beginning to become apparent, and already the disadvantages of overpopulation were starting to emerge.

THE THIRTY YEARS' WAR (1618–1648) intertwined toward the end with a series of revolutions that shook Catalonia, Portugal, Naples, France, and England: "War's burden on society was much heavier than in the past, and the active presence of the middle class was the new development in the revolutionary crisis, no longer polarized between the aristocratic conspiracy and the plebeian revolt."[17]

In Spanish-ruled Naples, the revolt took its name from Masaniello, a fishmonger originally from the Amalfi coast who, with behavior typical of a popular leader, but comforted by the guidance of the eighty-year-old abbot Giulio Genoino, was the protagonist of the first phase of the revolt, which broke out on 7 July 1647. Just ten days later, overwhelmed by the succession of events, he was killed.

"Long live the king of Spain, death to dishonest government!" This rallying cry characterized the revolt as a protest against the introduction of a commodity tax on fruit. The revolt involved the close alliance of groups of the middle class and intellectuals, artisans, merchants, the urban proletariat, and peasants, all arrayed against the viceregal government. That government, in keeping with the traditional approach, had allowed the barons a great deal of latitude, in order to win their favor at a time when the war then under way had led to flagrant plundering of the kingdom's resources. "The authority of the state and the sovereign, to which the lower classes had looked in the preceding period of Spanish rule as a guarantee of social equilibrium and progress, underwent a sharp decline."[18]

Although they were accompanied by a wave of violence against the aristocracy and the members of the Spanish government, the demands for reform put forward by the moderate wing of the movement—to wit, the abolition of all *gabelle,* or taxes on commodities, and the establishment of equal representation for populace and nobility in the city government (the so-called *sedili,* or seats), where there had been a fivefold dominance of the aristocratic vote—were accepted, and the revolt seemed to lessen in intensity. When it did flare up again, this time the demand was for independence from Spain, which the Neapolitans wanted to obtain for themselves, aspiring to the example of the United Provinces of the Netherlands. But the new revolutionary leaders internationalized the conflict, by turning for help to France, which was Spain's enemy number one. The opportunity offered on this occasion was seized less by the French government, then being run by Jules Cardinal Mazarin, than by the French nobleman Henry II, duc de Guise, who managed to have himself appointed head of the republic that was proclaimed in Naples in October 1647 under the title Serenissima Repubblica del Regno di Napoli, or Most Serene Republic of the Kingdom of Naples, which was understood "as a nation-state, not an institutional configuration."[19]

The Neapolitan Republic held out for many months (until 5 April

1648) against the fleet that had been sent by the Madrid government to restore order, and the armed bands that had been recruited by the barons of the kingdom. It stood firm in spite of the intrigues the duc de Guise employed to reinforce his personal power by dividing the mutineers' front. It was the first time, in a century and a half of Spanish domination in Italy, that a broad-based movement had arisen that was capable of attracting different classes of the populace in the name of causes that included both the institution of political and social reforms and independence from foreign rule. In this case as well, however, the call for French intervention constituted yet another manifestation of a bad old Italian habit.

———

IT HAS BEEN debated whether the naval victory achieved on 7 October 1571 against the Turkish fleet by the fleet of the Spanish, papal, and Venetian league at the mouth of the Gulf of Lepanto (a port town on the northern coast of the strait separating the Gulf of Patras and the Gulf of Corinth) was a Spanish victory or a Venetian victory, and therefore, in some sense, Italian. The fact remains, in any case, that without wheat, barley, and cheese from Italy, without wine from Naples, perhaps this victory would have been impossible, because Spain was suffering at the time from a very serious famine: "It was necessary to assemble and feed at the southernmost tip of Italy an entire city of soldiers and sailors, teeth and stomachs of the very first rank."[20]

When in Messina, on the point of assembly for the forces of the league, Don John of Austria, the son of Charles V and the commander in chief, succeeded in persuading the suspicious Venetians to allow four thousand soldiers, both Spaniards and Italians who were fighting at the orders of the king of Spain, to board their galleys, which had no soldiers of their own, the allied fleet seemed suddenly to have found a sense of unity. The rest was achieved on the day of the battle by the exceedingly accurate fire of the Venetian galleasses and the incomparable Spanish foot soldiers, remarkable protagonists in a battle that at a certain point changed from a sea battle to a land battle.

It has been ventured that Lepanto might perhaps have been a victory that was as pointless as it was widely proclaimed. Irony has been leveled at the out-of-date crusading enthusiasm that was artificially whipped up over the event. But if the fleet of the Holy League had been defeated, it is possible that the Turks might have gone on to attack Sicily and Naples. Certainly the Venetians learned, the day after the news of the victory at Lepanto arrived, that in the wake of the fall of Nicosia, Famagusta too, another stronghold on Cyprus that had been a Venetian possession since 1489, had fallen to the Turks. And the Venetians were soon wondering whether it had really been worthwhile for Venice to spend so much money. Above all, they wondered whether it had been worthwhile to run the risk that an alliance with the Catholic king of Spain entailed for this last bulwark of an independent Italy that had eluded Spanish dominion and influence. In March of 1573, Venice abandoned the Holy League. It had in fact been only a three-year commitment, but on account of the enthusiasm mentioned earlier, the Holy League was presented in the beginning as an "eternal pact."

The battle of Lepanto was not sufficient—and how could it have been?—to ward off the decline of the Mediterranean, which just a few years later, after a temporary renewal of aggressive hostilities on the part of the Turks, would no longer witness war—except for privateering—and would be practically abandoned. It was on the Atlantic that the fates of empires were being decided by that point. And from the Atlantic, English and Dutch sailing ships would soon overflow, through the Strait of Gibraltar, into the inland sea, coming to compete at the very doorsteps of Italian sailors, who thus a little later than the rest of the country slipped into that torpor which Benedetto Croce mentions in reference to Spanish Italy in general.

⎯⎯⎯

IN ORDER TO SAVOR, in person and on the spot, that *joie de vivre* whose meaning had been lost entirely in the countries engaged in the experiment with new and more personal forms of piety, a

Protestant queen renounced her crown, became a Catholic, and decided to spend the rest of her life in Italy—in Rome.

Felici faustoque ingressui: the inscription that conveyed to Christina, former queen of Sweden, wishes for a "happy and fortunate entrance" into the city of Rome, was dictated by Pope Alexander VII. It can still be made out, in abbreviated form, on the Porta del Popolo, which Gian Lorenzo Bernini decorated for the occasion. It was 23 December 1655. Christina, who was an experienced rider, was mounted on a magnificently saddled palfrey adorned in dark blue and silver, in spite of the horrible weather. It was one of the many gifts she had just received from the pope, clearly the gift that the former queen most appreciated. She was fond of dressing as a man. That day, she had on a simple gray outfit with a black scarf; she wore a plumed hat.

On St. Stephen's Day, before Christina left the Vatican to go to live in the Palazzo Farnese, Pope Alexander VII invited her to dine with him, making an exception to the rule that forbade women to eat at the pope's table. Chroniclers report that, to decorate the table for this queen who had intellectual ambitions, a number of Bernini's pupils made a sugar loaf sculpture of Minerva surrounded by the seven liberal arts. A distant whiff of the Renaissance emanated from that masterpiece of the Baroque pastry chef's art. Christina had come from afar in search of this very thing.

After having forced the Roman Curia to pay heavily—what with her whims, magnificent gestures, and endless series of escapades— for its generous initial overture, thought to be obligatory in the case of a Protestant queen who had unexpectedly converted to Catholicism, Christina died in Rome in the Palazzo Riario, the present-day Palazzo Corsini alla Lungara, at the foot of the Janiculum. Here she had built herself a home—with an adjoining museum of ancient statuary, a gallery of Renaissance canvases, and groves of orange and lemon trees—that was worthy at last of her ambitions and tastes for a refuge from her chilly homeland.

She left a written request to be buried in the church of the

Rotonda, which had been the Pantheon of the ancient Romans, a church that she loved. She wished to be buried without ceremony. Instead, she was interred in St. Peter's, to commemorate for all time a conversion to Catholicism that had provoked great astonishment. The funeral, solemn in keeping with the times, was held at the Chiesa Nuova of the Vallicella.

9

THE AUSTRIANS AND THE
LOMBARDO-VENETIAN KINGDOM

IN THE FIRST HALF of the eighteenth century, the "wars of succession" altered the geopolitical maps of Europe, and of Italy. Here, Austria replaced Spain as the hegemonic power. Moreover—and it was certainly a considerable if unlooked-for advantage—after having thought of themselves wrongly as superior to all others in civilization and culture (this was the withered bequest of the Renaissance), those Italians who were aware—that is, capable of looking around and seeing the world—began to feel a healthy sense of inferiority toward the foreign nations that were most advanced when it came to civility.[1]

The situation was triggered during the early years of the eighteenth century, to be precise, by the outbreak of a conflict in which the fate of the Spanish empire was at stake. This crisis on a European scale that had grown, as was customary, out of dynastic rivalries (the Bourbons of France and Spain against the Hapsburgs of Austria) inevitably came to involve the subject nations as well, including our own: "In those fifty years . . . Italy was conceived not as a mosaic of separate states, but as a single chess piece on the chessboard of European diplomacy; but that piece . . . was never considered to be anything more than a pawn."[2]

It was as if after the long years of the Spanish peace—interrupted only along the Po Valley by the Thirty Years' War—the times of the *guerres d'Italie* had suddenly returned, when the tables were turned and alliances upended every other day. In the meantime, however, the game had expanded in scope. With the Treaty of Utrecht (1713), the Austrians replaced the Spanish in Milan, Naples, and Sardinia. Not in Sicily, because their allies the English, whose trading activities in the Mediterranean were increasing continually, had ensured that the island's throne would be occupied by the monarch of a small state entirely free of maritime ambitions: the duke of Savoy, Victor Amedeus II (1684–1732), who was brought to Palermo by an English ship and promptly took the title of king of Sicily.

Just seven years later, the Austrians succeeded in forcing Victor Amedeus to exchange Sicily for Sardinia, and he shifted his previously acquired title of royalty to that island. The house of Savoy kept the title until 1861, when it acquired the Italian throne. Fourteen more years went by, and Naples and Sicily, once again united, both wound up under the rule of Charles VII (1734–1759), a monarch who belonged to the Spanish branch of the Bourbons but who was king over those two kingdoms alone—a sharp difference from the past. This was the Bourbons' skillful response to the threat of Austrian control over the peninsula as a whole.

The Hapsburgs quickly made their countermove. In Tuscany, where the Medici line had died out, they installed Duke Francis Stephen of Lorraine, the husband of Maria Theresa, who was in turn the daughter and heir of Emperor Charles VI of Hapsburg (1711–1740). That was followed by the Bourbons' counter-countermove: Philip, brother of Charles VII, king of Naples, obtained the Duchy of Parma, Piacenza, and Guastalla.

During this succession of events, the states and statelets of Italy failed to develop a common line of action. Once again, Italy was the passive object of the wishes of other states, which used the peninsula as a field of battle. In 1746, the revolt of the Genoans against the Austrians—a revolt that began with the "stone" thrown by the child Balilla—was nothing more than a brief flame, quickly snuffed out.

When peace returned, the foreigners—the Austrians—had a direct presence only in Lombardy (in Milan and Mantua). In Parma, Florence, and Naples the scions of the Bourbons and the Hapsburgs tended to operate on their own, keeping a healthy distance from the mother dynasty. Whether by the decree of others or out of deep-seated exhaustion, Italy was on its way to becoming a neutral nation, or perhaps we should say a neutralized nation. Experience shows, Victor Amedeus of Savoy wrote, "that arrogance in Italy had a considerable influence in bringing about universal equilibrium."[3] For Italy this was the basis of fifty years of peace.

It could also have been the basis for renewed slumber. That is not, however, what happened this time. In Milan, Florence, and Naples the recently established governments proved to be driven by the best intentions, in the spirit of the times that was sweeping through Europe: create order, rationalize.[4] And there was certainly no shortage of tasks to be accomplished: ecclesiastical privileges, expanded disproportionately in past centuries, to be pruned back; inefficient and corrupt public administrations to be reformed; fiscal systems to be rebuilt from the ground up, as regards both indirect taxes, collection of which was normally subcontracted out to private speculators, and direct taxes, whose collection was hindered by the network of privileges affording exemptions and the uncertainty over the actual substance and extent of landholdings—hence the push for the establishment of a "cadastre," which would allow a more equitable distribution of the fiscal burden.

The personnel of these new governments was highly composite and mobile: foreigners (Austrians, Spaniards, Frenchmen) who had arrived in the entourage of a prince, himself a foreigner, but always willing to enter the service of a different master if he was more amenable to their reformist zeal; or else Italians from different regions of the peninsula who, once they left their home region, felt like "outsiders" in the other regions. Without roots in the places where they worked, they possessed at the same time all the advantages and all the disadvantages of this situation. They were not hobbled by tradition. In places like Genoa and Venice where the old regimes still held sway, reforms were actually unthinkable. But they threatened to prompt insuperable resistance from the classes whose privileges were most directly threatened. These classes could always fall back on the inevitable "things were better when things were worse," that is, under the Spanish. And they could always dust off the old watchwords and use them against the newcomers, expressions like "Barbarians, go home!" with a mixture of arrogance and insolence. The fact remains, in any case, that nobles and churchmen at first had the upper hand.

The positive turn of events came after the middle of the century, when the "enlightened" monarchs found Italians willing to cooperate with them in a disinterested fashion, Italians who also had strong ties to various local situations and were capable of interpreting their requirements, if not acting as spokesmen.[5] Already in the first half of the century, when the Austrians had replaced the Spanish in Milan and Naples, their arrival had been greeted favorably by small groups of intellectuals, who saw Emperor Charles VI of Hapsburg as the heir to the Caesars of the Middle Ages, from Frederick II of Swabia to Henry VII of Luxembourg, who centuries and centuries ago had incarnated the hopes of Italian "Ghibellinism" and of Dante himself.[6] Those illusions, however, melted away quickly.

The subsequent generation of "enlightened" Italian intellectuals had their feet planted firmly on the ground and their eyes fixed not on the ancient or medieval past, but rather on contemporary Europe. Before returning to Milan, where he stayed, Pietro Verri—one of the leading figures—had gone to seek his fortune in Vienna. Many others, like him, had ventured beyond the borders of Italy to see how things were done elsewhere. And once they returned home, they offered comparisons abounding in lessons on what was to be done. For those who did not choose to travel, there were books and especially the "gazettes"—typical instruments of communication in the Age of Enlightenment—that supplied the information and data required to form an idea even from a distance of what was going on in other countries and societies.

The bitter results of this exploration—anything but theoretical—of the Europe of the time had already been anticipated, in 1747–1748, by Ludovico Antonio Muratori, who had refined his critical faculties through his studies of the medieval past, conducted directly on primary sources: "If we compare Italy with France, England, Flanders, Holland, or certain countries in Germany, we find that much of Italy remains inferior in industry and commerce to those north of the Alps." But it was not only in the fields of industry and trade that Italy had been left behind: "I looked back over years gone by, envious of those scholars north of the Alps who had with such clarity and precision and such liberty engaged in philosophy free of the vacuities of the barbarian years."[7]

North of the Alps, the "Quarrel between the Ancients and the Moderns" had long ago been resolved in favor of the moderns. In Italy, by contrast, the "ancients" remained firmly attached to their thrones, in part because the Church of the Counter-Reformation far preferred a discounted and calculated risk of paganism to the far more unsettling novelties of Protestantism and rationalism; in part because the ancients were also the Romans, and the Romans—as everyone knows—were our direct ancestors. The result of all this was that when the appropriate comparisons were made and the descendants of the "ancients" realized that they had been left many furlongs behind with respect to the descendants of the "barbarians," the dismay was such that the "ancients" were dethroned by those among the "moderns" who, in contrast to us, seemed to have all the credentials to aspire to succeed the former: the transalpine moderns—that is, foreigners.

In the dedication to the English consul at Venice of one of his plays, entitled *Il filosofo inglese* (*The English Philosopher*), first staged in Venice in 1753, Carlo Goldoni adopted this new prejudice, which here in Italy replaced the humanistic prejudice:

A philosopher is quite respectable—all the more so if plucked from the bosom of a nation that perhaps thinks and reasons more than others. Let us leave aside the great masters that you have produced, but all people who have any education recognize the merit of their good conduct through the inner seeds of philosophy; and I, who have had the good luck to have dealings with many in various parts of Italy, have almost invariably met with philosophers of the nature of this one of mine—that is to say, of a civil, discreet, and sociable philosophy.[8]

The very idea that there could be a nation on earth made up entirely of philosophers was a patent absurdity. But the fact remains that the "civil, discreet, and sociable" philosophy of the Enlightenment Italians, whether they had truly learned it at the schools of others or whether they had at least in part produced it themselves, rendered excellent service not only to the individual "enlightened" governments, but also to the nation at large, which in those decades regained part of the ground it had lost in previous years. In Austrian Milan, the collaboration between politicians and "philosophers" was especially productive. Foreigners and Italians worked together with some degree of success to build a more equitable and therefore more stable society.

———

THE VOYAGE IN ITALY—the grand tour, the great journey par excellence, as it was said at the time—became a rite of passage in the education of a foreigner who cherished any ambitions at all. What drove these foreigners to make the trip, though, was not an interest in the Italy of the time, but rather a series of artistic, poetic, and historic needs that could be satisfied only south of the Alps—here, where the Roman (and also Greek), Christian, and Renaissance past came forward and spoke to even the most unprepared visitor, not only from the ruins of the ancient monuments and from those monuments which remained relatively intact, but even from the cobblestones in the streets, from the walls of the houses:

[MALCESINE] 14 SEPTEMBER [1786]
As I planned, I went in the early morning to the old castle, which, having no gates or guards or keepers, is accessible to everyone. In its courtyard I sat down opposite the old tower built on and into the rocks; I thought I had found a very convenient little spot for drawing. . . . When the *podestà* arrived with his clerk I greeted him with-

out reticence and modestly answered his question as to why I was drawing their fortress by saying that I did not recognize this pile of masonry as a fortress. I pointed out to him and the people the decay of these towers and walls, the lack of gates, and, in short, the indefensibility of the whole thing, and I assured him that I had nothing else in mind except to see and draw a ruin.

His answer was, if it was a ruin, then what did I find remarkable about it? I answered, trying to gain time and favor, in great detail that they well knew how many travelers came to Italy only for the sake of its ruins, that Rome, the capital of the world, laid waste by the barbarians, was full of ruins which have been drawn many hundreds of times, and that not everything from antiquity was as well preserved as the amphitheater of Verona, which I also hoped to see soon.

ROME, 1 NOVEMBER [1786]
Not until I passed under the Porta del Popolo was I certain that Rome was mine. . . . Now I am here and calm—calmed, it would seem, for the rest of my life. . . . Now I see all my childhood dreams come to life; I see now in reality the first engravings that I remember (my father had hung the prospects of Rome in a corridor); and everything long familiar to me in paintings and drawings, copperplates and woodcuts, in plaster and cork, now stands together before me. Wherever I go I find something in this new world I am acquainted with; it is all as I imagined, and yet new. . . .

It is also morally very beneficial to me to live among these entirely sensual people, who have been the subject of so much talk and writing, whom every foreigner judges by the standards he brings along from home. I excuse everyone who criticizes and chides them; they are too unlike us, and a foreigner finds it tiresome and expensive to deal with them.

ROME, 24 NOVEMBER [1786]
The only thing I can say about this nation is that it is made up of primitive people who, under all their splendid trappings of religion

and the arts, are not a whit different from what they would be if they lived in caves or forests. What particularly strikes foreigners, and today again is the talk of the entire city—but only talk—is the homicides that take place so routinely. Just in the last three weeks four persons have been murdered in our district.[9]

The Italy of Goethe, even though he possessed a capacity for observation that he had patiently exercised on plants, stones, and men, "was an Italy outside of time, in all its serene, perfect immobility."[10]

The natives, for their part, also observed their foreign visitors with some curiosity. From these scattered observations, they derived characterizations of the various national types, which then became embedded as stereotypes that proved exceedingly hardy in certain cases.

In *La vedova scaltra (The Artful Widow),* staged in 1748, Goldoni has three foreign suitors buzzing around Rosaura: a Frenchman (Monsieur Le Blau), a Spaniard (Don Álvaro of Castile), and an Englishman (Milord Runebif). Here, taken wholesale, are some of the lines from the first act:

Monsieur Le Blau: "You Italians lack the fine French taste in dining."
Conte di Bosco Nero (an Italian): "Well, we have French cooks too."
Monsieur Le Blau: "Of course you do, but when they come to Italy, they forget how to cook fine food. Ah, you should see how they eat in Paris! That's where refinement is found."

. . . .

Rosaura: Tell me, dear Marionette. You were born in France and you were brought up in Paris. How would I be received there, among the fine French ladies?
Marionette (maidservant): You are spirited, and if you are spirited in France, you will be well received.
Rosaura: And yet I am not one of the most uninhibited; in Italy there are a great many women who are more exciting, quick-witted, and easygoing.
Marionette: Well, in Italy you might call them inspired, but we

might consider them possessed. In Paris, we like a restrained wit,
a mannered nonchalance, a sober hilarity, and a certain decency.
. . . .
Marionette: The English don't talk much, but they act.
Rosaura: Well, I don't like excessive seriousness.
Marionette: True, they may say a dozen words in a quarter of an
hour.
. . . .
Rosaura: Of course! If I had been born in Paris, I would be worth
something more, I suppose! I am proud to have been born in a
land where there is as much good taste as anywhere else. Italy today teaches the rest of the world how to live. She gathers all the
good from foreign nations, and avoids all the bad. This makes
her admirable, and when all the other nations come to spend
time in Italy, they fall in love with her.

The events that took place in Paris and France did not arrive like a
bolt out of the blue. On the eve of 1789, enlightened reformism had
already fallen into crisis, after doing all the good it was capable of
doing. Once again—and this time more than ever before—the push
for change in Italy came imperiously from without. At first, it was
the reports of what was happening in Paris, twisted and exaggerated
by distance, that awoke hopes or spread panic, depending on the situation. Then the armies of revolutionary France crossed the Alps
and descended on Italy, forcing governments and the governed to
make peremptory choices. There were those who had no doubts at
all, like Giovanni Fantoni, a Jacobin:

> Greeted by the sweet sound of the warlike trumpets of the libera-
> tors of nations, the dawn of liberty shone from the Alps into It-
> aly. . . . It all tended to form an imposing array of determination, re-
> sources, and forces, if the people of Italy had had the courage at that
> moment to proclaim their liberty and sovereignty in the face of the
> triumphant French army and to expel the fleeing German army

with the most sacred of oaths, the example of which would have shaken the neighboring cities, and quite quickly the French army and the Italian patriots would have decreed with weapons in hand that Italy was free.[11]

Instead of the single republic dreamed of by the minority to which Giovanni Fantoni belonged, in the territories that were said to have been "liberated," but which were actually occupied, by the French a profusion of republics sprang up, in keeping with the tradition, which had never diminished, of Italian particularism. Shocked at the excesses of every sort and the authentic atrocities committed by the Jacobins in France under Robespierre, most reformist intellectuals of the prerevolutionary period were thrust into more conservative positions. As for the Jacobins who took their place as the party of progress, it immediately became clear that they were incapable of establishing ties with the popular classes, and especially with the peasants. For that matter, the French occupying authorities, who held the real power, were by now taking orders from a government whose main concern was not to export the revolution, but rather to suppress social anarchy at home, and everywhere to reestablish the rule of law.

The deposed princes of the peninsula, including those who had been in the vanguard in encouraging reforms, with varying degrees of enthusiasm joined the array of coalitions with which the European powers were attempting to contain the expansionist drive of revolutionary France, a drive that was at the same time clearly subversive of domestic order in the various countries and of international equilibrium. War once again came to visit Italian lands. And these were wars fought with much greater enthusiasm and conviction by citizen soldiers than those had been which were once generally fought by professional armies. These were much bloodier wars.

Among the Italian Jacobin republics—the sister republics, as they were dubbed with reference to the older sister, the *grande nation,* France, whom they were all busy imitating—the Parthenopean Republic had the shortest and most troubled existence of them all. It lasted from January to June of 1799.

In Naples, the participation of the group of men of culture that had collaborated on the policies of reform of the preceding years was more extensive than elsewhere. Both in the capital and in the provinces, this class of men generally supported the new regime. But they failed to wage an effective fight against the so-called feudal abuses, which still held sway in the countryside. Seigneurial rights were in no way limited. Not a single reform capable of winning popular support for the republican government was actually instituted.[12]

Sensing the isolation in which she and her colleagues were working, a Jacobin leader, Eleonora Pimentel Fonseca, explored the possibility of spreading the new gospel in the countryside through simple speeches in dialect.[13] But no one had any patience for mere words! In the eyes of those who had nothing, the republican government, largely lacking that sacred aura which had surrounded the *ancien régime,* was nothing more than government by the usual and age-old exploiters of the people, now intent of amusing themselves with new ideas imported from France.

According to a folk saying,

> If you have no bread or wine
> You must become a Jacobin.[14]

The popular discontent, however, was skillfully manipulated and turned against the French and the Jacobins by emissaries of the Bourbons. Revolts broke out in many provinces, headed by impromptu leaders who were actually full-fledged and veritable brigands: Fra' Diavolo, Mammone, Sciabolone, Panzanera, Bizzarro, and Parafante. Guiding it all from behind the scenes was Cardinal Ruffo, who marched up the peninsula from Calabria with his "Christian army," to defend—as he roundly proclaimed—the Holy Faith from the godless Jacobins. Naples surrendered on 22 June 1799 in the face of the joint attack by Ruffo's army and insurrectionist local *lazzari*, or beggars.

The stout resistance of the Neapolitan patriots of 1799, their determination in the face of the repression that followed their defeat, made quite an impression in France, where until then serious doubts had been harbored about the revolutionary capabilities of the Italians in general, and especially the southern Italians. But in contrast with what was happening at the same time in northern Italy, where the Jacobin republics were falling amid the blows of the Austro-Russian army of the second anti-Napoleonic coalition, the Parthenopean Republic was overthrown after the French had already left, by a mass movement that prevailed by brute force over the best the kingdom had been able to offer since the end of Spanish domination.

The victory won by Napoleon at Marengo on 14 June 1800 over the armies of the second coalition marked the beginning of Italy's Napoleonic period. As never before, the peninsula was the theater of territorial reconfigurations and political and constitutional experiments undertaken by others, with the Italians as the subject. In those years for the first time as well, however, the topic of the independence and the unity of the Italian nation ceased to be merely a theme for more or less successful exercises in rhetoric and literary style and became a genuine political program. To implement that program, forces would contribute that were by and large new, and that emerged from the great reshuffling of the deck that took place precisely during the Jacobin and Napoleonic periods.

From this point on, at least until 1866 (annexation of Venetia to the Kingdom of Italy, created in 1861), the problem of the presence of the foreigners in the role of rulers in our own country as an obstacle to be eliminated in view of the construction of a nation-state had such an overwhelming influence on all other problems that it proves almost impossible to isolate it, as some have previously attempted to do. We shall therefore restrict ourselves to exploring a few aspects of the foreign presence in Italy during the period of the

Risorgimento and the events immediately preceding it, which are marginal yet significant, without any attempt to link them in a sequential consideration. Taking our leave of Napoleon for the moment, as he stands victorious on the battlefield of Marengo, we shall overlook, for instance, the good that came to us from this event, when all is said and done. Consider that during the Napoleonic period a number of the projects for reform of the enlightened governments of the eighteenth century, left unimplemented on the eve of 1789, were dusted off and carried out with the necessary degree of determination: equality of citizens before the law, the elimination of ecclesiastical and aristocratic privileges, guaranteed subsistence for all.

Instead, we shall explore the unrestrained passion for Italian artwork that led the first consul and president of the Italian Republic, later emperor and king of Italy, to become a highly unusual sort of collector of that art.[15] The plundering had begun in 1796, when the French military administration in Italy began to gather and ship northward across the Alps "the rich spoils of Italian culture": paintings, statues, ancient manuscripts. A French newspaper openly declared the ambitious goal that was being pursued: "We shall have the finest art gallery in Europe!" Napoleon echoed the sentiment: the museum that he intended to assemble would be "something fabulous, colossal, never seen before." In 1800, the first consul hailed the arrival in Paris of the Apollo Belvedere. In 1796, immediately after entering Milan, he had even proposed detaching Leonardo da Vinci's *Last Supper* from the walls of the convent of Santa Maria delle Grazie. The plan proved unworkable. And so he ordered an expert mosaicist to make an exact reproduction of the fresco. But the mosaic was completed when the emperor was already on his way out. It wound up being sent to Vienna, carefully packed in twelve separate crates, in the carts of the Austrian army.

In the spring of 1797, the presence of the French army in northeastern Italy had triggered a series of democratic "uprisings" in the cities of the Venetian *terraferma*. They managed to give the death blow to the Republic of Venice. A democratic municipality was established in the city of Venice, as well. The declaration of the extinction of the Venetian government was pronounced unilaterally by the Maggior Consiglio (Great Council) itself:

It might have been forty-five minutes past eight o'clock [on 12 May 1797] when the bell of the Maggior Consiglio pealed and I began to walk toward the Scala dei Giganti [Stairs of the Giants]. However eager the noble lords might have been to commit the great matricide, the comforts of [lying in] bed prohibited advancing the usual schedule by any more than a quarter of an hour. There were five hundred thirty-seven members present; the quorum was illegal, because an inviolable statute prohibits and nullifies any deliberations that are discussed in a meeting of fewer than six hundred members. Most of them were trembling with fear and impatience; they were in a hurry to be done, to get back home, to remove their togas, by now an exceedingly dangerous symbol of a fallen empire. Some clearly displayed their joy and confidence: they were traitors; others glowed with true contentment, with a winsome and generous pride at the sacrifice that in expelling them from the Golden Book made them free men and citizens. . . . In one corner of the hall twenty of the most patrician members stood wrapped in their togas, stiff and silent. A few venerable old men who had not made an appearance at the council in many years had come that morning to honor the fatherland with their final, impotent vote; among them were a few young men, honest young men who were inspired by the magnanimous sentiments of the grandfather of their own father's father-in-law. . . . They stood united, and almost bunched in a knot; they looked over at their fellow members with neither the arrogance of disdain nor the malice of hatred, but with the firmness and calm of martyrdom. . . . They were neither aristocrats nor tyrants, nor were they inquisitors; they were the grandsons of the Zenos and the Dandolos, who recalled to these royal halls for the last time the glories and virtues of their ancestors. . . . Throughout the hall rippled indistinct stirring, a whispering; only in that dark and secluded corner did melancholy and silence reign. . . . The doge [Lodovico Manin] rose pale and trembling before the sovereign body of the Maggior Consiglio, which he represented and to which he dared propose an unparalleled act of cowardice.[16]

With the Treaty of Campoformio (18 October 1797), which put an end to the first coalition, Napoleon ceded, however reluctantly, all the formerly Venetian territories to Austria, including Venice, where the municipality no longer had any legal or moral claim to aspire to take the place of the old aristocratic government:

Venice awoke, shivering with horror, from its lethargy, like a dying man regaining mental clarity on the very brink of death. The municipal government sent envoys to the Directory, to Bonaparte, asking for permission to defend itself. This phrase corresponded very nicely to the other phrase of the treaty mentioned above, in which the occupation of Venice was *allowed*. . . . But the municipals understood just how powerless they were, and they sought nothing more than to fool themselves right up until the last moment. . . . One fine morning, Villetard, lacrimose crocodile that he was, happened to announce in full assembly that Venice would have to sacrifice itself for the good of Europe as a whole . . . ; that the Cisalpine Republic offered a homeland, citizenship, and even a place for a new Venice to all those who were fleeing the new slavery.[17]

Some three centuries before, in 1499, Lodovico the Moor, duke of Milan, fleeing from his domain before the pursuing French army, had warned his subjects to surrender to the French or the Germans, rather than to the Venetians: "The former potentates are mortal, and the latter republic will never die." The Venetian Republic had had an extraordinarily long life, though perhaps not the eternity predicted by Lodovico the Moor. It died more of exhaustion than of violence, collapsing from within because of the hostility of cities on the mainland, Venetian possessions since the turn of the fifteenth century, toward Venice and because of obscure resentment of the provincial nobility toward the oligarchy that held all power.

On the very eve of the Risorgimento, a city fell that had been founded in the lagoon in the early centuries of the High Middle Ages, a city that had never known foreign domination. Venice was not to emerge from this painful ordeal, experienced after an astonishingly long delay, until five years after Italian unity was achieved. At the same time, a power that was continental by definition, Austria, was preparing to establish contact with the Adriatic Sea—from the Dalmatian Coast at Fiume, then with Trieste, and now with Venice—and thus finally achieve its belated vocation as a maritime power as well. The chief imperial port, however, continued to be Trieste, not Venice.

From 1815 on, the formerly Venetian territories were consolidated with Lombardy, which was once again Austrian, to form the Lombardo-Venetian Kingdom. Its autonomy, however, under the rule of Archduke Rainier, brother of the emperor of Austria Francis I (1804–1835), who had taken the title of viceroy, existed in name only. Two central gatherings, in Milan and Venice, and various provincial groupings composed of well-to-do citizens chosen by the emperor, with limited consultative roles on the subject of the distribution of the tributes in particular, at least gave the appearance of self-government. In reality, both in political and administrative affairs and in economic matters, everything was subject to the wishes and interests of Vienna. There were two especially sore points for the Italian subjects: the eight years of obligatory military service and the obstacles of various sorts that the royal imperial government raised to direct trade with markets other than those of the Austro-Hungarian Empire. In contrast with what was happening in other Italian states, in the Lombardo-Venetian Kingdom, absolute authority was accompanied by a fair and competent administration. Public education in particular was well run. At least at first, the officers were mostly Italian; only a minority were outsiders.[18]

If Austrian rule was so unpopular, it is not because it was actually so much worse than the others—if anything, the contrary is true—but only because the lack of tolerance for foreign domination was growing daily. If, however, we take in hand a book entitled *Il confortatorio di Mantova,* the diary of a priest named Luigi Martini, who served as the spiritual comforter in the prisons of Mantua for eleven Lombardo-Venetian patriots who were executed by firing squad or hanging at Belfiore between 1851 and 1855, it will not be hard to identify with the state of mind that united many Italians in hostility to the Austrians.

Among those arrested were also priests, and the Austrian governor had formally asked the bishop of Mantua to defrock one of them, Don Enrico Tazzoli, before his execution. The bishop, on his deathbed, had tried to resist the request, but the order came from Rome to proceed as requested by the civil authorities:

The terrible ceremony took place in the inspector's large room, which had been cleaned as was appropriate. A table had been covered with a white cloth, and on it stood a crucifix and four candelabra.

How the function was conducted I could not say, because as soon as I saw Don Enrico enter the room, dressed in priestly vestments, accompanied by the master of ceremonies, I felt the chill of death, and when he knelt before the bishop, I felt my heart burst. . . .

The master of ceremonies, with whom I spoke later, assured me that the defrocking took place according to the rules of the Roman Pontifical College. The bishop, however, failed to scratch his fingers with a piece of glass, but merely grazed them with a penknife, and instead of pushing the priest away with a kick, he embraced him lovingly. At that point, the priest tried to speak, but the bishop begged him to remain silent. Perhaps he wanted to tell him that though he may have been degraded, he still loved the bishop and revered him as his superior. . . .

The chancellor, once the dreary proceedings were complete, read the declaration; and since he was obliged to master his emotions and read in an exaggerated voice, it seemed as if he had not experienced the grief that had shaken everyone else present. But this was a mistake, because he felt Don Enrico's misfortune deeply in his heart and for some time he was sad and afflicted. I offer this testimonial to truth and I will confirm this more extensively elsewhere.[19]

The chilling aspect of these events is the respect for procedure on the part of a church that took a servile stance to the royal and imperial power.

―――

ABOUT TWENTY YEARS after the bloodiest and most decisive battle of the Risorgimento—"one of the great 'massacres in uniform' of the nineteenth century"[20]—a student of the psychiatrist and anthropologist Cesare Lombroso (1835–1909) decided to carry out a study of the skeletons of the numerous dead from that day, then being arranged in the ossuary of Solferino. The love of positive science won out in him over the sentiment of pity:

> In visiting the holy places that contained the bones of those killed on 24 June 1859 at Solferino and San Martino [mostly French allies of the Piedmontese defeated the Austrians in the first location, while most of the Piedmontese were engaged in the second location], among the memories and the pity that an Italian and a man takes from the somber spectacle, it was natural for a modest scholar of anthropological science to think that a treasure for science might perhaps be found in that broad expanse of skulls of different races from distant regions that the destiny of their peoples and death, the great leveler, had assembled and commingled there.

"They waged a horrifying battle, / Ten thousand fell dead here, / And the victors, mingled with the defeated / Are here as witnesses to themselves," the poet wrote. Now, "in that broad expanse of skulls of different races" (the word "race" already has a sinister sound), the scientist went in search of anatomical anomalies, with the intention, which he fulfilled, of displaying them separately in a special cabinet—in fact, a singular chapel—in the ossuary-cum-church of Solferino.

As the catalogue explains, four skeletons in their entirety were placed in the "Cabinet of Anomalies":

> One is notable for its exceptional stature. The reassembled skeleton measures 1.96 meters tall. The living person then must have been about 2 meters tall. He must have belonged to the Austrian army, because he was hit by a French bullet, which he still bears in the upper ridge of the left iliac bone. Second skeleton: It has been identified as that of a French officer, Philip Laporelle, captain of the *voltigeurs*. Third skeleton: Belongs to the Frenchman Joseph Epinquet, soldier of the line. Fourth skeleton: unknown victim.

It might seem to have been just one of the usual battles fought among foreigners on Italian soil—in one of Italy's loveliest corners, on the hills just behind Lake Garda. Instead, it was the fruit of Cavour's diplomatic masterpiece, which managed to bring into the war against Austria, the second war of independence, the emperor of the French people, Napoleon III (1808–1873). Alongside the roughly 60,000 Piedmontese fielded by Piedmont (instead of the 100,000 that had been promised), fought 130,000 Frenchmen (instead of the 200,000 promised).[21] Napoleon, who was the supreme commander, put an end to hostilities exactly when he pleased, and that was before the point agreed upon. But Milan and Lombardy were annexed by the Kingdom of Sardinia.

10

A PSEUDOCONQUEST AND A
TRUE LIBERATION

IN 1866, at the end of the third war of independence, fought as usual against Austria, the victory won on the field by our Prussian allies earned the newborn kingdom of Italy the right to annex Venetia as well. This further step toward unification, however, is accompanied by the bitter memory of two defeats produced by our lackluster conduct of the war: one defeat was on the sea, at Lissa; the other was on land, at Custoza.

The problem of Trentino and Trieste remained unresolved, but so above all did the problem of Rome, the perpetual *urbs regia,* to which the more enlightened pointed, in spite of all considerations of geography, as the only possible capital of a united Italy.

The road to Rome was blocked by those selfsame French who had been our allies during the second war of independence, in the critical moment of our Risorgimento. When Garibaldi attempted to force the situation in 1867, as he done successfully with his landing in Sicily seven years before, and invaded what still remained of the Papal States with his volunteers, he was in fact halted at Mentana by French soldiers sent to defend the last scrap of what had for more than eleven centuries been the temporal dominion of the popes. On this occasion the French, as enthusiasts of the military art like to point out, tested the breech-loading rifle that they had just been issued. At the end of the battle, considering the results, they pronounced it an excellent innovation.

Three years later, on 20 September 1870, the problem of providing the Kingdom of Italy with a capital was solved by regular troops through the use of force. Porta Pia, however, was not a real battle. The commemorative photograph with the *bersaglieri,* or sharpshooters, aiming their rifles toward the breach in that stretch of the Aurelian walls was further retouched to add a few extra silhouettes of men who had fallen in battle. It seemed distasteful that the reattachment of Rome to the new Italy should not have exacted an adequate cost in blood, while on the various fronts of the Franco-Prussian War then raging, rivers of blood were being spilled. Something very similar had happened fifteen years before at the time of the expedition in Crimea—with the difference that then there had been two thousand dead, but almost all owing to disease, so that "even that contribution was not sufficient to carry much weight in political terms, for it necessarily had to be put into perspective with the fourteen dead in combat and the fifteen dead as a result of wounds received: that is, losses no greater than the allied forces suffered every night in the operations before Sebastopol."[1]

A new and remarkable inferiority complex toward foreigners was thus becoming a part of the collective psychology of the Italians. The complex was cured only with the First World War.

—————

THE PROCESS that led to the creation of a nation-state in our country, if transcribed onto a succession of maps depicting the geographic steps in the territorial unification of the peninsula, seems to consist of progressive expansion of the Kingdom of Sardinia. The house of Savoy learned very well the art of turning to its own advantage what a metaphor taken from vegetable gardening, homely but effective, described as the "policy of the artichoke": one leaf after the other, until the whole artichoke had been swallowed. The very fact that the first parliament of the united Italy accepted the request of the first king of Italy, Victor Emmanuel, to continue to number himself even after 1861 as "the second," because that is how he had numbered his title—up until that significant moment, which might have deserved a signal of transition of some kind—as merely king of Sardinia, confirms the impression that one receives from the succession of maps.

This impression, however, is based merely upon appearances and is, in the final analysis, in no way linked to the truth. If at certain points it was set forth as a historical thesis, it is only because it was thought to offer a solution to the unsolved problems that faced us after the *cueillaison du rêve*—the achievement of the dream of political unity.

The vision of unification as the conquest of Italy by the Piedmontese took root first and foremost as a state of mind. Many Italians, especially in the south, in fact, felt they had been "conquered," not unified into a shared homeland. In their eyes, first Garibaldi and then Victor Emmanuel II appeared as foreign conquerors, no more and no less than all the others that had landed over the course of the centuries on the beaches of the *bel regno* ("beautiful kingdom") of Sicily. Meanwhile, in the eyes of the Italians who were most politicized in a democratic, and also republican, sense, whatever region of Italy they might have come from, the process that had led to unification nonetheless took the form of a "royal conquest," the product of a skillful and ruthless dynastic policy carried out in the style and with the methods of the *ancien régime*, which the French Revolution of 1789 had supposedly rendered unthinkable for all time.

FOR THAT MATTER, as late as the second war of independence, the soldiers of the Sardinian army, almost exclusively peasants and proletarians to whom the Piedmontese dialect was "the classical language," were "still not quite convinced that Piedmont was in Italy," and indeed they would often ask the volunteers from all the various regions of Italy, wisely sent by Cavour to reinforce the Sardinian army in view of the impending hostilities: "Do you come from Italy?"[2] But we need hardly point out that this was certainly something quite different from the decidedly "unitary" sentiment that characterized the liberal and democratic Piedmontese governing class and the numerous émigrés who had, fairly unsurprisingly, gravitated toward Turin from every corner of Italy after 1848–1849, along with the monarch of the house of Savoy himself, quite apart from the deep-rooted disagreements on timing and methods to be employed. Those disagreements persisted until the very end, understandably, given the composite nature of the coalition of forces.

In a few pages of a novel, a contemporary Italian writer (1901–1981) describes the last phases of the resistance of the Bourbon army in the fall of 1860, as they might have been experienced by a young officer loyal to his king till the very end:

Uneasily, from high on the cliff, Pino looked out over the sea. . . . Through the haze he could just make out the black shapes of the Piedmontese vessels, standing just off the vast gulf [the Gulf of Gaeta]. A broad semicircle of unfriendly ships, coming and going threateningly. . . . They had appeared the day before in place of the departing French fleet—the French fleet that was supposed to guard the right flank of the Bourbon army, deployed in a defensive position along the banks of the Garigliano River. This had been the promise made by Napoleon III to the king [Francis II of Bourbon], but then he had broken that promise, and now the lines of the royal army were vulnerable, irremediably exposed to cannon fire all along one flank. The men had been forced to retreat to Mola, giving up their positions without a fight. . . .

Along the harbor and up and down the Appian Way, the ancient consular road, there was only the lightest screen of troops between Traetto and Mola. . . . Now they were facing not Garibaldi and his men, but the powerful, well-equipped army of Victor Emmanuel. . . .

On the far side of the Garigliano, the mist began to dissipate, and the freshening breeze revealed masses of men, dark and dense, and a sheen of weapons. A number of little cannons, like so many toys, began to fire. At whom? . . . . At whom were they shooting, if there were no soldiers on this side of the river? But wait, because on this side of the river, as well, among the green reeds, a single shaft of sunlight picked out a glitter of bayonets, and a burst of musket fire crackled. . . .

It was a handful of men stubbornly taking on an army. The Piedmontese, in fact, were about to cross the river, not over the old iron bridge, which they assumed was mined, but over two new raft bridges that they were building downstream. The big black barges, seen from up there, looked like cockroaches on tinfoil. . . .

That handful of men refused to pull back. They wanted to show the Piedmontese gentlemen, victors in the battles of San Martino and Castelfidardo who had beaten the Austrians and the pope's handpicked international Zouaves, just how well the humble folk of Naples knew how to die. And so the musket fire echoed along the riverbanks and amid the drifting smoke, which seemed diaphanous from this distance; red flares flickered.

And then the fleet opened fire on that small band of men; the Piedmontese really were in a hurry.[3]

We should not be surprised that the end of the Kingdom of the Two Sicilys should have been viewed by Alianello's Pino, and by many others, in this way. Instead, what was serious was that, given the failures and broken promises of the Unified State, the slightly pathetic, and in the final analysis harmless, nostalgia that enlivened the parlor debates of the veterans of the dissolved Bourbon army should have been transformed into a grim resentment against the alleged foreign conquerors, accused of having brought poverty and desolation to the flourishing countryside of southern Italy. The first ones to react against this absurd legend were those southerners who had preserved a sense of reality. In 1899, Giustino Fortunato (1848–1932), a southern partisan *(meridionalista)* who was himself quite the opposite of a *piagnone* [literally, "crybaby," a pejorative term that refers to the enforcers of morals of that period and which harked back to the overly zealous followers of Girolamo Savonarola in late fifteenth-century Florence—Trans.] wrote to Pasquale Villari:

> I don't know who could be more pessimistic than I. And yet, no one views the future as safer and more untroubled, *as long as Italian unity holds up.* Because it is possible to see the "present" of southern Italy as grim, just as I see it, exceedingly grim; but everything, everything encourages me to hope, or at least to have faith, when I let my thoughts turn to the "past." . . . Progress, thanks to unification, moral progress has been astounding. And for that reason I am and I have been one of the very few who laugh in the face of the *piagnoni,* as long as the *piagnoni* have shed tears over the so-called decadence. Decadence there may have been, perhaps, in the rest of Italy: but not here, a hundred and again a hundred times no. . . . But regrets for the past, no; but regrets over lost faiths, no, never. We were not acquainted in 1860, and it took us years and years to become acquainted: even now we don't know each other. This is the source of many of our political, economic, financial, and administrative mistakes, which have brought us to the sad crossroads of today. Let us ensure that Italy survives, and that for a decade she lives unassumingly, honestly, and very parsimoniously. A decade would be enough, perhaps not to solve the question, but to ward off the danger of a fatal division. The danger exists, and it is very serious. It is no accident that there are those who say—and I am quoting my father!—that the unification of Italy was a sin against history and geography. . . . My poor father, dead now the last twenty years, with the grief, with the moral certainty of the subjection of these provinces by the "foreigner"![4]

Not *piagnone,* but exceedingly pessimistic by nature, Fortunato had no illusions about quick and easy solutions to what would on the agenda of the governments of a unified Italy from then on be known, and is still described, as the "southern question," possibly because Italy in the meantime lived neither "unassumingly," at least under Fascism, nor "honestly" nor "very parsimoniously," even after Fascism. But Fortunato was right about the fact that whatever solution might be available entailed a rejection once and for all of that mistaken belief that the southern provinces would always be dominated by "foreigners," the belief with which his father had died, the viewpoint, that is, of what Fortunato called the "fatal separation."

In Rome, despite the presence (which was impossible to ignore) of the pope—a prisoner, as he liked to describe himself, in the Vatican—the arrival of the Piedmontese produced less of a trauma. Certainly, "the rather harsh and peremptory manners of certain of the new government staff," wrote Diomede Pantaleoni in a memo for the minister for foreign affairs, Emilio Visconti Venosta (1829–1914), "generated great dissatisfaction. . . . People called it an invasion, a conquest."⁵ With greater serenity, other Romans just laughed at the strange words used by the newcomers, like *chiel* and *parei,* words that echoed among the ruins of the Roman Forum. As a joke, or as a form of ridicule, the new arrivals were dubbed *buzzurri.* But quite soon, *forestieri* (outsiders, no longer *stranieri,* or foreigners!) and local folk found ways of getting along, engaging together in speculation on the construction contracts for public buildings and new neighborhoods. Without foreign armies at the gates, without the red glare of flames, a new Sack of Rome began to take shape.

Of course, there were problems: the speculation in construction, the banking scandals, electoral clientelism (especially in the south), the pitfalls of an overambitious colonial policy, the warning signs of the transformation of national feeling into nationalism (fatherland and liberty). Still, taken as a whole, the first forty-five years of an Italy unified at last, free of foreign "preponderance" or "domination" and rule, were years of civil progress and economic development. As a result, the country that was the last to appear on the European stage was able to survive the ordeal of the First World War—a test that culminated in victory, though it was overshadowed by the ruinous defeat of Caporetto (24 October 1917) at the hands of the Austro-German army:

The artillery piece near the mountain stream was firing its last shots against the sky. Last of all, Maritza's line, which was not working, rang: "Hello?" "Hello," a calm, relaxed voice replied. "Am I speaking with Italy?" and rang off. The enemy appeared rapidly, incredibly, even ready to make jokes. An ambulance loaded with wounded men had come back down the Caporetto Road because it had taken rifle fire. This confirmed what I had reported to headquarters: we were cut off; maybe, just maybe, there was a path through the woods. And the order was given to retreat, under cover of night. . . .

Near the house, a captain in the Carabinieri in a loud voice was ordering the women to run away. The women were in tears. "I am telling you for the last time, the Austrians will be here soon. Listen to me—it's not going to be pretty. Go on! Get out of here!" And a little girl, her head bowed over her knees, was sobbing on the doorstep: "Ahi! Ahi! Ahi!" The captain, impatient, whipped the air with his swagger stick and quickly turned on his heel to catch up with the colonel, already striding through the fields.[6]

On 28 October 1917, Udine was occupied. It seemed that Venice was ready to fall from one day to the next. Nothing was holding together any longer. It was the Italy of the Risorgimento that seemed on the verge of crumbling after three years of war, three years of harsh suffering, that had swallowed up the nation's moral and material resources. Other nations engaged in the conflict also suffered bruising defeats, sudden rollbacks from the front. For the Italians, the conquest of independence and unity was something still too new for the return of armed foreigners, after a battle shamefully lost, not to awaken the memory of how foreigners used to lord it over us as masters in our own house. But then came [the battles of] the Piave and Vittorio Veneto, and it appeared that independence and unity had been confirmed and even strengthened by our successful passage through such a severe ordeal.

Other ordeals awaited us, however, this time inflicted not by foreign armies but by those whom Saint Ambrose (333–334 or 339), refer-

ring to the crisis of the Roman Empire, placed on a par with the barbarians for dangerousness, calling them *hostes interni,* the internal
enemies, whom he distinguished from the others—the "external enemies." As a Christian bishop, he meant to refer to the passions
that poison the heart of man and via this path manage to threaten
the health and salvation of an entire community. The internal enemies of the Italy that emerged from the Risorgimento, even though
they claimed merely that they wished to complete the job, were the
Fascists.

Italian schoolchildren were taught, and Italian adults were reminded to the point of bored tears, that "foreigners"—all "foreigners"—were their enemies. Italians should have a sense of pride and
honor that they have so many enemies in the great world out there.
And then they singled out from the mass of foreigners and identified
as our friends and natural allies the only foreigners toward whom
many Italians harbored a deep-seated prejudice dating back to the
years of the Great War—the Germans (in the sense of inhabitants
of Germany, not of German-speakers). Now, the Germans had
even been our allies from time to time during the years of the
Risorgimento. After the *Anschluss* (annexation) of Austria in 1938,
however, they were solidly fused with our most direct enemies, both
from the Risorgimento and from the Great War. They were being
rewarded for having followed us down the wrong road, the dead-end
street, that we had marched blindly down in 1922. And for that matter, they would soon overtake us and leave us in their dust.

The war we lost with Germany as our ally, the Allied invasion, the
war of liberation waged against the Germans and the Italian Fascists
of the Republic of Salò, are all events at which many Italians can still
claim to have been eyewitnesses or participants. Reviewed in light of
the theme that we have set for ourselves in this book, *Italy and Its Invaders,* they smack of the paradoxical at first glance, unless of course
we hasten to conclude that they simply reflect the unreliability and
fickleness that is characteristic of our country: allies who become invaders or who are considered invaders by many of us Italians, and

who were even fought, weapons in hand, by a great number of us; enemies who are greeted as liberators by the great majority of the Italians, and attacked fiercely by a die-hard majority willing to fight to the death. But this is no paradox. One need only call to mind the very specific nature of the conflict—a war more between opposing ideologies than between different states—of the Second World War. In this context we shall limit ourselves to offering two examples of how the Italians of the time experienced, with varying degrees of awareness, what might seem to have been role-playing: one example takes place in Sicily, the other in Rome.

In a short story, Leonardo Sciascia (1921–1989) evokes the astonishing and unsettling promptitude with which in July 1943, immediately after the Allied landing on the island, the Sicilians were able to distinguish in their own way between the two foreign armies fighting for control of their land (the Italian army had already melted away entirely), in welcoming the Anglo-Americans as their liberators:

> Filippo's father was a carpenter. He'd been a Socialist, and was often taken to the barracks and held for several days for questioning. Seeing the militia, Filippo always cursed, "Bastards!" and awarded them the decoration of spit on their backs whenever he could. So he was waiting for the Americans; his father wanted to relish showing . . . those bastards who had him taken to the barracks [a thing or two]. . . . I was waiting for the Americans, as well. My mother told me about America, that she had a sister there who was rich and had a large store and four children, one already grown up, a son who might be one of the soldiers we were waiting for. For me, America was my aunt's large store, a shop as full of good things as Piazza del Castello, with clothes, coffee, and cuts of meat, and my aunt's son was a soldier who was bringing those good things with him, and he was good at fighting of course, at telling us about the store in America and letting fly punches at the bastards pointed out to him by Filippo's father.
>
> But the Americans didn't come. Perhaps they'd stopped at the

neighbouring town and were lying on their camp beds, playing games like our soldiers, calling out numbers, shooting their fingers out from clenched fists, and who cursed, saying they would end up as prisoners. . . .

That day when they'd said the Americans were coming, and there were the two Germans passing instead, the news spread mysteriously through the town. My father and uncle set to, burning their Fascist Party cards, portraits of Mussolini, pamphlets on the Mediterranean and the Empire. . . . But the next day, equally mysteriously, word spread that the Germans, seriously this time, were driving the Americans back to the sea, between Gela and Licata. The political secretary who, prudently, had stayed at home for several days, came out again. . . .

We were walking over the roof when suddenly we were surprised by a loud, confused shouting, just as if the radio had been switched on in the middle of a football match, when someone's about to score a goal. . . .

There was a huge crowd yelling and clapping in the piazza, but there was one voice which rose above all the others, that of Dagnino, the lawyer, a tall robust man, whom I used to admire for the way he cried out the Fascist hurrahs, "Eia, eia, alalà," who was now clapping his hands and shouting, "Long live the United States!" People were swigging wine, which was passed from hand to hand over the crowd. Following in their direction we reached the Americans, five of them there were; they wore dark glasses and had long rifles.[7]

The lawyer who cried, "Eia, eia, alalà" louder than all the others, and who now led the crowd in applauding the Americans, is still among us. All that has changed is garb and gesture. He is still our number one "internal enemy." If Sicily and the rest of Italy survived the ordeal of the "liberation," as well, it was owing to the fact that as they slowly and determinedly marched north, the Allies not only were supported by units of the Italian army that had miraculously returned intact after the general dissolution of our armed forces that followed the armistice of 8 September, but were greeted by Italians, also jubilant, but some of whom had fought against the Germans and the Italian Fascists behind the front lines. These Italian soldiers enjoyed the material and moral support of many others who were not waiting to see how it all turned out before taking a stand on the side of justice and right, even if they did not actually carry a machine gun to do so. And yet even this would not have been enough to redeem us in the eyes of the world for our vacillating stance if in truth the Italy that emerged from the Risorgimento had been nothing more than a territory that had been conquered by a foreign king through the "policy of the artichoke," at a negligible cost in human lives, and not rather one that had been unified, even if perhaps by only a minority, but a minority that was after all representative of the nation as a whole.

Rome, too—in contrast to Naples, where if nothing else the *scugnizzi,* before being reduced to the *sciuscià* of Vittorio De Sica's film by that name, or to an episode of Roberto Rossellini's *Paisà,* had been able to cause the retreating Germans considerable difficulties— did nothing when the time came:

> The people of Rome, by a large majority, preferred to adopt the wait-and-see attitude of the Church, rather than the interventionism of the armed resistance, which . . . had for its part been at its best in the early months of the Occupation . . . and, when the time came, had been bled white. Things being what they were, we should not speak of a "failed insurrection," but rather of a "noninsurrection" accepted, if not actually stipulated, by all the forces involved.[8]

Among them, the Church got the best of the others, as if it were in some sense a harbinger of the future and was already busy preparing for it. "Soothe and cut off, Reverend Father: cut off and soothe"—Manzoni's Uncle Count had suggested to the Capuchin provincial father in warning against the risks of destabilization inherent in excessive repression of thugs and hooligans. What prevailed in Rome during the days immediately preceding its liberation from foreigners and their local accomplices was the deplorable wisdom of a typical representative of the old Italy of *I promessi sposi (The Betrothed)*.

But there were also those who experienced that arrival and that departure with the degree of understanding required by the nature of the event that they were witnessing. A historian of antiquity who, felicitously, also became a memoirist recalled his impressions of that

event of such great historic and military import, which . . . almost no one, and especially no Roman, seems to remember, as if this city had any recent claim to recognition other than this—that is, having been the site of one of the most important battles of the twentieth century (a remarkable century for battles) and therefore the cause of the death, wounding, and annihilation of many thousands of young men from distant and very distant lands who had never felt any need for this battle or its object, and indeed had intended to do anything rather than allow themselves to be butchered or blinded just so that they could march day and night under the windows of the residents of this city. The truly remarkable fact . . . is that the night, on that occasion, took on the special quality of a *time of liberty*, which, although it has never again manifested itself with the same degree of intensity, has never entirely been lost over the years, naturally enough. In effect, he [the narrator] remembers that night as *a logical and historical premise,* so to speak, for everything that came after, all the way up to the present time (whose description is, of course, out of the question here):

From the window that they kept nonchalantly, and in truth recklessly, open (for they [the Ferraras] lived on the ground floor, and so if you leaned out the window, you were no more than two-and-a-half meters above the sidewalk), it was possible to see toward the right (south), if you looked carefully, the entire length of the Via Flaminia, ending almost imperceptibly at the Porta del Popolo. . . . As sunset approached . . . , he [still the narrator] walked down into the silent and deserted street to go fill a flask with water from the public fountain at the corner of the palazzo, . . . and as he was waiting to fill his bottle . . . , he saw coming toward him from the distant Porta del Popolo a great mass of vehicles of every sort, and just as he was walking back in through the front door, that endless line began to pass quickly in front of the palazzo. He remembered that the line consisted of trucks and carts of every sort, size, and variety, military and civilian—ambulances and garbage trucks, ancient and picturesque wine carts and market wagons pulled by bedraggled horses. All of them were flying white flags with the red cross, and on those vehicles, lying down or seated, were hundreds and thousands of soldiers in bloody bandages. Some of them noticed him as he was slipping in through the front door, and they waved their helmets as if in greeting. . . . And as that very long line of wounded and dying men moved down the street, clearly fleeing the city, along either side of the road two lines of soldiers began to move past *in full battle dress,* as the expression goes, tall and strong, looking in no way . . . beaten, though clearly in retreat, marching swiftly and in orderly fashion, serving as . . . a rear guard protecting the German army corps that had in the meantime withdrawn along other roads (in all likelihood, the famous paratroopers of the First Paratrooper Division. . . . In any case, these were the first young soldiers perfectly equipped to do battle and actually engaged in a battle that he had ever had the opportunity to see and hear—the noise of their hobnailed boots, their mutterings and grunting under the heavy loads, their weapons and their backpacks. . . .

He remained gazing through the crack in the blinds . . . until he was distracted by . . . a sort of very faint *whispering tread* that right then and there was inexplicable, but then was quickly identifiable, from its beat, as a *march step.* . . . It was impossible to tell whose footsteps they were, even if it was easy to guess, because they were moving by directly under the window and he could not see down through the crack in the blind. Then his brother suddenly pulled the strap of the roll-up blinds. The two of them leaned out to look and saw that beneath them soldiers were moving by, silently (he under-stood it immediately and remained astonished) because of their rub-ber-soled combat boots, which right away struck him as an indica-tion of how absolutely different these soldiers were, as they moved swiftly by, how different from the soldiers who many hours before had marched past on the same sidewalk, in the exact same marching order . . . ; those soldiers' hobnailed boots had signaled their rhyth-mic step from afar, and now he thinks that this was the distinctive trait of this new army that was passing by beneath his windows, and it always would be: this was a *rubber-soled army.* . . .

He remembers that sensation *of an end and a beginning* which he experienced, so strange and unrepeatable, as if in the time between sunset and dawn something unique had been consummated, a de-parture and an arrival that had in a certain sense an absolute value, as he sees it today.[9]

Giovanni Ferrara's book was published in 1995. It is 2004 as of this writing. During the sixty years that have passed since June 1944, nei-ther hobnailed foreign armies nor foreign armies with a rubber tread have touched the soil of our country. The foreigners that have come to visit us have been for the most part peaceful tourists and, espe-cially in recent years, pilgrims, who have arrived in great numbers not so much to garner indulgences as to acclaim a pope who after 455 years of exclusively Italian popes in unbroken succession, is a for-eigner like them. But it is not only tourists and pilgrims.

Among the many whoppers that Mussolini told was that we had no need for aircraft carriers because the entire Italian peninsula, projecting as it does way out into the Mediterranean Sea, was itself an aircraft carrier. We Italians, meanwhile, have discovered—if we had not noticed before—that the Italian peninsula has, along its 7,456 kilometers of more or less jagged coastline, countless landing spots for the rubber rafts or vessels of every size and shape used by those trying to flee wars, tyranny, underdevelopment, and massacres in the Balkans, the Middle East, or the Maghreb. The refugees come here to seek the promised land in our midst, or else only stay long enough to rest before venturing across the Alps in search of another promised land. As to whether we should welcome them with open arms or, without thinking twice, send them—or at least some of them—back where they came from opinions differ. Opinions differ, as they always do when deep-rooted and conflicting emotions and interests are at play. It is therefore entirely natural that the history we have surveyed in certain of its most basic features will have nothing to teach us. The lessons of the past never allow us to engage in anything more than very general considerations.

Even if we Italians are particularly exposed as a way station, the problem is not limited to Italians alone but extends to all the peoples living in the European territory of Western civilization. On the eve of the Second World War, in the passage we quoted concerning the "last invasions" (ninth and tenth centuries), Marc Bloch wrote that from that time on, "Western society would certainly have its clashes; but they would take place within a closed arena." Shortly thereafter, he would witness one of those clashes, as devastating as it could possibly have been, which would rapidly spread well beyond those boundaries. The process of European unification now under way allows us to hope that it may have been the last of its kind. Bloch added that having since the year 1000 been "uninterrupted by any attack from without or any influx of foreign settlers" had given the West itself "the possibility of a much more regular cultural and social evolution," at least by comparison with Eastern Europe, "trampled underfoot until modern times by the peoples of the steppes and by the Turks." He could certainly not have foreseen that at the end of the second millennium and the turn of the third the West, although it had a break, at least for the time being, from "the interruption of attacks from without," would experience an "influx of foreign settlers" on a vast and ever-increasing scale. Bloch also believed, as we have seen, that the "new Western civilization" had been formed a few centuries before the "last invasions," and specifically "in the fiery crucible of the Germanic invasions"; he considered them, in contrast with the last invasions, a positive contribution from abroad.[10] Is it too much to hope that a brand-new Western civilization might be formed in the crucible of the invasions, up until now relatively peaceful, during which we are bewildered spectators? For the moment on the horizon we see no effective social glue comparable with Christianity. Spreading gradually from the east where it was born into the provinces of the Western Roman Empire, on the solid common substrate of the civilization that that empire had transmitted, Christianity was able to incorporate that heritage within the limits of what was possible and compatible, thereby cushioning the impact between the now senescent old world and the new arrivals, supplying a buffer in what would otherwise have been a catastrophic collision.

NOTES

1. From the Sack of Rome to Odoacer, "King of the Nations"

1. Procopius of Caesarea (ca. 500–ca. 565), *Le guerre persiana vandalica gotica*, ed. M. Craterì (Turin: Einaudi, 1957), vol. 5, bk. 1, 344ff. These were the wars fought and won by the emperor Justinian. Procopius, *History of the Wars*, vol. 3, bks. 5 and 6, trans. H. B. Dewing (Cambridge: Harvard University Press, 1941), 7–9.

2. For the Sack of Rome of 410 and the passages quoted, see P. Courcelle, *Histoire littéraire des grandes invasions germaniques* (Paris: Hachette, 1948), 19–55.

3. Orosius, *Le storie contro i pagani*, ed. A. Lippold, trans. A. Bartolucci, 2 vols. (n.p.: Fondazione Lorenzo Valla, Mondadori, 1976), 1.159–163 (II, 19). Paulus Orosius, *The Seven Books of History against the Pagans*, trans. Roy J. Deferrari (Washington, D.C.: Catholic University of America Press), 1964, 75–76.

4. Orosius, *Le storie*, 2.267–269 (VII, 7); *Seven Books of History*, 298–299.

5. Orosius, *Le storie*, 2.383 (VII, 39); *Seven Books of History*, 354.

6. Procopius, *Le guerre*, vol. 3 (III, 2); Procopius, *History of the Wars*, vol. 2, bks. 3 and 4, 17.

7. See L. Storoni Mazzolani, *Galla Placidia* (Milan: Rizzoli, 1975).

8. Orosius, *Le storie*, 2.399–401 (VII, 43); *Seven Books of History*, 361–362.

9. Ammianus Marcellinus, *Histoire*, ed. G. Sabbah (Paris: Les Belles Lettres, 1999), 6.98–101 (XXXI, 2, §1–11).

10. A. Momigliano, "La caduta senza rumore di un impero nel 476 d.C."

(1973), vol. 1, Momigliano, *Sesto contributo alla storia degli studi classici e del mondo antico* (Rome: Edizioni di Storia e Letteratura, 1980), 159–179.

2. Ostrogoths, Romans of Italy and Romans of the East

1. S. Ferri, "Per la storia del Mausoleo di Teoderico," in *I Goti in Occidente: Problemi* (Spoleto: Settimane di studio del Centro italiano di studi sull'alto medioevo, 1956), 3:57–64.

2. Cassiodorus Senator, *Variae*, ed. Th. Mommsen, in *Monumenta Germaniae historica, AA.* (1894), 12.55f. (II, 16).

3. A. Momigliano, *L'età del trapasso fra storiografia antica e storiografia medievale, 320–550 d.C.*, in *La storiografia altomedievale*, 2 vols. (Spoleto: Settimane di studio del Centro italiano di studi sull'alto medioevo 7, 1976), 1:114; A. Momigliano, "Cassiodoro," in *Dizionario biografico degli italiani*, 21 (Rome: n.p., 1978), 495–503, esp. 496.

4. Cassiodorus, *Variae*, 292 (IX, 25).

5. Jordanes, *De origine actibusque Getarum*, ed. F. Giunta and A. Grillone, in *Fonti per la storia d'Italia* 117 (1991): 48 (108).

6. P. Lamma, *Teoderico* (Brescia: La Scuola, 1961), 76f.

7. Ibid., 64.

8. *Anonymus Valesianus II*, ed. R. Cessi, in *Rerum italicarum sciptores*, vol. 2, 24/4 (1912–1913), 20 (28).

9. Dante Alighieri, *Convivio*, ed. C. Vasoli and D. De Robertis, in Dante, *Opere minori*, I/2, *La letteratura italiana: Storia e testi* (Milan: Riccardo Ricciardi, 1988), 18f. (I, ii, 13). Dante Alighieri, *Dante's Il Convivio (The Banquet)*, trans. Richard Lansing (New York: Garland Publishing, 1990), 7–8.

10. Lamma, *Teoderico*, 185.

11. Boethius, *De consolatione philosophiae*, ed. T. Venuti De Dominicis (Grottaferrata: S. Nilo, 1912), 2.16f. (I, 44). Boethius, *The Consolation of Philosophy*, trans. Wilbraham Villiers Cooper (London: J. M. Dent, 1902). *http://etext.lib.virginia.edu/etcbin/toccer-new?id=BoePhil&images=images/modeng&data=/texts/english/modeng*.

12. Cassiodorus, *Variae*, 246 (VIII, 15).

13. Procopius, *Le guerre*, 556 (VII, 9). Procopius, *History of the Wars*, bks. 6 and

7 (vol. 4), trans. H. B. Dewing (Cambridge: Harvard University Press, 1942), 221–223.

14. Procopius, *Le guerre*, 557 (VII, 9). Procopius, *History of the Wars*, bks. 6 and 7 (vol. 4), 225.

15. Procopius, *Le guerre*, 538 (VII, 1). Procopius, *History of the Wars*, bks. 6 and 7 (vol. 4), 161.

16. S. Mazzarino, "Si può parlare di rivoluzione sociale alla fine del mondo antico?" in *Il passaggio dall'antichità al medioevo in Occidente* (Spoleto: Settimane di studio del Centro italiano di studi sull'alto medioevo, 1962), 9:410–425.

17. *La Regola di san Benedetto e le Regole dei Padri*, ed. S. Pricoco, Fondazione Lorenzo Valla (Milan: Mondadori, 1995), 233–235 (LIII). *The Rule of Benedict*, trans. Monks of Glenstal Abbey (Dublin: Four Courts, 1994), 246–248. The opening citation from the Bible is Matt. 25:35.

3. The Longobards in War and Peace and the Origins of the Temporal Dominion of the Popes and of Venice

1. *Leges Langobardorum, 643–866*, ed. F. Beyerle, in *Germanenrechte, N.F., Westgermanisches Recht* [9], 2d ed. (1962), 212 (Adelchis Principis Capitula).

2. Paulus Diaconus, *Storia dei Longobardi*, ed. L. Capo, Fondazione Lorenzo Valla (Milan: Mondadori, 1992), 169 (III, 32); Paul the Deacon, *History of the Lombards*, trans. William Dudley Foulke (Philadelphia: University of Pennsylvania Press, 1974), 145.

3. S. Gasparri, *La cultura tradizionale dei Longobardi: Struttura tribale e resistenze pagane* (Spoleto: Centro italiano di studi sull'alto medioevo, 1989), 11.

4. Paulus Diaconus, *Storia dei Longobardi*, 115 (II, 31); Paul the Deacon, *History of the Lombards*, 86.

5. Paulus Diaconus, *Storia dei Longobardi*, 115–117 (II, 32); Paul the Deacon, *History of the Lombards*, 86–93.

6. G. Volpe, "Lambardi e Romani nelle campagne e nelle città: Per la storia delle classi sociali, della Nazione e del Rinascimento italiano" (sec. 11–15), in Volpe, *Origine e primo svolgimento dei Comuni nell'Italia Longobarda: Studi preparatori* (Rome: Giovanni Volpe, 1976), 3–168.

7. Gregory the Great, *Dialogi libri 4*, ed. U. Moricca, in *Fonti per la storia d'Italia* 57 (1924; lithographic reprint 1990), 135–139 (III, 1).

8. Paulus Diaconus, *Storia dei Longobardi*, 161–165 (III, 30); Paul the Deacon, *History of the Lombards*, 137–140.

9. G. P. Bognetti, *Appunti per una storia dei Longobardi*, in Bognetti, *L'età longobarda*, 4 vols. (Milan: Giuffrè, 1966–1968), 4:645.

10. P. Delogu, "Il regno longobardo," in *Longobardi e Bizantini*, vol. 1 in *Storia d'Italia*, ed. G. Galasso (Turin: UTET, 1980), 1–216, esp. p. 125 and n. 4.

11. Paulus Diaconus, *Storia dei Longobardi*, 349 (VI, 48); Paul the Deacon, *History of the Lombards*, 288–289.

12. Paulus Diaconus, *Storia dei Longobardi*, 363–365 (VI, 58); Paul the Deacon, *History of the Lombards*, 306–308.

13. Paulus Diaconus, *Storia dei Longobardi*, xxix.

14. Gregory I, *Registrum epistolarum*, in *Monumenta Germaniae historica, Epistolae*, 1/1–2 (1887–1891), 325 (V, 38).

15. Paulus Diaconus, *Storia dei Longobardi*, xv.

16. Gregory I, *Registrum*, 43 (I, 29).

17. *Leges Langobardorum*, 118 (Liutprandi Leges, Anni 11 [733], chap. 3).

18. Y. Congar, "Neuf cents ans après: Notes sur le 'Schisme oriental,'" in *1054–1954: L'Église et les églises—Neuf siècles de douloureuse séparation entre l'Orient et l'Occident* (Chevetogne, Belgium: Collection Irénikon, 1954), 1:3–95.

19. *Liber pontificalis*, ed. L. Duchesne, 2 vols. (Paris: De Boccard, 1886–1892), 1.406.

20. In *Epistolae langobardiacæ selectae*, in *Monumenta Germaniae historica, Epistolae*, ed. W. Gundlach (1892), 3.702.

21. Thomas F. X. Noble, *The Republic of St. Peter: The Birth of the Papal State, 680–825* (Philadelphia: University of Pennsylvania Press, 1984).

22. *Leges Langobardorum*, 194 (Ahistulfi Leges Anno 1 [750]); *Liber pontificalis*, 1.435.

23. See O. Bertolini, "Il primo 'periurium' di Astolfo verso la Chiesa di Roma, 752–753," in Bertolini, *Scritti scelti di storia medievale* (Leghorn: Il Telegrafo, 1968), 1:127–169.

24. *Liber pontificalis*, 1.444.

25. N. Machiavelli, *Istorie fiorentine*, in Machiavelli, *Tutte le opere storiche e*

letterarie, ed. G. Mazzoni and M. Casella (Florence: Barbera, 1929), 388 (I, 9); http://www.gutenberg.net/dirs/etext01/hflit10.txt.

26. L. Duchesne, *I primi tempi dello Stato pontificio*, 2d ed. (Turin: Einaudi, 1967 [1898]), 27 n. 1.

27. See P. Classen, *Karl der Grosse, das Papsttum und Byzanz: Die Begründung des karolingischen Kaisertums* (Sigmaringen, Germany: Thorbecke, 1968), 23.

28. *Liber Pontificalis*, 1.401.

29. Cassiodorus, *Variae*, 380 (XII, 24).

30. Duchesne, *I primi tempi*, 18.

4. In the Empire of Charlemagne and within the Shelter of the City Walls

1. See P. E. Schramm, *Kaiser, Könige und Päpste: Beiträge zur allgemeinen Geschichte, I/1: Von der Spätantike bis zum Tod Karls des Grossen (814)* (Stuttgart: Anton Hiersemann, 1968), 201.

2. A. Manzoni, *Adelchi*, ed. A. Giordano (Milan: Rizzoli, 1976), 133–134 (from the chorus of the third act). Alessandro Manzoni, *Two Plays*, trans. Michael J. Curley (New York: Peter Lang, 2002), 184–185.

3. *Collectio Sangallensis*, ed. K. Zeumer, in *Monumenta Germaniae historica, Formulae* no. 39 (1886), 1.421.

4. M. Bloch, *La società feudale*, 1939–1940 (Turin: Einaudi, 1965), 3–4, 273ff. Marc Bloch, *Feudal Society*, trans. L. A. Manyon (Chicago: University of Chicago Press, 1961).

5. F. L. Ganshof, *Qu'est-ce que la féodalité?* (Neuchâtel, Switzerland: Éditions de la Baconnière, 1947), 30ff.

6. R. S. Lopez, "Silk Industry in the Byzantine Empire," *Speculum* 20 (1954): 38.

7. See P. Delogu, *Mito di una città meridionale: Salerno, secoli 8–11* (Naples: Liguori, 1977).

8. B. Croce, *Storia del Regno di Napoli*, 3d ed. (Rome-Bari: Laterza, 1944), 21–23. Benedetto Croce, *History of the Kingdom of Naples*, trans. Frances Frenaye (Chicago: University of Chicago Press, 1970), 25–27.

9. See G. Galasso, *Mezzogiorno medievale e moderno* (Turin: Einaudi, 1965), 63–135.

10. A. Guillou, *L'Italia bizantina: Douleía e oikeiōsis*, in Guillou, *Studies on Byzantine Italy* (London: Variorum Reprints, 1970), 1:5.

11. *Libellus de imperatoria potestate in urbe Roma*, ed. G. Zucchetti, in *Fonti per la storia d'Italia* 55 (1920), 200. The *Libellus* was drawn up in 880/910.

12. W. Ohnsorge, *Das Zweikaiserproblem im früheren Mittelalter* (Hildesheim: August Lax, 1947).

13. G. Levi Della Vida, *Gli Arabi nella storia*, in Della Vida, *Arabi ed Ebrei nella storia* (Naples: Guida, 1984), 284.

14. P. Cammarosano, *Storia dell'Italia medievale: Dal VI all'XI secolo* (Rome-Bari: Laterza, 2001), 271, 307 n. 3.

15. F. Gabrieli, *L'Islàm nella storia: Saggi di storia e storiografia musulmana* (Bari: Dedalo Libri, 1966), 52.

16. Cammarosano, *Storia*, 206.

17. *Annales Casinates*, ed. G. H. Pertz, in *Monumenta Germaniae historica, SS, 3* (1839), 172.

18. *Liber pontificalis*, 2.123f. See R. Krautheimer, *Rome: Profile of a City, 312–1308* (Princeton, N.J.: Princeton University Press, 1980), 119; and Krautheimer, *St. Peter's and Medieval Rome* (Rome: Unione internazionale degli istituti di archeologia, storia e storia dell'arte in Roma, 1985).

19. Bloch, *La società feudale*, 15, 72; Bloch, *Feudal Society, 3*, 56.

20. G. Tabacco, *La dissoluzione medievale dello stato nella recente storiografia* (Spoleto: Centro italiano di studi sull'alto medioevo, 1979).

21. *Liber pontificalis*, 2.123f.

22. *Poésie latine chrétienne du moyen âge*, ed. H. Spitzmüller (n.p.: Desclée de Brower, 1971), 1208–1210.

23. On the *incastellamento*, or castle-building, in Latium, see P. Toubert, *Les structures du Latium médiéval: Le Latium méridional et la Sabine du IXe siècle à la fin du XIIe siècle*, 2 vols. (Rome: École française de Rome, 1973), 1:303–368.

24. For an Italian definition of "contradiction in the attribute" *(contraddizione nell'attributo)*, see *Vocabolario della lingua italiana* (Rome: Istituto dell'Enciclopedia italiana, 1986), 1:922.

25. "Liutprandi Cremonensis Antapodosis," in *Eiusdem Opera omnia*, ed. P. Chiesa, in *Corpus Christianorum continuatio mediaevalis*, 156 (1998): 6f. (I, 3); translation into Italian, also by Chiesa, forthcoming.

26. M. Maccarrone, *Il pellegrinaggio a S. Pietro: I "Limina Apostolorum,"* in Maccarrone, *Romana ecclesia: Cathedra Petri* (Rome: Herder, 1991), 1:258.

27. M. Sot, *Pèlerinage*, in *Dictionnaire raisonné de l'Occident médiéval*, ed. J. Le Goff and J.-C. Schmitt (Paris: Fayard, 1999), 892–905.

28. *Liber pontificalis*, 2.6. For the translation into Italian, see L. Bianchi, *Ad limina Petri: Spazio e memoria della Roma cristiana* (Rome: Donzelli, 1999), 101.

29. *Poésie latine chrétienne*, 1210–1212.

5. Germans at Legnano, Normans in Southern Italy and Sicily

1. See R. Elze, *Die "Eiserne Krone" in Monza*, in P. E. Schramm, *Herrschaftszeichen und Staatssymbolik* (Stuttgart: Anton Hiersemann, 1955), 2:450–479; H. Zug Tucci, "Henricus coronatur corona ferrea," in *Il viaggio di Enrico VII in Italia* (Città di Castello: Edimont, 1993), 29–42.

2. Quoted in G. Miccoli, *Chiesa gregoriana: Ricerche sulla Riforma del secolo 11* (Rome: Herder, 1999), 144 n. 36.

3. See G. Miccoli, *Francesco d'Assisi: Realtà e memoria di un'esperienza cristiana* (Turin: Einaudi, 1991), 3–32.

4. See G. Dagron, *Empereur et prêtre: Étude sur le "césaropapisme" byzantin* (Paris: Gallimard, 1996).

5. *Opus Caroli regis contra synodum (Libri Carolini)*, ed. A. Freeman, in *Monumenta Germaniae historica*, Conc., 2, supplement 1 (1998), 98.

6. See G. De Vergottini, *I giuristi bolognesi a Roncaglia*, in De Vergottini, *Scritti di storia del diritto italiano* (Milan: Giuffrè, 1977), 695–792.

7. Radulfi di Biceto, in *Imagines Historicarum*, ed. F. Liebermann and R. Pauli, in *Monumenta Germaniae historica*, SS, 27 (1885), 268.

8. Archipoeta, *Carmina*, ed. H. Watenphul and H. Krafeld (Heidelberg, 1958), 69.

9. See G. Volpe, *Albori della nazione italiana*, in Volpe, *Momenti di storia italiana* (Florence: Vallecchi, 1952), 35–38.

10. For the concept of "imported feudalism" see M. Bloch, *La società feudale, 1939–1940* (Turin: Einaudi, 1965), 216–218.

11. *Storia de' Normanni di Amato di Montecassino volgarizzata in antico francese*, ed. V. De Bartholomaeis, in *Fonti per la storia d'Italia* 76 (1935), 24 (I, 19).

12. J. M. Martin, *Italies normandes: XIe-XIIe siècles* (Paris: Hachette, 1994), 39.

13. Goffredo Malaterra, "De rebus gestis Rogerii Calabriae et Siciliae Comitis et Roberti Guiscardi Ducis fratris eius, ed. E. Pontieri," in *Rerum italicarum sciptores,* vol. 2, 5/1 (1928), 25 (I, 5).

14. Ibid., 50 (II, 42).

15. Martin, *Italies normandes,* 71f. (Henry II Plantagenet was king of England from 1154 to 1192; Philip Augustus was king of France from 1180 to 1223– Trans.)

16. Ibid., 42f.

17. Benedetto Croce, *Storia del Regno di Napoli* (Rome-Bari: Laterza, 1944), 6. Benedetto Croce, *History of the Kingdom of Naples,* trans. Frances Frenaye (Chicago: University of Chicago Press, 1970), 11.

18. Croce, *Storia del Regno,* 11–13; Croce, *History of the Kingdom,* 16–18.

19. D. Abulafia, *Federico II: Un imperatore medievale* (Turin: Einaudi, 1990), 11; David Abulafia, *Frederick II: A Medieval Emperor* (New York: Oxford University Press, 1988), 19.

6. The Meteor Frederick II and the Bitter "Chickpeas" of the French in Sicily

1. D. Abulafia, *Federico II: Un imperatore medievale* (Turin: Einaudi, Turin 1990), 64; David Abulafia, *Frederick II: A Medieval Emperor* (New York: Oxford University Press, 1988).

2. Benedetto Croce, *Storia del Regno di Napoli* (Rome-Bari: Laterza, 1944), 13; Benedetto Croce, *History of the Kingdom of Naples,* trans. Frances Frenaye (Chicago: University of Chicago Press, 1970), 18.

3. *Lieux de mémoire,* vol. 3: *Les France;* vol. 1: *Conflits et partages* (Paris: Gallimard, 1992).

4. E. Sestan, *Le origini delle signorie cittadine: Un problema storico esaurito?* in Sestan, *Italia medievale* (Naples: Edizioni scientifiche italiane, 1966), 193– 223, esp. 221.

5. Walther von der Vogelweide, *Poesie,* Ital. trans. G. Zamboni (Florence: Vallecchi, 1963), 135; *Single-Stanza Lyrics,* trans. Frederick Goldin (New York: Routledge, 2003), 175, poem 44.

6. Abulafia, *Federico II,* 185; Abulafia, *Frederick II,* 222.

7. Abulafia, *Federico II*, xi–xii; Abulafia, *Frederick II*, 1–2.

8. Dante Alighieri, *De vulgari eloquentia*, ed. P. V. Mengaldo, in Dante, *Opere minori*, vol. 2, *La letteratura italiana: Storia e testi* (Milan: Riccardo Ricciardi, 1979), 101 (I, xi); Dante Alighieri, *A Translation of the Latin Works of Dante Alighieri*, trans. A. G. Ferrers Howell (New York: Greenwood Press, 1969), 38–39.

9. See Frederick II of Swabia, *De arte venandi cum avibus*, 1:7, 14, 40; Federico II di Svevia, *L'arte di cacciare con gli uccelli*, Italian trans. A. L. Trombetti Budriesi (Rome-Bari: Laterza, 2000), 24, 30, 52–54.

10. J.-L.-A. Huillard-Bréholles, *Historia diplomatica Friderici secundi*, vol. 5, bk. 1 (Paris, 1857), 161–162.

11. See also, for the text of the letter and the inscription, M. Guarducci, "Federico II e il monumento del Carroccio in Campidoglio," *Xenia* 8 (1984): 83–94; Guarducci, "L'iscrizione sul monumento del Carroccio in Campidoglio e la sua croce radiata," *Xenia* 11 (1986): 75–84.

12. J.-L.-A. Huillard-Bréholles, *Historia diplomatica Friderici secundi*, vol. 6, bk. 2 (Paris: Plon, 1861), 737f., 738f.

13. N. Kamp, "Clemente IV," in *Enciclopedia dei papi*, vol. 2 (Rome: Istituto dell'Enciclopedia italiana, 2000), 401–411, esp. 406.

14. See G. Galasso, "Carlo I d'Angiò e la scelta della capitale," in Galasso, *Napoli capitale: Identità politica e identità cittadina. Studi e ricerche, 1266–1860* (Naples: Electa, 1998), 46–60, esp. 49.

15. G. Galasso, *Intervista sulla storia di Napoli*, ed. P. Allum (Rome-Bari: Laterza, 1978), 38.

16. See A. Barbero, *Il mito angioino nella cultura italiana e provenzale fra Duecento e Trecento* (Turin: Biblioteca storica subalpina CCI, 1983).

17. See D. Abulafia, "La caduta di Lucera Saracenorum," in *Per la storia del Mezzogiorno medievale e moderno: Studi in memoria di J. Mazzoleni* (Rome: Ministero per i beni culturali e ambientali, Ufficio centrale per i beni archivistici, 1998), 1:171–186. See also G. B. Gifuni, *Origini del Ferragosto lucerino*, 2d ed. (Lucera, Italy: T. Pesce, 1933), 5ff.

18. M. Amari, *La guerra del Vespro siciliano*, 8th ed., 2 vols. (Florence: Le Monnier, 1876 [1842]).

19. See E. Dupré Theseider, *I papi d'Avignone e la questione romana* (Florence: Le Monnier, 1939).

20. M. Maccarrone, "Ubi est papa, ibi est Roma" in Maccarrone, *Romana ecclesia: Cathedra Petri* (Rome: Herder, Rome 1991), 1:1137–1156.

21. Francesco Petrarca, *Sine nomine: Lettere polemiche e politiche,* ed. U. Dotti (Rome-Bari: Laterza, 1974), 20–23 (letter 2).

22. See A. Frugoni, *Il giubileo di Bonifacio VIII,* ed. A. De Vincentiis (Rome-Bari: Laterza, 1999).

23. Jacopo Stefaneschi, *De centesimo seu iubileo anno,* ed. C. Leonardi, Italian trans. A. Placanica (Tavarnuzze, Italy: Edizione nazionale dei testi mediolatini, SISMEL-Edizioni del Galluzzo, 2001), 3–5.

24. A. Tartaro, "Il giubileo di Dante," *La Cultura* 39 (2001): 396.

25. See Giovanni Villani, *Nuova cronica,* ed. G. Porta, 3 vols. (Parma: Fondazione Pietro Bembo, 1990–1991), 1:57f.

26. Stefaneschi, *De centesimo seu iubileo anno,* 13.

7. The Chalk of Charles VIII and the Lance of Fieramosca

1. Quoted in M. Del Treppo, *I mercanti catalani e l'espansione della corona d'Aragona nel secolo XV,* 2d ed. (Naples: University of Naples, Seminario di storia medioevale e moderna 4, 1972), 596f.

2. F. Guicciardini, *Considerazioni intorno ai discorsi del Machiavelli sopra la prima deca di Livio,* in Guicciardini, *Scritti politici e ricordi,* ed. R. Palmarocchi (Rome-Bari: Laterza, 1933), 23 (I, 12); *The Sweetness of Power: Machiavelli's 'Discourses' and Guicciardini's 'Considerations,'* trans. James B. Atkinson and David Sices (DeKalb, Ill.: Northern Illinois University Press, 2002), 404.

3. F. Guicciardini, *Storia d'Italia,* ed. S. Seidel Menchi (Turin: Einaudi, 1971), 1:5f. (I, 1); Francesco Guicciardini, *The History of Italy,* trans. Sidney Alexander (Princeton, N.J.: Princeton University Press, 1984 [1969]), 3–4.

4. F. De Sanctis, *Storia della letteratura italiana,* rev. ed. B. Croce, vol. 1, *Scrittori d'Italia* (Rome-Bari: Laterza, 1925), 385; Francesco De Sanctis, *History of Italian Literature,* trans. Joan Redfern (New York: Barnes and Noble, 1968), 427.

5. De Sanctis, *Storia della letteratura italiana,* 390; De Sanctis, *History of Italian Literature,* 433.

6. Machiavelli, "Proemio," *Istorie fiorentine,* in Machiavelli, *Tutte le opere*

storiche e letterarie, ed. G. Mazzoni and M. Casella (Florence: Barbera, 1929), 378; *http://www.gutenberg.net/dirs/etext01/hflit10.txt*.

7. Machiavelli, "Proemio," *Istorie fiorentine*, 409; *http://www.gutenberg.net/dirs/etext01/hflit10.txt*; G. Sasso, *Niccolò Machiavelli*, vol. 2: *La storiografia* (Bologna: Il Mulino, 1993), 47–159; *http://www.gutenberg.net/dirs/etext01/hflit10.txt*.

8. Machiavelli, *Istorie fiorentine*, 407 (I, 39); *http://www.gutenberg.net/dirs/etext01/hflit10.txt*.

9. Machiavelli, *Istorie fiorentine*, 407; *http://www.gutenberg.net/dirs/etext01/hflit10.txt*.

10. For the reliance upon mercenary militias and the phenomenon of *condottierismo*, see F. Chabod, "Del 'Principe' di Niccolò Machiavelli," in Chabod, *Scritti su Machiavelli* (Turin: Einaudi, 1964), 74–80, esp. 78.

11. N. Machiavelli, *De principatibus*, in Machiavelli, *Tutte le opere*, ed. G. Mazzoni and M. Casella (Florence: Barbera, 1929), 25 (in chap. 12).

12. Philippe de Commynes, *Memorie*, trans. M. A. Daviso di Charvensod (Turin: Einaudi, 1960), 413f. (VII, 9, 2).

13. Luigi da Porto, *Lettere storiche*, ed. B. Bressan (Florence: Le Monnier, 1857), 138–141. The Vicentine Luigi da Porto is known primarily as the author of the novella *Giulietta e Romeo* (Romeo and Juliet).

14. P. Pieri, *Il Rinascimento e la crisi militare italiana del Rinascimento* (Turin: Einaudi, 1952), 612.

15. See Sasso, *Niccolò Machiavelli*, 2:152–159.

16. Guicciardini, *Storia d'Italia*, 522–525 (V, 13).

17. See also, for the passages quoted, G. Procacci, *La disfida di Barletta: Tra storia e romanzo* (Milan: Bruno Mondadori, 2001), 53f., 72f.

18. L. Febvre, *Martin Lutero* (Rome-Bari: Laterza, 1969), 68.

19. Guicciardini, *Storia d'Italia*, vol. 3 (XVIII, 1); Guicciardini, *History of Italy*, 376.

20. Guicciardini, *Storia d'Italia*, 1856–1858 (XVIII, 8). Guicciardini, *History of Italy*, 382–384.

21. F. Gregorovius, *Storia della città di Roma nel medioevo*, trans. A. Casalegno (Turin: Einaudi, 1973), 3:2518 (XIV, 6). Gregorovius's *Storia* was first published in eight volumes between 1859 and 1872.

22. R. Ridolfi, *Vita di Francesco Guicciardini* (Rome: Angelo Belardetti, 1960), 314f.

23. Ibid.

8. Milan and Naples in the Castilian Empire

1. B. Croce, *Storia dell'età barocca in Italia: Pensiero—Poesia e letteratura—Vita morale* (Rome-Bari: Laterza, 1957), 45 and passim.

2. See R. Villari, *Mille anni di storia: Dalla città medievale all'unità dell'Europa* (Rome-Bari: Laterza, 2000), 181.

3. Croce, *Storia dell'età barocca*, 14, 487, 48.

4. A. Manzoni, *I Promessi sposi*, ed. A. Asor Rosa (Milan: Feltrinelli, 1960), 3 (Introduction), 12f. (chap. 1); *The Betrothed (I Promessi sposi)*, trans. Archibald Colquhoun (London: Folio Society, 1969), 34.

5. Manzoni, *I Promessi sposi*, 148f. (chap. 9); *The Betrothed*, 158–159.

6. Manzoni, *I Promessi sposi*, 185 (chap. 10); *The Betrothed*, 193.

7. In B. Croce, *La Spagna nella vita italiana durante la Rinascenza* (Rome-Bari: Laterza, 1949), 273–293.

8. Villari, *Mille anni di storia*, 97.

9. F. Chabod, "Lo Stato di Milano e l'impero di Carlo V (1934)," in Chabod, *Lo Stato e la vita religiosa a Milano nell'epoca di Carlo V* (Turin: Einaudi, 1971), 60.

10. Villari, *Mille anni*, 168.

11. Quotation in Chabod, "Lo Stato di Milano," 68.

12. For a largely negative assessment of Spanish Naples, see Villari, *Mille anni di storia*, 174f.

13. For the various phases in the relations between the central authority and the barons of the kingdom see G. Galasso, *Intervista sulla storia di Napoli*, ed. P. Allum (Rome-Bari: Laterza, 1978), 40ff.

14. Ibid., 39.

15. Ibid., 58.

16. Ibid., 63.

17. Villari, *Mille anni*, 242.

18. Ibid., 251–253; R. Villari, *La rivolta antispagnola a Napoli: Le origini, 1585–1647*, 4th ed. (Rome-Bari: Laterza, 1994 [1967]).

19. R. Villari, *Per il re o per la patria: La fedeltà nel Seicento* (Rome-Bari: Laterza, 1994), 29.

20. F. Braudel, *La Méditerranée et le monde méditerranéen à l'époque de Philippe II* (Paris: Armand Colin, 1986 [1949]), 2:391; for the Battle of Lepanto and its consequences, see 384–398; Fernand Braudel, *The Mediterranean and the*

Mediterranean World in the Age of Philip II, trans. Siân Reynolds (Berkeley: University of California Press, 1995).

9. The Austrians and the Lombardo-Venetian Kingdom

1. Stuart J. Woolf, "La storia politica e sociale," in *Storia d'Italia*, vol. 3, *Dal primo Settecento all'Unità* (Turin: Einaudi, 1973), esp. 22.
2. Ibid., 7.
3. Quotation ibid., 11.
4. Ibid., 49ff.
5. Ibid., 81ff.
6. See F. Venturi, *Settecento riformatore: Da Muratori a Beccaria* (Turin: Einaudi, 1969), 18ff.
7. Quotations ibid., 186, 533.
8. C. Goldoni, *Il filosofo inglese*, ed. P. Roman, *Edizione Nazionale delle Opere di C. Goldoni* (Venice: Marsilio, 2000), 79.
9. J. W. Goethe, *Viaggio in Italia*, Italian trans. E. Castellani (Milan: Mondadori, 1983), 29–30, 137–139, 158; J. W. Goethe, *Italian Journey*, trans. Robert Heitner (Princeton, N.J.: Princeton University Press, 1994), 30–31, 103–104, 117.
10. F. Venturi, "L'Italia fuori d'Italia," in *Storia d'Italia* (Turin: Einaudi, 1973), 1104.
11. Quoted in Woolf, "La storia politica e sociale," 185.
12. Ibid., 182f.
13. Ibid., 170.
14. Quotation ibid., 187.
15. See Venturi, "L'Italia fuori d'Italia," 1133.
16. I. Nievo, *Confessioni di un italiano*, ed. F. Ruffilli, 2 vols. (Milan: Garzanti, 1996), 1:450f.
17. Ibid., 2:488.
18. Woolf, "La storia politica e sociale," 251–253.
19. L. Martini, *Il confortatorio di Mantova*, ed. A. Zorzi (n.p.: Cappelli, 1961), 76–78.
20. R. Romeo, *Cavour e il suo tempo*, 3 vols. (Rome-Bari: Laterza, 1969–1984), 3:571.
21. Ibid., 572.

10. A Pseudoconquest and a True Liberation

1. R. Romeo, *Cavour e il suo tempo*, 3 vols. (Rome-Bari: Laterza, 1969–1984), 3:169f.
2. Ibid., 573 and n. 126. The observations in quotation marks were made by a volunteer.
3. C. Alianello, *L'alfiere* (Milan: Feltrinelli, 1964), 459–462.
4. G. Fortunato, *Carteggio, 1865–1911*, ed. E. Gentile (Rome-Bari: Laterza, 1978), 68f.
5. Quoted in Chabod, *Storia della politica estera italiana dal 1870 al 1896*, 2d ed. (Rome-Bari: Laterza, 1962 [1951]), 186 n. 1.
6. G. Comisso, *Giorni di guerra* (Milan: Longanesi, 1961), 134–144.
7. L. Sciascia, *La zia d'America*, in Sciascia, *Gli zii di Sicilia*, in *Opere, 1956–1971*, ed. C. Ambroise (Milan: Classici Bompiani, 2000), 179–181; Leonardo Sciascia, *Sicilian Uncles*, trans. N. S. Thompson (Manchester, N.Y.: Carcanet, 1986), 12–15.
8. E. Forcella, *La resistenza in convento* (Turin: Einaudi, 1999), 195.
9. G. Ferrara, *Il senso della notte* (Palermo: Sellerio, 1995), 30f., 34–36, 53–54, 56.
10. Marc Bloch, *La società feudale* (Turin: Einaudi, 1965), 72, 15.

INDEX